POLISH MUSIC

MUSIC RESEARCH
AND INFORMATION GUIDES
(VOL. 12)

GARLAND REFERENCE LIBRARY
OF THE HUMANITIES
(VOL. 1093)

MUSIC RESEARCH AND INFORMATION GUIDES

POLISH MUSIC
A Research and Information Guide

William Smialek

GARLAND PUBLISHING, INC. • NEW YORK & LONDON
1989

Library of Congress Cataloging-in-Publication Data

Smialek, William.
    Polish music.

    (Music research and information guides; vol. 12)
(Garland reference library of the humanities; vol.
1093)
        Discography: p.
        Includes index.
        1. Music—Poland—History and criticism—
Bibliography. I. Title. II. Series. III. Series:
Garland reference library of the humanities; vol. 1093.
ML120.P6S6 1989 016.78'09438 89-11965
ISBN 0-8240-4614-5 (alk. paper)

Printed on acid-free, 250-year-life paper
Manufactured in the United States of America

To Molly
and our sons, Andrew and Adam

CONTENTS

FOREWORD

This bibliography had its genesis as long as a decade ago, when I was beginning my doctoral dissertation. In the summer of 1978 I traveled for the first time to Poland to attend a six-week intensive language course at Nicolas Copernicus University in the city of Toruń. My intention was to begin studying the Polish language, but I was also prepared with a stack of index cards from which I hoped to begin my work on the nineteenth-century composer Ignacy Feliks Dobrzyński. I soon discovered that Polish scholars had produced a number of fine reference works and bibliographies, enabling me to complete my preliminary research with a limited command of the Polish language. Years later I realized that I had acquired experience with sources on nineteenth-century music in Poland but was not as aware of key differences in other periods of music history and related subjects. A reference work that gives some comment describing the entry and its appended materials, such as musical examples, lists, and indexes, was necessary. There are Polish bibliographies that are more comprehensive than this research guide, but they are not annotated. Also, a problem exists in gathering citations to books and articles in western languages on the subject of Polish music. For this research and information guide I have selected references that I find to be the most useful and important Polish writings and sources in western publications. My main intention is that the bibliography will be useful to scholars, both specialists on the music of Eastern Europe and others whose research takes a sudden turn east into Poland. I also hope that this book will be helpful to a more general music audience for its information on twentieth-century Polish composers, who are becoming increasingly notable to an international audience. Perhaps other musicians will find that the book leads them to new performance repertory. Indeed, the less technical references will be of use to those interested in Slavic studies, whatever their knowledge and background in music.

The 600 included references were selected from among over 2,000 collected citations for their value to the projected audiences. The language of many of the sources is Polish, which will be inaccessible to many users of this reference. I have tried, however, to make note of summaries in English and other western languages, usually French or German. In some cases I discovered that Polish scholars had published articles in the West which generalized on the research that they previously had issued in Polish journals. In this instance, I tried to trace the historiography of the research and offer in this bibliography the best citation for my prospective audiences. Another factor in the selection process was the availability of the source in the United States. I purposely limited myself to two major Polish music journals, the scholarly journal *Muzyka* and the more popular chronicle of Polish musical activity *Ruch Muzyczny*. Nevertheless, even access to these serials is somewhat restricted, especially to earlier issues. The bibliography contains references to Polish music that were published through 1987. In another major decision about the nature of this bibliography, I decided to exclude all but the most general reference material on Chopin because soon after beginning work on this project I discovered that Chopin really deserved to be addressed in a separate volume.

The references are categorized into broad topics based generally on the format of *RILM Abstracts*. Sources on the history of Polish art music are grouped by historical period. This is followed by other topics of musical interest, and a discography of selected recordings is placed at the end. The intention of this list of recordings is not comprehensiveness; it is to serve as an addendum to other composer discographies, which may be found in the index. Although consistency in the selection and annotation process was my ideal, I know that there was some variance in my thinking from the beginning to the end of the project, and the depth and breadth of the annotations may vary accordingly. During the review process I tried to maintain the perspective of someone not fluent in the Polish language and especially made note of the presence of translated summaries of the literature. I have reviewed each item personally, except for several dissertations which I annotated from *Dissertation Abstracts.* The index will allow the user to find material by an author's name and also by subject.

In reviewing the results of my efforts to catalog references on Polish music, several observations have come forward. While it is rewarding to note that American scholarship on Polish topics has increased greatly in the 1980s, as judged from doctoral dissertations, most of this research is focused on the music of the twentieth century. Even the Polish journals are including less research on early Polish music and increasing their coverage of more mainstream European topics. Presumably, this represents the direction of research by younger scholars. Nevertheless, it could signify that the intense interest in studying the remains of Polish culture after the destruction of World War II has reached the point of diminishing returns. To some degree, this reference work anticipates a new stage of research devoted to criticism of sources and reinterpretation of prior scholarship. In the area of performance repertory, the discography makes very clear the limited interest in Polish composers to date, four or so names excluded.

The greatest part of my work on this bibliography was accomplished in only a few libraries. Closest to home are the library of the University of Texas at Tyler and also the Tyler Public Library. As a academic scholar it was a delight for me to discover the effectiveness of the interlibrary loan system at my disposal through the Tyler Public Library, and I wish to thank the staff of this institution for the assistance I received in gaining access to the necessary materials. Another collection that served my research needs on a regular basis was the Music Library at the University of North Texas. I thank my friends on the staff for both their assistance and encouragement. Considerable work toward the completion of this bibliography was accomplished in an intense two-week period at the University of Illinois, made possible through a Summer Research Associateship at the Russian and East European Center in the summer of 1988. To a lesser extent, I also utilized the libraries of the University of Texas at Austin, the Boston Public Library, and the Biblioteka Narodowa in Warsaw. Finally, I extend special thanks to my wife, Molly McCoy, who read the manuscript and offered many

corrections and suggestions, and to Deborah Finley, who spent many
hours proofreading the final typescript.

William Smialek
Jarvis Christian College

Polish Music

REFERENCE AND RESEARCH MATERIALS

General Polish Reference Materials

An encyclopedia is often useful for questions of general
history and culture.

1. *Wielka encyklopedia powszechna PWN* [Great universal
     encyclopedia], 13 vols. Warszawa: Polskie
     Wydawnictwo Naukowe, 1962-1970. DK 404.P695

   Short articles on composers and truncated bibliographies.
   May be a good source for non-music facts, dates, or
   questions related to research projects.

There are several general bibliographies which can be of use
in locating the latest specialized literature.

2. American Association for the Advancement of Slavic
     Studies. *American Bibliography of Slavic and East
     European Studies*. Columbus: American Association
     for the Advancement of Slavic Studies, 1967- .
     ISSN 0094-3770   Z 2483.A65

   References to Polish music are found under music in
   Eastern Europe.

3. Biblioteka Narodowa, Instytut Bibliograficzny.
     Bibliografia zawartości czasopism [Bibliography of
     the contents of periodicals]. Warszawa: Biblioteka
     Narodowa, 1947- . AI 15.B45

   A monthly publication classified by subject. Section
   XXIII *Sztuka* [art] contains references to *Muzyka* [music]
   and subheadings such as *Festiwale muzyczne* [music
   festivals]. Section XXIIIa *Nuty* refers to printed music.

1

Compiles a list of music articles in Polish serials with
cross references to other sections of the bibliography.
There is a subject and author index at the end of each
issue.

4. Estreicher, Karol. *Bibliografia polska*, 34 vols.
    Kraków: Polskie Akademia Umietętności, 1870-1951.
    Z 2521.E85

    Includes the publications of composers through the ages.
    Compiled in different series, such as the 19th century,
    and 15th-18th centuries, which renders the structure
    somewhat confusing.

5. *European Bibliography of Soviet, East European and
    Slavonic Studies*, ed. M. Armand, M. Aymard, Cl.-L.
    Charbonnier. Paris: Éditions de l'École des Hautes
    Études en Sciences sociales, Institut d'Études
    slaves, 1975- . Z 2483.E94 DJK9

    An annual bibliography of material published in Europe.
    Music is listed in category 11.10.

6. *Przewodnik bibliograficzny; Urzędowy wykaz druków
    wydanych w Polskiej Rzeczypospolitej Ludowej*
    [Bibliographic guide; official list of issued
    printed matter in the Polish Peoples' Republic].
    Warszawa: Biblioteka Narodowa, 1945- .
    ISSN 0033-2518 Z 2523.P93

    A weekly publication of Polish publishing activity
    organized by subject categories. Category 78 is
    designated for books about music, with 78.089 reserved
    for printed music (*nuty* in Polish). Information
    provided includes ISBN, pagination, extra features
    outside of text, and the number of copies in the print
    run (*Egz.*). Polskie Wydawnictwo Muzyczne, the state
    music publishing house centered in Cracow also issues
    catalogs of music publications.

Polish-English dictionaries

7.   Bulas, Kazimierz, Lawrence L. Thomas, and Francis J.
         Whitfield. *The Kościuszko Foundation Dictionary*,
         2 vols. The Hague: Mouton and Company, 1961.
         1037, 772 pp. PG 6640.K6

8.   Stanisławski, Jan, ed. *Wielki Słownik Polsko-Angielski/*
         The Great Polish-English Dictionary, 2 vols.
         Warszawa: Państwowe Wydawnictwo Wiedza Powszechna,
         1977. 800, 928 pp. PG 6640.S842

General histories of Poland

9.   *The Cambridge History of Poland*, 2 vols., ed. W.F.
         Reddaway *et al.* Cambridge: The University Press,
         1941; reprinted by Octagon Books, 1978. DK 414.C3

     Collected essays on Polish history by a great number of
     scholars. Gives some attention to cultural history.

10. Davies, Norman. *God's Playground: A History of Poland*,
         2 vols. New York: Columbia University Press, 1982.
         ISBN 0231043260 DK 4140.D38

     Offers a comprehensive survey in English which is meant
     to be impartial and without an ideological agenda.
     Reviews of the book and the subsequent events in Davies'
     academic career would suggest that he was not completely
     successful in this regard. Takes a different approach
     to the issue of Polish nationalism than native scholars.
     Intersperses chronology with extracts from historical
     documents and references to cultural history, making
     the book more enjoyable to read than most historical
     surveys. Provides many plates of key Polish art works,
     maps of regions under discussion, and a good index.

     Reviews: Stanisław Barańczak, *New Republic* 187
     (November 15, 1982): 25; Leszek Kolakowski, *New York
     Times Book Review* (April 15, 1982): 6; Martin Malia,
     New York Review of Books 30 (September 29, 1983): 18;
     Ronald Modras, *America* 147 (December 18, 1982): 394;
     Gustaw Moszcz, *New Statesman* 103 (May 21, 1982): 2;

Olga A. Norkiewicz, *History* 68 (1983): 126; Hugh
Seton-Watson, *Times Literary Supplement* (March 19,
1982): 297; Piotr Wandycz, *American Historical Review*
80 (April 1983): 437; *Economist* 282 (March 6, 1982):
104.

11. Wandycz, Piotr S. *The Lands of Partitioned Poland,
    1795-1918.* Vol. 7 of *A History of East Central
    Europe.* Seattle: University of Washington Press,
    1974. 431 pp. ISBN 0295953519 DJK4.S93 v. 7

    Presents a chronological survey of nineteenth-century
    Poland focusing on local institutions and the growth of
    nationalism. Considers the various roles of social and
    ethnic groups, such as the nobility, Jews, and
    intelligentsia. A bibliographical essay assesses the
    relative merits of reference material in Polish and
    Western European languages, but is limited to only five
    references related to cultural history.

Several surveys of Polish literature, particularly useful for
studying vocal music, have been published in English.

12. Krzyżanowski, Julian. *A History of Polish Literature,*
    trans. Doris Ronowicz. Warszawa: Polskie
    Wydawnictwo Naukowe-Polish Scientific Publishers,
    1978. 807 pp. PG 7012.K78

    Covers Polish literature from the Middle Ages to about
    World War II. Relates the major themes of Polish
    literature with discussion of specific examples within
    the relative historical context. There is a series of
    plates of famous Polish writers. Includes a bibliography,
    list of Polish literature in English translation, and
    index.

13. Miłosz, Czesław. *The History of Polish Literature,* 2nd
    ed. Berkeley and Los Angeles: University of
    California Press, 1983. 583 pp. ISBN 0520044657
    PG 7012

    Surveys Polish literature from the Middle Ages through
    about 1970. Covers prose, poetry, drama, historical
    writing, the novel, short stories, and essays written in

Latin and the Polish language. Treats writers in groups
and movements, tending to isolate only the major figures
for individual detail, but places the history of Polish
literature within the context of general Polish history.
Not supplemented with a great deal of examples.
Includes a short essay "On Polish Versification." The
bibliography is classified by period and includes
translations of Polish works into English and other
European languages.

Watermark studies have not been prominent in studies of
Polish music, but there are catalogs for references to papers
produced in Poland.

14. Siniarska-Czaplicka, Jadwiga. *Filigrany papierni
    położonych na obszarze rzeczypospolitej polskiej od
    początku XVI do połowy XVIII wieku* [Watermarks
    deriving from the territory of the Polish Republic
    from the beginning of the sixteenth to the first
    half of the eighteenth centuries]. Wrocław-
    Warszawa-Kraków: Zakład Narodowy im. Ossolińskich
    Wydawnictwo PAN, 1969. Z 237.S5

    Catalogs watermarks of various Polish paper mills.
    Includes an introduction to Polish watermarks and the
    production of paper in Poland.

15. _____. *Katalog filigranów papierni polskich 1500-
    1800 r.* [Catalog of Polish watermarks from 1500-
    1800]. Łódź: Stowarzyszenie inżynierów i techników
    przemyslu papierniczego w Polsce, 1983.

    Continues the watermark study of paper mills in the
    Polish Republic published in 1969 (item 14). Extends
    the catalog of known watermarks to the years 1750 to
    1800.

Libraries, Museums, and Other Collections

16. Benton, Rita, gen. ed. *Directory of Music Research
         Libraries. RISM C5.* Kassel: Bärenreiter, 1985.
         267 pp. ISBN 3761807406 ML 113.I6 C5

         "Poland," pp. 111-175, compiled by James B.
         Moldovan.

     Lists 59 Polish music libraries with such information
     as the address; availability of microfilm readers,
     photocopiers, and other equipment; size and strengths
     of the collection; and hours. This is prefaced by a
     general essay giving national holidays, interlibrary
     loan requirements, deposit of materials according to
     Polish copyright law, a map of Poland, and a general
     bibliography. Index.

17. Jenkins, Jean, ed. *International Directory of Musical
         Instrument Collections.* Buren: Frits Knuf, 1977.
         166 pp. ML 462.I57

     Lists 20 collections in Poland. The most important
     instrument collection is in Poznań: Muzeum Narodowe
     w Poznaniu, Muzeum Instrumentów Muzycznych, containing
     755 instruments. A bibliography pertaining to this
     collection is included.

18. Musioł, Karol. *Opracowanie rzeczowe zbiorów muzycznych*
         [The subject catalogs of the music library]. Prace
         Biblioteki Państwowej Wyższej Szkoły Muzycznej w
         Katowicach, no. 6. Katowice: PWSM, 1965. 161 pp.
         ML 111.M88

     Introduces the subject classification system used in
     Polish music libraries.

Encyclopedias and Dictionaries

19. Dziębowska, Elżbieta, gen. ed. *Encyklopedia muzyczna,*
    PWM [Music encyclopedia]. Kraków: Polskie
    Wydawnictwo Muzyczne, 1979- . ISBN 8322401124
    ML 100.E56

    Contributes a new music encyclopedia with most of the
    leading figures in Polish musicology serving on the
    editorial committee and/or writing articles. The
    Encyklopedia muzyczna is a reference work not limited
    to Polish music, although East European musicians little
    known in the West are strongly represented. Contains
    plates, lists of works, and references. To date, only
    three volumes of the biographical section have been
    issued. Major articles in the A through G section
    include the contribution of Mieczysław Tomaszewski on
    Chopin. See item 107. The *Encyklopedia muzyczna* can
    be difficult to read due to the use of numerous
    abbreviations adopted to save space.

    Reviews: Władysław Malinowski, *Muzyka* 27, no. 1-2
    (1982): 83-99; *Ruch Muzyczny* 29, no. 7 (1985): 22-23;
    Ruch Muzyczny 29, no. 17 (1985): 10-12.

20. Grigg, Carolyn Doub. *Music Translation Dictionary.*
    Westport, Conn.: Greenwood Press, 1978. 336 pp.
    ML 108.G855

    Contains in a polyglot format musical terms in Polish
    and other Polish equivalents applicable in rehearsal
    or discussion about music. The page layout is somewhat
    confusing because of the code numbers used in the
    process of computer sorting. Other languages included
    are English, Czech, Danish, Dutch, French, German,
    Hungarian, Italian, Portuguese, Russian, Spanish and
    Swedish.

21. Instytut Sztuki PAN. *Słownik muzyków polskich*
    [Dictionary of Polish musicians], 2 vols., ed.
    Józef Chomiński. Kraków: Polskie Wydawnictwo
    Muzyczne, 1962. ML 106.P7 S6

    Continues the coverage of earlier biographical
    dictionaries by expanding the entries to include the

nineteenth and twentieth centuries. Features detailed
lists of composers' works, and biographical entries
include Polish musicologists. Other noteworthy contributions are a list of organists categorized by church
position (*organiści*) and an extensive listing of chapel
ensembles and associated musicians (*kapele*, vol. 1,
pp. 216-61). The latter compilation is the standard of
information which much of the subsequent periodical
literature on court orchestras in Poland then updates.
This dictionary represents the collective effort of the
many Polish scholars who were contributors.

Reviews: Hieronim Feicht, *Muzyka* 10, no. 2 (1965): 78-
81; *Ruch Muzyczny* 9, no. 10 (1965): 18; *Ruch Muzyczny*
12, no. 2 (1968): 17-18.

22. Kallmann, Hellmut, Gilles Potvin, Kenneth Winters, eds.
       Encyclopedia of Music in Canada. Toronto:
       University of Toronto Press, 1981. 1076 pp.
       ISBN 0802055095 ML 106.C36E52

"Poland": short article on Polish traditional music
which includes a list of musicians of Polish origin or
descent. Other references to Polish music are
scattered throughout the volume.

23. *The New Grove Dictionary of Music and Musicians,* 20
       vols., ed. Stanley Sadie. London: Macmillan, 1980.
       ISBN 0333231112 ML 100.N48

In addition to major articles on "Poland" and "Warsaw,"
the *New Grove* contains information on Polish music in
almost 500 entries. Includes entries for many little-
known Polish composers and musicians. The bibliographies in these articles are quite useful.

24. Polska Akademia Nauk, Instytut Sztuki. *Słownik
       biograficzny teatru polskiego 1795-1965*
       [Biographical dictionary of Polish theater, 1795-
       1965]. Warszawa: Polskie Wydawnictwo Naukowe, 1973.
       905 pp. PN 2859.P65 S58

Includes biographies of opera singers which concentrate
on major roles. Entries include a bibliography.

25. Śledziński, Stefan, ed. *Mała encyklopedia muzyki*
     [Short encyclopedia of music], 3rd ed. Warszawa:
     Państwowe Wydawnictwo Naukowe, 1981. 1278 pp.
     ML 100.M18

     Provides a general encyclopedia of names and musical
     terms, including Polish artists and musical genres.
     Includes a list of names and index of compositions.

     Review: *Ruch Muzyczny* 13, no. 11 (1969): 17-19.

26. Sowinski, Albert. *Les musiciens polonais et slaves*.
     Paris: Librarie Adrien Le Clere, 1857; reprint New
     York: Da Capo, 1971. 599 pp. ML 106.P7 S7

     Offers a biographical dictionary of Polish composers
     and musicians to the mid-nineteenth century. Devotes
     long articles to major figures of Polish music history
     with some musical examples and lists of works. The
     dictionary is prefaced with a short essay on the history
     of Polish music to the nineteenth century, which
     includes such topics as dance rhythms, dramatic music,
     military music, and instruments found in Poland.

     Reviews: Karl Laux, *Musik und Gesellschaft* 24, no. 6
     (June 1974): 368-70; John Tyrell, *Musical Times* 113
     (June 1972): 567.

27. Szulc, Zdzisław. *Słownik lutników polskich* [Dictionary
     of Polish violin makers]. Poznań: Nakładem
     Poznańskiego Towarszystwa Przyjaciół Nauk, 1953.
     264 pp.

     Catalogs known string instrument makers. Also provides
     plates of makers' markings in actual instruments and
     photographs of a number of instruments. Summaries and
     translations are provided in French, English, German,
     and Russian. Indexes of names and places.

Catalogs and Indexes

28. Biblioteka Narodowa. Stacja Mikrofilmów i Zakład
    Muzyczny. *Katalog mikrofilmów muzycznych* [Catalog
    of musical microfilm], 3 vols. Warszawa: Biblioteka
    Narodowa, 1956-1965. ML 113.K3

    A list of manuscripts from various locations in Poland
    which have been microfilmed and added to the microfilm
    archive in Warsaw. Microfilm can be ordered from the
    Biblioteka Narodowa by catalog number.

    Review: Adam Sutkowski, *Muzyka* 7, no. 4 (1962): 106-7.

29. Biegański, Krzysztof. *Biblioteka muzyczna Zamku w
    Łańcucie. Katalog* [Music library of the castle at
    Łancut. Catalog]. Kraków: Polskie Wydawnictwo
    Muzyczne, 1968. 430 pp. ML 138.L3y

    Organizes the contents of this collection into lists of
    books on theory and pedagogy, vocal-instrumental works,
    and instrumental music. Indexes composers, arrangers,
    publishers, and titles. Includes an index of textual
    incipits.

30. Bogdany, Wanda, ed. *Gazeta Muzyczna i Teatralna 1865-
    1866; Przegląd Muzyczny 1877.* Bibliografia polskich
    czasopism muzycznych, no. 4. Kraków: Polskie
    Wydawnictwo Muzyczne, 1955. 93 pp. ML 5.G2875

31. _____. *Muzyka 1950-1956.* Bibliografia polskich
    czasopism muzycznych, no. 15. Kraków: Polskie
    Wydawnictwo Muzyczne, 1976. 189 pp. ML 5.M9979

32. _____. *Muzyka Polska 1934-1939.* Bibliografia polskich
    czasopism muzycznych, no. 12. Kraków: Polskie
    Wydawnictwo Muzyczne, 1967. 193 pp. ML 5.M9928

33. Bogdany, Wanda and Kornel Michałowski, eds. *Ruch
    Muzyczny 1857-1862.* Bibliografia polskich czasopism
    muzycznych, no. 3. Kraków: Polskie Wydawnictwo
    Muzyczne, 1957. 333 pp. ML 157.P3

34. Dziki, Sylwester. *Muzyka w polskich czasopismach
    literackich i społecznych 1831-1863* [Music in Polish
    literary and social journals, 1831-1863].
    Bibliografia muzyczna polskich czasopism
    niemuzycznych, no. 2. Kraków: Polskie Wydawnictwo
    Muzyczne, 1973. 169 pp. ML 120.P6 B5

    References are classified by subject. Approximately
    225 periodicals have been indexed. A name index adds
    to the accessibility of the information. The
    reproduction from a typed manuscript is difficult to
    read.

35. Espina, Noni. *Repertoire for the Solo Voice, a Fully
    Annotated Guide to Works for the Solo Voice
    Published in Modern Editions and Covering Material
    from the 13th Century to the Present*, 2 vols.
    Metuchen, N.J.: Scarecrow Press, 1977. ML 128.S3 E8

    Annotates some Polish works in the volume devoted to
    vocal literature of the nineteenth and twentieth
    centuries (volume 2). Composers represented include:
    Chopin, M.K. Ogiński, Paderewski, Panufnik, Poldowski,
    Serocki, Szulc, and Szymanowski. Ironically, none of
    the songs of Moniuszko are represented.

    Review: Stephen M. Fry, *Notes* 34, no. 3 (1978): 620.

36. Hodgson, Julian. *Music Titles in Translation: A
    Checklist of Musical Compositions*. Hamden, Conn.:
    Linnet Books, 1976. 370 pp. ML 111.H7

    Contains a few Polish titles to works by well-known
    composers such as Chopin and Moniuszko.

37. International Music Centre. *Music in Film and
    Television: An International Selective Catalog
    1964-1974*. Paris: Unesco Press, 1975. 197 pp.
    ML 128.M7 I63

    Includes two entries for Polish television operas:
    Tadeusz Baird, *Jutro* (1973); Krzysztof Meyer,
    Cyberiada (1970). The address to contact about Polish
    films: Polskie Radio i Telewizja, Woronicza 17,
    pok. 144, Warszawa 12.

38. Kielanowska-Bronowicz, Maria. *Kwartalnik Muzyczny*
    1911-1914, 1928-1933, 1948-1950; Polski Rocznik
    Muzykologiczny 1935-1936. Bibliografia polskich
    czasopism muzycznych, no. 8. Kraków: Polskie
    Wydawnictwo Muzyczne, 1963. 211 pp. Z 6815.P6 K5

39. Michałowska, Maria. *Ruch Muzyczny 1945-1949, 1957-*
    1959, 2 vols. Bibliografia polskich czasopism
    muzycznych, no. 14. Kraków: Polskie Wydawnictwo
    Muzyczne, 1981. ML 118.M5

40. Michałowski, Kornel. *Muzyka w czasopismach polskich*
    1919-1939. Bibliografia muzyczna polskich
    czasopism niemuzycznych, no. 5. Kraków: Polskie
    Wydawnictwo Muzyczne, 1979. 468 pp.
    ISBN 8322401221 ML 120.P6 M5

41. _____. *Gazeta Teatralna 1843-1844.* Bibliografia
    polskich czasopism muzycznych, no. 2. Kraków:
    Polskie Wydawnictwo Muzyczne, 1956. 74 pp.
    ML 5.G288

42. _____. *Muzyka 1924-1938,* 2 vols. Bibliografia
    polskich czasopism muzycznych, no. 9. Kraków:
    Polskie Wydawnictwo Muzyczne, 1967. 188, 127 pp.

43. _____. *Opery polskie* [Polish operas]. Materiały do
    bibliografii muzyki polskiej, no. 1. Kraków:
    Polskie Wydawnictwo Muzyczne, 1954. 277 pp.
    ML 128.04 M5

    Catalogs operas in two sections: works of Polish
    composers or composers active in Poland, and operas
    of other composers performed in Poland. Entries include
    some information in the following areas: librettist,
    translator, premiere, dates of composition, manuscript
    location, publishing information. Operas are indexed
    by composer and in a chronological table by first
    performance (1778-1953). Although the original authors
    are given for the many works which are translations,
    only the titles of the Polish versions are provided.

44. Mietelska-Ciepierska, Agnieszka. "Rękopisy polskich
    kompozytorów XIX wieku w zbiorach Biblioteki
    Jagiellońskiej" [Manuscripts of nineteenth-century
    Polish composers in the collections of the
    Jagiellonian Library]. *Muzyka* 27, no. 1-2 (1982):
    65-82.

    Presents a history of the manuscript collection and
    then discusses the most interesting examples from the
    collection. Most of the manuscripts can be considered
    "trivial music."

45. Mrygoń, Adam and Maria Burchard. "Katalog poloników
    muzycznych w zbiorach austriackich" [Catalog of
    Polish musical materials in Austrian collections].
    Szkice o kulturze muzycznej XIX wieku, 5 (1984):
    161-324. See item 296.

    Expands and supplements the version of this catalog
    published in *Muzyka* in 1970. Includes manuscripts and
    printed music of Polish composers now found in Austria.
    Utilizes a cumbersome classification system which
    considers manuscripts and prints separately, with
    subdivisions by genre. Presents the items alphabetically
    within each group. Identifies the library or archive
    source and shelf number. Includes an alphabetical
    author index and index of publishers.

    Review: William Smialek, *Notes* 44, no. 4 (1988): 720-
    22.

46. *Music Index,* 1949- . ISSN 0027-4348

    Currently indexes the Polish music journals *Muzyka,*
    Polish Music/Polnische Musik, and *Ruch Muzyczny.* Also
    lists books reviewed in these publications.

47. Neuer, Adam, ed. *Polish Opera and Ballet of the
    Twentieth Century: Operas, Ballets, Pantomines,
    Miscellaneous Works.* Kraków: Polskie Wydawnictwo
    Muzyczne, 1986. 132 pp. ISBN 8322403003
    ML 1736.5.P6413

Combines a publisher's catalog with bibliography to
continue item 43 into the twentieth century.
Alphabetically lists 262 works for stage, radio, or
television, all of which are available for performance.
Provides information on an opera's instrumentation,
plot, duration of performance, prizes and awards,
recordings, and availability of score and parts.
Includes black and white photographs of stage works,
indexes of composers and librettists, and a chronology
of works cited.

48. Nowak-Romanowicz, Alina. "Polonika w bibliotekach
     czechosłowackich" [Polish works in Czechoslovak
     libraries]. *Muzyka* 20, no. 1 (1975): 100-103.

     Reports on works in the Hudební Oddělení in Prague.
     Collection includes manuscripts of Bohdanowicz (two
     violin duets and a flute sonata) and three partitas
     for six wind instruments by Lessel. Czech collections
     also contain other nineteenth-century works.

49. Papierz, Stanisław. *Muzyka w polskich czasopismach
     niemuzycznych w latach 1800-1830.* Bibliografia
     muzyczna polskich czasopism niemuzycznych, no. 1.
     Kraków: Polskie Wydawnictwo Muzyczne, 1971. 349 pp.
     ML 120.P6 B5

50. Podejko, Paweł. "Na marginesie dotychczasowych wzmianek
     o życiu muzycznym na Jasnej Górze w Częstochowie"
     [A sidenote to what has been mentioned to this time
     about the musical life at Jasna Góra in Częstochowa].
     Muzyka 12, no. 1 (1967): 37-43.

     Adds or corrects information on musicians and musical
     life at the Jasna Góra monastery already published in
     item 166.

51. Porębowiczowa, Anna, ed. *Młoda Muzyka 1908-1909;
     Przegląd Muzyczny 1910-1914, 1918-1919.*
     Bibliografia polskich czasopism muzycznych, no. 7.
     Kraków: Polskie Wydawnictwo Muzyczne, 1964.
     232 pp. ML 5.M445

52. Poźniak, Włodzimierz, ed. *Echo Muzyczne 1877-1882;*
     Echo Muzyczne, Teatralne i Artystyczne 1883-1907,
     2 parts. Bibliografia polskich czasopism
     muzycznych, no. 5. Kraków: Polskie Wydawnictwo
     Muzyczne, 1972-1973. 503, 473 pp. ML 106.E18

53. Rich, Maria F., ed. *Who's Who in Opera.* New York:
     Arno Press, 1976. 684 pp. ML 102.06 W5

     Includes biographical entries for a number of Polish
     artists, as well as a profile of the Teatr Wielki in
     Warsaw.

54. *RILM Abstracts of Music Literature.* 1967- .
     ISSN 0033-6955

     Provides bibliographic citations and short abstracts of
     literature in Polish and other languages. Polish
     consultants have included references to the more obscure
     journals published in Poland and not readily available
     in the West. Includes information on the publication
     of Polish translations of prominent Western texts.

     Reviews: Elżbieta Szczepańska, *Muzyka* 21, no. 1 (1976):
     141-46; Jerzy Gołos, "Glosa do recenzji z 'RILM
     Abstracts of Music Literature. Cumulative Index I-V.'
     [A gloss to the review of RILM]." *Muzyka* 22, no. 4
     (1977):92-93; Elżbieta Szczepańska, "W odpowiedzi na
     glosę Jerzego Gołosa." [In answer to the gloss of Jerzy
     Gołos]. *Muzyka* 22, no. 4 (1977): 93-94.

55. Stempniewicz, Mirosława, ed. *Przegląd Muzyczny*
     Poznański 1925-1931; Życie Muzyczne i Teatralne
     1934-1935. Bibliografia polskich czasopism
     muzycznych, no. 11. Kraków: Polskie Wydawnictwo
     Muzyczne, 1966. 252 pp. ML 106.P7 S8

56. Strumiłło, Dobrochna, ed. *Tygodnik Muzyczny 1820-1821;*
     Pamiętnik Muzyczny Warszawski 1835-1836.
     Bibliografia polskich czasopism muzycznych, no. 1.
     Kraków: Polskie Wydawnictwo Muzyczne, 1955. 114 pp.
     ML 5.T945

57. Szczawińska, Elżbieta, ed. *Muzyka w polskich
     czasopismach literackich i społecznych 1864-1900*
     [Music in Polish literary and social journals,
     1864-1900]. Bibliografia muzyczna polskich
     czasopism niemuzycznych, no. 3. Kraków: Polskie
     Wydawnictwo Muzyczne, 1964. 399 pp.
     ML 120.P6 B5 t.3

58. _____. *Muzyka w polskich czasopismach literackich i
     artystycznych 1901-1918* [Music in Polish literary
     and artistic journals, 1901-1918]. Bibliografia
     muzyczna polskich czasopism niemuzycznych, no. 4.
     Kraków: Polskie Wydawnictwo Muzyczne, 1971. 364 pp.
     ML 120.P6 B5 t.4

59. Szwedowska, Jadwiga. *Muzyka w czasopismach polskich
     XVIII wieku. Okres saski (1730-1764)* [Music in
     Polish periodicals of the eighteenth century. The
     Saxon period (1730-1764)]. Kraków: Polskie
     Wydawnictwo Muzyczne, 1975. 152 pp. ML 120.P6 S95

     Uses a simple classification system of five headings:
     biography, opera, instrumental music, vocal music, and
     dance-ballet. Each category is separated into Polish
     and foreign references. The information has been taken
     from five newspapers of the period; the full reference
     has been reproduced in this catalog. Includes indexes
     of places, people, and instruments. Reproduction from
     typescript can be difficult to read.

     Review: Maria Burchard, *Muzyka* 21, no. 4 (1976): 84-
     91.

60. _____. *Muzyka w czasopismach polskich XVIII wieku.
     Okres stanisławowski (1764-1800)* [Music in Polish
     periodicals of the eighteenth century. The Stanisław
     period, (1764-1800)]. Kraków: Polskie Wydawnictwo
     Muzyczne, 1984. 335 pp. ISBN 832240266X
     ML 120.P6 S96

     Follows the same format as item 59, but is typeset.
     Selects references from 20 serials in Polish, French,
     and German. Both volumes have extensive introductions
     on the period, especially newspaper publishing of
     the eighteenth century.

61.   Turska, Irena. *Przewodnik baletowy* [Ballet guide].
      Kraków: Polskie Wydawnictwo Muzyczne, 1973.
      412 pp. GV 1790.A1 T87

      A handbook of both Polish and foreign works giving
      information about the music, libretto, characters, and
      choreography. Supplies a history of each ballet,
      summary of plot, and other comments. Dates of premieres
      are also included.

Catalogs, Thematic

62.   Burhardt, Stefan. *Polonez: katalog tematyczny* [The
      Polonaise: thematic catalog], vol. 2 (1792-1830).
      Kraków: Polskie Wydawnictwo Muzyczne, 1976. 663 pp.

      A catalog of 3439 polonaises by Polish composers and
      others. Information on manuscripts, printed versions,
      and documentation. The book begins with an essay on
      the polonaise by Karol Hławiczka, which together with
      the comments on editorial method is printed in English.

63.   _____. *Polonez: katalog tematyczny* [The Polonaise:
      thematic catalog], vol. 3 (1831-1981). Kraków:
      Polskie Wydawnictwo Muzyczne, 1985. 818 pp.
      ISBN 8322402465

      Catalogs 1508 polonaises alphabetically by composer.
      Most entries include a musical incipit, the date of
      composition, manuscript data, information on printed
      editions, and references to pertinent literature. The
      introduction provides an overview of the history of the
      polonaise in this period and a statement of the research
      methodology followed to compile the volume.

      Reviews: Vol. 2: *Fontes artis musicae* 24, no. 1 (1977):
      49; *Ruch Muzyczny* 22, no. 17 (1978): 17. Vol. 3: *Ruch
      Muzyczny* 29, no. 16 (1985): 24; *Ruch Muzyczny* 30, no. 12
      (1986): 22.

64. Chmara-Żaczkiewicz, Barbara, Andrzej Spóz, and Kornel
         Michałowski. *Mieczysław Karłowicz: Katalog
         tematyczny dzieł i bibliografia* [Thematic catalog
         of works and bibliography]. Kraków: Polskie
         Wydawnictwo Muzyczne, 1986. 294 pp.
         ISBN 8322402759 ML 134.K284 A15

     Provides extensive information on Karłowicz's musical
     works and writings, including the facts of composition,
     manuscripts, printed editions, transcriptions,
     performances, recordings, literature, and reviews.
     Uses many abbreviations which are given in a table at
     the front of the volume, along with English
     translations. The foreword is translated into English.
     Assembles an extensive bibliography of literature on the
     composer. Includes photographs; lists of works,
     publishers, and libraries holding manuscripts; and an
     index of names and titles.

65. Michałowski, Kornel. *Karol Szymanowski 1882-1937:
         katalog tematyczny dzieł i bibliografia* [Karol
         Szymanowski 1882-1937: Thematic catalog of works
         and bibliography]. Kraków: Polskie Wydawnictwo
         Muzyczne, 1967. 348 pp. ML 134.S995 M5

     A list of works arranged chronologically by completion
     date. Includes information about each composition,
     extant manuscripts, editions, recordings, and
     performances. Thematic incipits are provided for each
     work. The introduction and contents are printed in
     English and German, as well as Polish. Other aspects
     of the catalog include a list of incomplete works and
     list of Szymanowski's writings. The bibliography of
     over 1,600 citations is categorized, but not annotated.
     Includes a name index.

66. Szweykowski, Zygmunt M., ed. *Musicalia vetera: katalog
         tematyczny rękopiśmiennych zabytków dawnej muzyki w
         Polsce* [Thematic catalog of early musical
         manuscripts in Poland]. Kraków: Polskie Wydawnictwo
         Muzyczne, 1969- . ML 135.M87

         Volume 1, fascicles 1-6. *Zbiory muzyczne
         proweniencji wawelskiej* [Musical collections of
         Wawel provenance]. Kraków: Polskie Wydawnictwo
         Muzyczne, 1969-1983.

Volume 2, fascicle 1. *Zbiory muzyczne proweniencji podkrakowskiej* [Musical collections from the surroundings of Cracow]. Kraków: Polskie Wydawnictwo Muzyczne, 1970.

Presents an inventory and full-voiced musical incipits of manuscript materials. Formatted with English translations of the textual material.

Reviews: Charles Cudworth, *Musical Times* 111 (January 1970): 49; Tadeusz Maciejewski, *Muzyka* 23, no. 1 (1978): 111-15.

Bibliographies and Discographies

67. Bennett, John R., ed. *Melodiya: A Soviet Russian L.P. Discography*. Discographies, no. 6. Westport, Conn.: Greenwood Press, 1981. 832 pp. ML 156.2.B44

Includes the music of major Polish names, such as Chopin, Moniuszko, Paderewski, and Wieniawski.

68. Cabanowski, Marek and Henryk Choliński. *Polska dyskografia jazzowa 1955-1972*. Warszawa: Polski Stowarzystwo Jazzowe, 1974. 186 pp.

Reviews: *Jazz Research* 8 (1976): 237; *Jazz Forum* no. 32 (December 1974): 71.

69. Croucher, Trevor, ed. *Early Music Discography from Plainsong to the Sons of Bach*, 2 vols. London: The Library Association, 1981. ML 156.2.C76

Catalogs recordings of early Polish music on Muza and other labels. The actual discography is found in volume 1, where recordings are classified by historical period. Recordings of Polish music can often, but not consistently, be found under the subheading for Eastern Europe. Volume 2 comprises the indexes of composers, plainsong recordings, anonymous works, and performers. An overview of recordings containing examples of early Polish music is difficult without searching for the works of specific composers.

Reviews: Martin Elste, *Musikforschung* 37, no. 4 (1984):
299-300; *Early Music* 10, no. 2 (1982): 245; *Musical
Times* 123 (July 1982): 477.

70. Heskes, Irene. *The Resource Book of Jewish Music: A
          Bibliographical and Topical Guide to the Book and
          Journal Literature and Program Materials.* Westport,
          Conn.: Greenwood Press, 1985. 302 pp.
          ISBN 0313232512 ML 128.J4H48

     Incorporates about twenty references to Jewish music in
     Poland. Provides annotations of literature.

71. Idaszak, Danuta and Maria Burchardt. "Discographie de
          la musique polonaise 1 mai 1966 - 20 nov. 1971."
          La Musique en Pologne 8 (1972): 61-104.

     Lists works on Polish record labels.

72. Kondracki, Miroslaw, Marta Stankiewicz, and Frits C.
          Weiland. *International Diskographie elecktronischer
          Musik.* Mainz: Schott, 1979. 174 pp. ML 156.4.E4 K6

     Lists the works of electronic music by several Polish
     composers, each entry including author, title,
     publishing information, and recording studio where the
     composition was completed. Contains introductory notes
     in German, English, and French, as well as lists of
     record companies, electronic music studios, and an index
     of represented composers.

     Reviews: Martin Elste, *Musikforschung* 33, no. 1 (1980):
     65-66; Paul Griffiths, *Musical Times* 121 (May 1980):
     319; D. Laszlo, *Computer Music Journal* 6, no. 3 (1982):
     78-79; Rainer Wehinger, *Musica* 34, no. 3 (1980): 298;
     Fritz Winckel, *Neue Zeitschrift für Musik* 142, no. 1
     (January-February 1981): 89.

73. Lerski, George J. and Halina T. Lerski. *Jewish-Polish
          Coexistence, 1772-1939: A Topical Bibliography.*
          Bibliographies and indexes in world history, no. 5.
          New York: Greenwood Press, 1986. Z 6373.P7 L47

Includes eight citations concerning Jewish music in
Poland in the chapter on culture and the arts.

74. Michałowski, Kornel. *Bibliografia polskiego
    piśmiennictwa muzycznego* [Bibliography of Polish
    writings on music]. Materiały do bibliografii
    muzyki polskiej, no. 3. Kraków: Polskie Wydawnictwo
    Muzyczne, 1955. 280 pp. ML 120.P6 M5

    Covers the period from the sixteenth century to 1954
    and Polish dissertations from 1917 to 1954. Includes
    publications in Polish and works by Polish authors
    published in other languages. Categorizes 1,837
    citations by subject matter, but citations are not
    annotated. Includes author index.

75. _____. *Bibliografia polskiego piśmiennictwa muzycznego*.
    Suplement I [Bibliography of Polish writings on
    music]. Materiały do bibliografii muzyki polskiej,
    no. 4. Kraków: Polskie Wydawnictwo Muzyczne, 1964.
    203 pp. ML 120.P6 M5

76. _____. *Bibliografia polskiego piśmiennictwa muzycznego*.
    Suplement II [Bibliography of Polish writings on
    music]. Materiały do bibliografii muzyki polskiej,
    no. 5. Kraków: Polskie Wydawnictwo Muzyczne, 1978.
    464 pp. ML 120.P6 M5

77. _____. "Bibliography 1980-1984 [Books]." *Music in
    Poland* 1985, no. 1: 31-44.

78. _____. "Polish Dissertations in Musicology 1947-
    1974." *Polish Musicological Studies* 1 (1977): 261-
    69. See item 131.

    The Assistant-Professor dissertation is better known as
    a *praca habilitacyjna*. Polish dissertations and
    magister theses can be difficult to consult because
    often the only copies are in institute libraries.

79. _____. "Polish Dissertations in Musicology 1973-
             1977." *Polish Musicological Studies* 2 (1986):
             341-44. See item 131.

     Extends prior listing in *Polish Musicological Studies* 1
     (1977). See item 78.

80. _____. "Polish Musicological Literature: A Selected
             Bibliography 1970-1974." *Polish Musicological
             Studies* 1 (1977): 270-332. See item 131.

     A classified listing of Polish literature, books, and
     periodicals, not only on Polish subjects. Titles are
     translated into English.

81. _____. "Polish Musicological Literature 1975-1977."
             Polish Musicological Studies 2 (1986): 345-94.
             See item 131.

     Continues the bibliography in *Polish Musicological
     Studies* 1 (1977), item 80. Categorization of references
     is somewhat different.

82. Mrygoń, Adam and Ewa Mrygoń. *Bibliografia polskiego
             piśmiennictwa muzykologicznego (1945-1970)*
             [Bibliography of Polish musicological writing, 1945-
             1970]. Warszawa: Polskie Wydawnictwo Naukowe, 1972.
             208 pp. ML 120.P6 M8

     A classified bibliography of about 3,400 citations.
     Some of the literature cited was published outside of
     Poland. Includes the work of Polish musicologists, not
     only writings about Polish music. References are in
     scholarly journals as well as congress reports and more
     popular periodicals. The citations are not annotated.
     Includes an author index. (In the original Polish the
     authors names are given in the plural as Adam i Ewa
     Mrygoniowie.)

     Review: Maria Prokopowicz, *Muzyka* 22, no. 3 (1977):
     125-27.

83. Wescott, Steven D. *A Comprehensive Bibliography of
    Music for Film and Television.* Detroit Studies in
    Music Bibliography, no. 54. Detroit: Information
    Coordinators, 1985. 432 pp. ISBN 0899900275
    ML 128.M7 W47

    Does not list Poland (or Polish) in the index, but does
    contain a number of items specifically concerning Polish
    music for film and television.

Iconographies

84. Banach, Jerzy. *Tematy muzyczne w plastyce polskiej.
    I. Malarei plastik* [Musical themes in Polish
    plastic art. I. Painting]. Kraków: Polskie
    Wydawnictwo Muzyczne, 1956. 128 pp. N 8226.B2

    The 93 illustrations in this book cover Polish art of
    the twelfth to twentieth centuries. An introduction
    gives background on representations of music in Polish
    paintings.

85. _____. *Tematy muzyczne w plastyce polskiej. II.
    Grafika i rysunek* [Musical themes in Polish plastic
    art. II. Graphics and drawings]. Kraków: Polskie
    Wydawnictwo Muzyczne, 1962. 195 pp. N 8226.B2

    _____. *Die Musik in den bildenden künsten Polens,*
    2 vols. Kraków: Polskie Wydawnictwo Muzyczne, 1957,
    1965. N 8226.B315

    Begins with an introduction on iconography in Polish
    music. The album consists primarily of 225 illustrations
    from the sixteenth to the twentieth centuries.
    Instruments represented in the art works are listed in
    an index.

    Reviews: Krystyna Wilkowska-Chomińska, *Muzyka* 2, no. 2
    (1957): 87-89; Narcissa Williamson, *College Music
    Symposium* 8 (1968): 155-6.

86. Gołos, Jerzy. "Zapisy muzyczne w plastyce" [Musical
        writings in art works]. *Muzyka* 14, no. 4 (1969):
        106-9.

     Examines two art works for incorporation of musical
     notation. The art works are: Leżajsk, choir fresco
     from the Bascilica of the Bernardine Fathers (18th
     century); and a portrait of the Reverend Florian
     Gieczyński (c. 1840). Transcribes the music into modern
     notation.

87. Rozanow, Zofia. *Muzyka w miniaturze polskiej* [Music in
        Polish miniatures]. Kraków: Polskie Wydawnictwo
        Muzyczne, 1965. 152 pp. ML 85.R68

     Reproductions of 41 art works. The text discusses
     themes in Polish iconography supported by the
     illustrations. Begins in the Middle Ages. The examples
     show instrumental and vocal music, as well as symbolism
     in Polish art works. Includes a list of illustrations
     with the sources.

     Reviews: Jerzy Morawski, *Muzyka* 11, no. 1 (1966): 99-
     100; *Ruch Muzyczny* 10, no. 8 (1966): 19.

88. _____. "Średniowieczna ikonografia muzyczna" [Medieval
        musical iconography]. *Musica medii aevi* 2 (1968):
        93-114.

     The study begins with an overview of iconography as a
     discipline within Polish scholarship. Specific attention
     is paid to representation of St. Gregory, funeral
     rituals, liturgical drama, and dance scenes. Gives
     description of specific illustrations.

89. Sutkowski, Adam. "Les sujets musicaux dans les
        miniatures médiévales en Pologne." In *Mélanges
        offerts à René Crozet*, 2 vols., ed. Pierre Gallais
        et Yves-Jean Riou, 1341-43. Poitiers: Société
        d'Études Médiévales, 1966. 1420 pp. D 119.M5

     Discusses Polish iconography and the diversity of
     iconographic examples. Examines specific medieval
     manuscripts. Reproduces 10 plates as examples.

Periodicals

90. *Annales Chopin/Rocznik chopinowski.* 1956- .
    ML 410.C54 A55

    Reviews: Volume 2, Reinhold Sietz, *Musikforschung* 14,
    no. 1 (1961): 90-92; vols. 12-13, *Ruch Muzyczny* 27,
    no. 5 (1983): 18; vol. 14, *Ruch Muzyczny* 28, no. 10
    (1984): 25-26.

91. *Chopin Studies* 1 (1985)- . ISSN 0239-8567
    ML 410.C54 S933

    Reprints selected materials from *Rocznik chopinowski*
    in English translation.

92. *Jazz Forum.* 1967- . ISSN 0021-5635

    English language magazine of the International Jazz
    Federation, edited in Warsaw. Each issue includes a
    column devoted to international jazz events, often
    providing information on Polish jazz activities.

93. *Musica medii aevi.* 1965- . ISSN 0077-247X.

    Studies on medieval Polish music. Extended articles
    are printed on repertories and contents of specific
    manuscripts. Some of the volumes have English
    summaries.

    Reviews: Volume 1, Krzysztof Biegański, *Muzyka* 11,
    no. 2 (1966): 156-62; Michel Huglo, *Revue de musicologie*
    52, no. 2 (1966): 241-42; vol. 2, Tadeusz Maciejewski,
    Muzyka 13, no. 4 (1968): 92-98; *Ruch Muzyczny* 13, no. 16
    (1969): 17-18; vol. 2-3, Henri Musielak, *Revue de
    musicologie* 61, no. 2 (1975): 329-33; vol. 3, Maria
    Pamuła, *Muzyka* 19, no. 4 (1974): 82-85; *Ruch Muzyczny*
    14, no. 9 (1970): 17-18.

94. *Musik des Ostens.* ML 570.S9

    Reviews: Volume 2, Rudolf Stephan, *Neue Zeitschrift für
    Musik* 128, no. 10 (October 1967): 424-26; Franz Zagiba,

Musikforschung 19, no. 4 (1966): 441-43; *Beiträge zur
Musikwissenschaft* 8, no. 1 (1966): 79-80; vol. 3,
Rudolf Stephan, *Neue Zeitschrift für Musik* 128, no. 10
(October 1967): 424-26; Miloš Velimirović, *Musikforschung*
21, no. 1 (1968): 89-91; *Musica* 20, no. 4 (1965): 195-
96; vol. 4, Dieter Lehmann, *Beiträge zur Musikwissen-
schaft* 8, no. 1 (1966): 79-82; Walter Salmen,
Musikforschung 22, no. 3 (1969): 380-81; Rudolf Stephan,
Neue Zeitschrift für Musik 129, no. 12 (December 1968):
552-53.

95. *La Musique en Pologne; Music in Poland* 1966-1981.
       ISSN X003-1892   ML 5.M9874

Contains general articles on Polish music and musical
life. Also includes current events, bibliography,
premieres of compositions, and music published.
Published from a typescript.

96. *Muzyka. Kwartalnik poświęcowy historii i teorii muzyki.*
       ISSN 0027-5344.

The major musicology journal in Poland. Articles are in
Polish, but often summaries in English or another
Western European language (French or German) are
provided. Translated summaries have been inconsistent
over the publishing history of the journal, as has
their position in the layout of the serial. (Summaries
have been noted in the annotations to individual
articles.) *Muzyka* also prints book reviews and reviews
of conferences. The public defense of Polish
musicological dissertations is also noted. A survey of
recent volumes of the journal will reveal that Polish
musicology is moving away from studies of Polish music
toward integration into the study of mainstream European
music. There are occasional articles outside of
historical musicology, most often in the area of
ethnomusicology. Examples of the earlier volumes of
Muzyka are limited to only a few libraries in the
United States.

97. Szczepańska-Malinowska, Elżbieta. *Bibliografia
       zawartości "Muzyka" 1956-1973.*   80 pp.

Presents a classified ordering of articles published in the Polish musicological journal *Muzyka* (item 96). Includes an author index.

98. _____. *Bibliografia zawartości "Muzyka" 1974-1978.* 33 pp.

Both indexes use the same classification system to organize the contents of the journal for easy reference.

99. *Notes.* 1943- . ISSN 0027-4380

The section entitled "Books Recently Published" often includes a selection of titles in Polish, with ISBN and LC numbers.

100. *Polish Music/Polnische Musik.* ISSN 0032-2946

Articles on historical aspects of Polish music, but more oriented toward current musical events. Covers new compositions, publications, and festivals such as Musica Antiqua Europae Orientalis and Warsaw Autumn. Information on current activities of contemporary composers and specific compositions.

101. *Polish Music/Polnische Musik. 1966-1974. List of Contents,* ed. Wanda Skoraczyńska. Warszawa: Author's Agency, [1975]. 54 pp.

A classified index to the periodical.

102. *Res facta,* ed. Michał Bristiger. Kraków: Polskie Wydawnictwo Muzyczne, 1967- . ML 197.R47

Collected essays on twentieth-century music. Not all the articles concern Polish composers and their compositions. Some of the contributions are translations into Polish.

Reviews: Volume 1, Marianna Kotyńska, *Muzyka* 13, no. 1 (1968): 101-2; vol. 2, *Muzyka* 14, no. 2 (1969): 112-14; vols. 3-6, *Muzyka* 19, no. 2 (1974): 80-86; vols. 6-7,

Hudební věda 12, no. 2 (1975): 182-84; vol. 8,
Hudební věda 16, no. 4 (1979): 77-79; vol. 9, Oldřich
Pukl, *Hudební věda* 21, no. 2 (1984): 183-84.

103. *Ruch Muzyczny.* 1957- . ISSN 0035-9610

A bi-weekly publication intended for a popular
audience of music lovers. Includes some new research,
but most of the serious articles are summaries of
research already published in the scholarly literature.
Often presents groups of articles on facets of music
history, both of Polish music and European music.
There are interviews with composers and performers,
announcements of current activities, reviews of
concerts, and record and book reviews.

Reference Materials on Frédéric Chopin

Bibliography

104. Melville, Derek. *Chopin: A Biography, with a Survey
    of Books, Editions and Recordings.* London: Clive
    Bingley, 1977. 108 pp. ISBN 0208015426
    ML 410.C54 M47

Begins with a short biography of Chopin and then has
a bibliographic essay of materials in English. Covers
editions of Chopin's music. Includes a discography
and index.

105. Michałowski, Kornel. *Bibliografia chopinowska: Chopin
    Bibliography 1849-1969.* Kraków: Polskie
    Wydawnictwo Muzyczne, 1970. 267 pp. ML 410.C54 D6

Focuses on the Polish literature devoted to Chopin
since the year of his death and the more recent
literature in other European languages selected from
both scholarly and popular publications. The 3,970
citations concentrate on Chopin's life and works, but
sections of the bibliography address the interpretation
and reception of Chopin's music. Although the
citations are not annotated, translations and reviews
are noted. The table of contents and introduction

are translated into English; subject, work, and
author indexes are provided.

Reviews: Eveline Bartlitz, *Beiträge zur Musikwissenschaft* 13, no. 3 (1971): 224-26; Arnfried Edler,
Musikforschung 32, no. 2 (1979): 198-99.

106. _____. "Bibliography 1970-1983." *Chopin Studies* 1
(1985): 181-296.

Lists citations, with English translations, of writings
on Chopin published since Michałowski's 1970
bibliography (see item 105). Includes a general index.

107. Tomaszewski, Mieczysław. "Chopin," *Encyklopedia
muzyczna PWM CD,* ed. Elżbieta Dziębowska, 108-92.
Kraków: Polskie Wydawnictwo Muzyczne, 1984.
See item 19.

Provides an extensive biographical and analytical
article which includes a list of works and chronology
of activities. Appropriate bibliography and
discography are placed in the margins of each page,
deviating from the general page layout of the volume.

Catalogs

108. Brown, Maurice J.E. *Chopin: An Index of His Works in
Chronological Order,* 2nd ed. New York: Macmillan,
1972. 214 pp. ISBN 0333135350 ML 134.C54 B84

Presents each composition with a musical incipit,
publication history, and dedication. Includes
additionally the appropriate background information on
manuscripts and other facts of interest. Appendixes
include a chronological list of publications, list of
editions, and a list of dedications.

Reviews: Willi Kahl, *Musikforschung* 16, no. 3 (1963):
299-300; Hans F. Redlich, *Music Review* 23, no. 1
(1962): 67-68.

109. Kobylańska, Krystyna. *Rękopisy utworów Chopina:*
        katalog, 2 vols. Kraków: Polskie Wydawnictwo
        Muzyczne, 1977.

        _____. *Frederic Chopin: Thematisch-Bibliographisches*
        Werkverzeichnis. München: G. Henle Verlag, 1979.
        362 pp. ISBN 3873280299 ML 134.C54 A315

        Includes more information in the Polish version; for
        example, volume 2 reproduces plates of manuscripts
        that are not in the German version of the catalog.
        Polish edition does not include musical incipits. See
        Kallberg review in the *Journal of the American*
        Musicological Society for a detailed comparison of the
        Polish and German editions.

        Reviews: Jean-Jacques Eigeldinger, *Fontes artis*
        musicae 26, no. 2 (1979): 142-44; L. Michael Griffel,
        Notes 37, no. 4 (June 1981): 847-49; Jeffery Kallberg,
        Journal of the American Musicological Society 34,
        no. 2 (1981): 357-65; Jeffery Kallberg, *19th Century*
        Music 3, no. 2 (1979): 163-64; Zofia Lissa, *Muzyka* 23,
        no. 2 (1978): 85-88; *Ruch Muzyczny* 21, no. 19 (1977):
        15-16.

Collections of correspondence

110. Kobylańska, Krystyna, ed. *Korespondencja Fryderyka*
        Chopina z rodziną [Chopin's correspondence with his
        family]. Warszawa: Państwowy Instytut Wydawniczy,
        1972. 413 pp. ML 410.C54 A238

111. Sydow, Bronisław Edward, ed. *Korespondencja Fryderyka*
        Chopina, 2 vols. Warszawa: Państwowy Instytut
        Wydawniczy, 1955. ML 410.C54 A283

        _____. *Correspondance de Frédéric Chopin*, 3 vols.
        Paris: Richard-Masse, 1953-1960. 324, 416, 479 pp.
        ML 410.C54A2837

        Includes 793 letters arranged chronologically, some
        with explanatory notes. The original language of each
        letter is marked.

112.   _____. *Selected Correspondence of Fryderyk Chopin,*
            trans. and ed. Arthur Hedley. London: Heissemann,
            1962; reprinted 1979. 400 pp. ML 410.C54 A2835

        Selected letters from the collection *Korespondencja
        Fryderyka Chopina* (see item 111) and translated into
        English from the French edition of letters by Sydow.
        Letters selected for general readers of music biography
        provided without lengthy footnotes. The controversial
        issue of letters to Delfina Potocka is addressed in an
        essay in the appendix. The editor provides a
        chronological table of correspondence and its
        relationship to Chopin's life. 348 letters are
        printed.

Editions

113.   Higgins, Thomas. "Whose Chopin?" *19th Century Music*
            5, no. 1 (1981): 67-75.

        Reviews seven editions of Chopin's music, citing
        specific errors and inconsistencies. Finds the
        Henle Urtext edition to be the most satisfactory, yet
        concludes that there is a need for a better edition.

HISTORY, POLISH ART MUSIC

The Discipline

114. Chodkowski, Andrzej. "Les études musicologiques en Pologne." *La Musique en Pologne* 2 (July 1967): 17-22.

    Musicology in Poland dates from 1911 and the Jagiellonian University's granting of a position to Jachimecki. Chodkowski traces the development of musicology as a discipline in the early twentieth century with three university programs and the conferring of 30 doctorates by 1939. The programs after World War II produced 24 doctorates and 266 magister diplomas by 1966. The article also outlines the musicology curriculum and thesis requirements for degrees.

115. Krush, Joseph Martin. "History of Harmony and Counterpoint, Volume II: The Renaissance by Józef M. Chomiński: A Translation, Evaluation, and Critique." Ph.D. diss., Michigan State University, 1981. 598 pp. (*Dissertation Abstracts* 42 (1981): 4969-A)

116. Lissa, Zofia. "Kazimierz Kelles-Krauz: Początki marksistowskiej myśli muzycznej w Polsce" [Kazimierz Kelles-Krauz: the beginning of Marxist musical thought in Poland]. *Muzyka* 11, no. 2 (1966): 8-35.

    Lissa underscores the significance of little-known Kelles-Krauz (1872-1905) in the crystallization of Polish Marxist thought in music. Discusses the independence of his ideas in the period 1900 to 1905 and his publications concerning economic factors on music.

117.   _____. *Wstęp do muzykologii* [Introduction to
        musicology]. Warszawa: Państwowe Wydawnictwo
        Naukowe, 1974. 227 pp. ML 3797.L5

        Designed as an introduction for university students.
        Polish musicologists have a broad definition of
        musicology which includes all that is written about
        music. This book reveals Lissa's Marxist approach
        to studying music. Includes a section on musicology
        departments in the various Polish universities.
        Bibliographies follow each subject presented in the
        book.

        Review: *Sovetskaya Muzyka* 39 (November 1975): 125-26.

118.   Maciejewski, Tadeusz. "Musica antiqua polonica:
        Achievement of the past 30 years." *Polish Music* 8,
        no. 3-4 (1973): 21-28.

        Reviews the work completed since World War II in the
        production of publications and search for archival
        materials. Maciejewski notes that the new discoveries
        in early music failed to introduce new concepts into
        Renaissance studies. Reviews salient issues in Polish
        musicology. The organization of festivals and
        appearance of new publications were also a highlight
        of the period.

119.   _____. "Poland: An Appraisal of the Musicological
        Work in Poland in the Post-War Years." *Current
        Musicology* No. 22 (1976): 14-21.

        Focuses on the growth of the discipline since World
        War II, giving important publications and research
        projects. Considers each historical period until the
        present century from the viewpoint of new discoveries.

120.   Morawska, Katarzyna. "Historical Studies of Old
        Polish Music during the Thirty Years of the Polish
        Peoples' Republic." *Polish Musicological Studies* 2
        (1986): 198-340. See item 131.

        Summarizes the research of Polish musicologists between
        1945 and 1975 on Polish music of the Middle Ages through
        the eighteenth century. One factor in the

musicological work of this period was the redevelopment
of musicology as a discipline after World War II. Work
on editions of early Polish music was a main emphasis.
The article also presents major directions in the
writings of specific scholars. A bibliography of 804
references, with titles translated into English, is
appended to the commentary.

121. Perz, Mirosław. "Die Publikationen alter Musik in
        Polen." In *Beiträge zur Musikgeschichte Osteuropas*,
        ed. Elmer Arro, 38-55. Wiesbaden: Franz Steiner
        Verlag, 1977. 446 pp. ISBN 3514021574 ML 240.B35

      Presents the historiography of printed editions of
      Polish music prepared in the nineteenth and twentieth
      centuries. Includes a list of the contents of the
      following editions:

      Wydawnictwo dawnej muzyki polskiej
      Źródła do historii muzyki polskiej
      Antiquitates musicae in Polonia
      Monumenta Musicae in Polonia
      Muzyka polskiego odrodzenia
      Muzyka w dawnym Krakowie
      Muzyka staropolska
      Muzyka antiqua polonica

      Also provides indexes of names, subjects, and editors.

122. Pociej, Bohdan. "The Art of Editing." *Polish
        Perspectives* 16, no. 3 (March 1973): 64-69.

      Describes a post-graduate program of study at the
      Cracow Conservatory in music editing. Gives a
      description of the curriculum and philosophy of the
      course. The School of Music Editing is under the
      leadership of Mieczysław Tomaszewski.

123. Pociej, Bohdan and Olgierd Pisarenko. "O warszawskiej
        muzykologii mowią Anna Czekanowska, Zofia Helman,
        Andrzej Chodkowski, Mirosław Perz" [Anna
        Czekanowska, Zofia Helman, Andrzej Chodkowski, and
        Mirosław Perz talk about Warsaw musicology]. *Ruch
        Muzyczny* 18, no. 6 (March 17, 1974): 3-6.

Four scholars review the activities, experiences, and history of the Musicology Institute at Warsaw University. They mention professors and former students by name. The discussion expresses the objectives and strengths of Warsaw University's musicology program.

History, General

124. Abraham, Gerald. "The Early Development of Opera in Poland." In *Essays on Opera and English Music in Honour of Sir Jack Westrup*. Oxford: Clarendon, 1975. See item 125.

Begins with the introduction of Italian opera in Poland in the reign of Władysław IV. Mentions several Italian operas performed in Polish. Stage works of the eighteenth century are set against the background of foreign opera. Carries through to the institution of Polish opera at the end of the eighteenth century. Details the music of *Nędza uszczęśliwiona* and notes the incorporation of Polish melodies in *Żółta szlafmyca albo Kolęda na Nowy Rok* [The Yellow Nightcap or A Present for New Year]. Other early operas considered in detail include Stefani's *Krakowiacy i Górale* and the works of Elsner and Kurpiński. Offers unusual insight in placing opera within the context of political events and general musical styles.

125. _____. *Essays on Russian and East European Music*. Oxford: Clarendon, 1985. 193 pp. ISBN 0193112086 ML 60.AZ

Reprints several essays on Polish music. Includes a name index. Selected articles include:

"Some Eighteenth-Century Polish Symphonies," pp. 113-21. See item 264.
"The Early Development of Opera in Poland," pp. 122-40. See item 124.
"Polish Song," pp. 141-55. See item 126.
"The Operas of Stanisław Moniuszko," pp. 156-80.

126.   _____. "Poland." In *A History of Song*, ed. Denis
            Stevens, rev. ed., 323-37. New York: Norton, 1960.

        Abraham's essay begins the coverage of Polish vocal
        solos in the seventeenth century, but finds an emphasis
        in nineteenth-century art song, principally works by
        Elsner, Chopin, and Moniuszko. In the early twentieth
        century contributions by Szymanowski and Karłowicz are
        highlighted.

        Review: Hans F. Redlich, *Music Review* 23, no. 1 (1962):
        65-67.

127.   _____. "Slavonic Music and the Western World."
            Proceedings of the Royal Musical Association 87
            (1960-1961): 45-56.

        Abraham begins with the thesis that limited knowledge
        of Slavic languages presents a barrier to comprehending
        vocal music, and consequently the instrumental music
        of Eastern Europe is better known. Abraham then
        acknowledges that the Czechs and Poles have always
        shared a common culture with Western Europe. Noting
        that Slavic vocal music has been influenced by the West,
        he shows that instrumental music, particularly Polish
        melodic elements, passed in the opposite direction.
        He concludes by urging more knowledge of musical
        development in Slavic countries.

128.   Belza, Igor'. *Istoriya pol'skoy muzykal'noy kul'tury*
            [The history of Polish musical culture], 3 vols.
            Moskva: Gosudarstvennoe Muzykal'noe Izdatel'stvo,
            1954-1972. ML 306.B44

        The first volume covers Polish musical history from the
        Middle Ages. The other two volumes are devoted to
        nineteenth-century Polish music and the music of Chopin,
        which are the main areas of Belza's interest.

129.   Chaniecki, Zbigniew. "Dyskantyści w kapelach polskich
            od XVI do XVIII wieku (cz. I). Pueri cantores"
            [Discantists at Polish chapels from the sixteenth to
            eighteenth centuries (Pt. 1)]. *Muzyka* 18, no. 4
            (1973): 28-43.

Formulates a view of the place and duties of boy
singers in Polish chapel choirs. Many locations,
cities, and chapels are incorporated into this
comprehensive choir study.

130. _____. "Dyskantyści w kapelach polskich od XVI do
     XVIII wieku (cz. II). Discantistae castrati"
     [Discantists at Polish chapels from the sixteenth
     to eighteenth centuries (Pt. 2)]. *Muzyka* 19, no. 1
     (1974): 35-53.

Continues the study of singers at Polish chapels by
considering the role of castrati and focusing on
specific singers. High male voices were replaced with
women beginning in the eighteenth century.

131. Chechlińska, Zofia and Jan Stęszewski, eds. *Polish
     Musicological Studies*, 2 vols. to date. Kraków:
     Polskie Wydawnictwo Muzyczne, 1977- .
     ISBN 8322402635 ML 5.P644

An irregular serial publication which translates
important Polish research into English. The
translations are often rather stiff. In volume 2
further examples to cover the articles by Witold
Lutosławski, Ludwik Bielawski, and Anna Czekanowska
are found on pp. 303-40. This is not represented in
the Table of Contents. The book also carries a
separate score of Lutosławski's *Jeux vénitiens*. The
section "Lectures, Classes, Seminars" includes a list
of faculty and addresses of the various musicological
departments in Poland. A directory of members of the
Musicological Section of the Polish Composers Union
and a calendar of musicological events is also appended
to each volume of studies.

Reviews: Detlef Gojowy, *Musikforschung* 32, no. 3
(1979): 329; Stefan Jarociński, *Muzyka* 25, no. 4
(1980): 110-14; *Ruch Muzyczny* 22, no. 7 (1978): 19.

132. Chwałek, Jan. "Księga rachunkowa kapeli kolegiackiej
      w Sandomierzu" [An account book of the collegiate
      chapel in Sandomierz]. *Muzyka* 18, no. 3 (1973):
      130-31.

      Analyzes archival expense records from the years 1682
      to 1811.

133. _____. "Muzycy kapeli kolegiackiej w Sandomierzu w
      latach 1682-1812" [Musicians of the collegiate
      chapel in Sandomierz in the years 1682-1812].
      Muzyka 19, no. 4 (1974): 70-72.

      Offers an alphabetical listing of musicians with dates
      of activity and specific role.

134. Djuric, Jelena M. *The Music of Eastern Europe.*
      Columbus, Ohio: American Association for the
      Advancement of Slavic Studies, 1978. 66 pp.
      ML 420.D6

      Poland, pp. 39-44. A concise history which names only
      major Polish composers from the Middle Ages through
      Baroque. Skips to the nineteenth century and the
      composers Chopin, Moniuszko, and Wieniawski.

135. Dobrzycki, Jerzy. *Hejnał krakowski* [The Bugle Call of
      Cracow], 2nd ed. Kraków: Polskie Wydawnictwo
      Muzyczne, 1983. 105 pp. ISBN 8322400063
      ML 297.8.K7 D6

      A popular book recalling the story of the well-known
      hejnał [trumpet call] heard daily in Cracow. It is
      printed with many photographs and includes summaries
      in English and German.

136. Dufourq, Norbert, ed. *Larousse Encyclopedia of Music.*
      New York: World Publishing Co., 1971. 576 pp.
      ML 160.L34

      Two sections are devoted to music in Poland. Pages
      303-312 cover "Polish music from earliest times to the
      end of the nineteenth century" by identifying major

composers and types of pieces. The information
spanning the Renaissance through eighteenth century is
scanty, but Chopin and other better known Polish
composers are addressed in the section on Romanticism.
The twentieth century is the focus of pages 461-463:
"Central European music: Poland." This short overview
concentrates on the group Young Poland and Szymanowski,
with some space provided to post-war composers.

137. Dworzyńska, Wiesława. "Kultura muzyczna Warszawy w
     okresie średniowiecza i renesansu" [The musical
     culture of Warsaw in the Middle Ages and Renaissance].
     In *Studia Hieronymo Feicht septuagenario dedicata,*
     ed. Zofia Lissa, 190-197. Kraków: Polskie
     Wydawnictwo Muzyczne, 1967.

     Presents information on early music in Warsaw at both
     church and court. Focuses on the music at the
     Cathedral of St. John as this church rose in importance
     through the centuries. Also describes instrumental
     music at court and the increase of musical activity
     that accompanied the move of the Royal Court to
     Warsaw.

     Review: Andrzej Chodkowski, *Muzyka* 15, no. 3 (1970):
     98-111.

138. Dziębowska, Elżbieta, Zofia Helman, Danuta Idaszak,
     Adam Neuer. *Studia Musicologica: aesthetica,
     theoretica, historica.* [Lissa Festschrift.]
     Kraków: Polskie Wydawnictwo Muzyczne, 1979. 440 pp.
     ISBN 8322401051   ML 55.L52

     The introduction to this volume outlines the career of
     the musicologist Zofia Lissa, including also a
     bibliography of her writings. Articles authored by an
     international representation of music scholars appear
     in English, German, Italian, Polish, or Russian. Only
     a few of the contributions relate directly to Polish
     music.

139. Erhardt, Ludwik. *Music in Poland.* Warsaw: Interpress
     Publishers, 1975. 164 pp. ML 306.E7313

Summarizes the history of Polish music, giving
attention only to prominent composers and important
compositions. Supplements each chapter with a
discography of Muza recordings of music in that period.
The short book is relatively strong on twentieth-
century achievements for its size. Supplies a window
on musical life in the 1970s.

Review: Henri Musielak, *Revue de Musicologie* 61, no. 2
(1975): 350-51.

140. Gablenz, Thomas. "Organ Building in Poland."
      Diapason 53, no. 6 (May 1962): 8-9; 28-29; 53, no. 7
      (June 1962): 36-37.

This short history of organ building and builders in
Poland concentrates on specific instruments rather
than attempting a comprehensive treatment of the
subject. Stop lists are provided for these selected
historical instruments. The main criterion for
inclusion appears to be the availability of information
as provided by Polish organists.

141. Giełżyński, Wojciech. *Culture in Poland*. Warsaw:
      Interpress Publishers, 1975. 93 pp. DK 4115.G53

The single chapter on music presents a very short
survey of the history of Polish music through the first
half of the twentieth century. There is also
information provided on concert organizations,
festivals and competitions, music schools, and popular
music. The book was printed in English, French,
German, Russian, and Spanish, as well as Polish.

142. Gołos, Jerzy. "Liber Missarum z Archiwum Kapituły
      Warszawskiej" [A mass book from the archives of the
      Warsaw Chapterhouse]. *Muzyka* 18, no. 1 (1973): 40-
      50.

A descriptive essay on Archiwum Akt Dawnych
Archdiecezji Warszawskiej *Ms. M4*, which originated at
Warsaw's Collegiate Chapel. Diagrams the structure
and contents of the manuscript and provides a thematic
catalog of the contents.

143. _____. "Modern Organ Music in Poland." *Polish
      Music* 3, no. 3 (1968): 16-20.

Surveys nineteenth- and twentieth-century organ music,
as well as prominent organists after 1900. Further
mentions active composers and their musical styles,
organ competitions, and the state of organ instruction.

144. _____. "Muzykalia biblioteki klasztora karmelitów na
      piasku w Krakowie" [Music in the library of the
      Carmelite Monastery in Cracow]. *Muzyka* 11, no. 3-4
      (1966): 86-97.

Presents 28 liturgical manuscripts from the fourteenth
to eighteenth centuries, 5 theoretical treatises, and
three prints all found in the chapter library.
Catalogs the contents of the manuscripts, treatises, and
prints, and additionally offers two examples of polyphony from a 1747 Missal. Three facsimiles are
published with the article. Includes an English
summary.

145. _____. "Old Polish Organ Music." *Polish Music* 3,
      no. 2 (1968): 3-8.

Reviews music from sixteenth-century Polish tablatures.
Explains the Italian elements in Polish organ music of
the seventeenth century. Catholic music of the early
period features alternative settings of liturgical
items. In the sixteenth century, Polish organ music
was second only to the music of Germany in forming a
distinctive keyboard style.

146. Görlich, Joachim Georg. "Deutsch-polnische Beziehungen
      in der Musik." *Musik des Ostens* 5 (1969): 49-68.

Covers musical contact between Poland and Germany from
the sixteenth century, beginning with a quote from
Agricola's *Musica instrumentalis deudsch*. Considers
both Polish musicians' influence in Germany and German
musicians' activities to the east. As the chronology
approaches the nineteenth century, more detail is
recorded. In the twentieth century the many occasions
for travel and contact undermine the significance of
their note.

147. Jachimecki, Zdzisław. *Muzyka polska w rozwoju
      historycznym* [Polish music in historical develop-
      ment], 2 vols. Kraków: Nakładem Księgarnii
      Stefana Kamińskiego, 1948.

      An outdated history of Polish music from the medieval
      song Bogurodzica through the works of Chopin. The book
      remains of some value, nevertheless, for the musical
      examples, some of which are in the original notation,
      and for references to nineteenth-century sources
      which existed before September 1939.

148. _____. "Polish Music." *Musical Quarterly* 6 (1920):
           553.

      This article, written to relate the history of Polish
      music to American readers, concentrates on the late
      Renaissance and early Baroque periods, continuing into
      the nineteenth century with Chopin, Moniuszko,
      Wieniawski, and Szymanowski. Jachimecki emphasizes
      Polish connections with Western Europe, such as the
      exportation of the polonaise and mazurka. The
      information contained in this article has been
      corrected, expanded, and refined by subsequent
      research.

149. Jarociński, Stefan. *Antologia polskiej krytiki
      muzycznej XIX i XX wieku* [Anthology of Polish music
      criticism of the nineteenth and twentieth
      centuries]. Kraków: Polskie Wydawnictwo Muzyczne,
      1955. 523 pp. ML 306.J27

      Jarociński begins with an introduction on music
      criticism and its background in Poland. He presents
      the writings of fourteen critics, taken mostly from
      newspaper articles and reviews. Music criticism of
      the nineteenth century is the most heavily represented.

      Review: Jan Prosnak, *Muzyka* 1, no. 1 (1955): 164-67.

150. _____. *Polish Music.* Warszawa: Polskie Wydawnictwo
      Naukowe, 1965. 327 pp. ML 306.J28

Histories of each period were supplied by specialists
in the area. Unfortunately, the book is a short
music history without much discussion of the music,
often resulting in a chronology of the most important
names and pieces. Some of the authors do add their
own concepts and interpretations of Polish music
history. In the twentieth-century section, composers
are featured with short biographies and Polish musical
life is explained. The English translation is quite
good. Illustrative plates can be found throughout the
book. A substantial bibliography is arranged by
historical period.

Reviews: Czesław R. Halski, *Music and Letters* 47,
no. 4 (1966): 339-41; François Lesure, *Revue de
musicologie* 52, no. 2 (1966): 240-41; Irena Poniatowska,
Muzyka 12, no. 1 (1967): 102-4; *Ruch Muzyczny* 10, no. 7
(1966): 17-18.

151. Kański, Józef. "Le Grand Théâtre de Varsovie." *La
     Musique en Pologne* 6/7 (1970-1971): 14-18.

Describes the opera tradition from the beginning of
opera in seventeenth-century Poland. The article
considers the achievements of nineteenth-century opera
in Warsaw, the presentation of Moniuszko's *Halka* in
1858, and more recent twentieth-century activities.
Mentions specific productions, music directors, and
foreign tours of the Teatr Wielki company.

152. Kański, Józef, ed. *Teatr Wielki w Warszawie* [The
     Great Theater in Warsaw]. Warszawa: Wydawnictwa
     Artystyczne i Filmowe, 1965. Not paginated.
     ML 1740.8.W4 T44

This album was compiled to celebrate the opening of
the rebuilt theater following World War II. Offers
photographs of the theater's history and an extensive
essay on the history of opera in Warsaw beginning
before the opening of the original building in 1833.
Includes a table of directors of the opera over its
history. Only the introduction is translated into
English.

153. Kozłowski, Józef. *Śpiewy proletariatu polskiego*
      [Songs of the Polish proletariat]. Kraków: Polskie
      Wydawnictwo Muzyczne, 1977. 197 pp. ML 2851.P6 K69

      A general history of socialist songs from 1882 onwards,
      placed within the context of revolutionary and
      workers' songs of the nineteenth and twentieth
      centuries. Specific songs are presented with the music
      and full text. Interspersed are photographs of music
      prints and related documents. The author connects the
      popularity of the music to the movement of socialism
      in Poland.

      Review: Elżbieta Illasiewicz, *Muzyka* 23, no. 2 (1978):
      96-98.

154. Kratzenstein, Marilou. "A Survey of Organ Literature
      and Editions: Hungary and Poland." *Diapason* 67
      (October 1976): 14-15, 18.

      Reviews monuments of Polish organ music chronologically
      from the sixteenth through twentieth centuries.
      Mentions organ builders and foreign musicians in Poland.
      Includes a list of editions and collections of organ
      music by Polish composers.

155. Lissa, Zofia, ed. *The Book of the First International
      Musicological Congress Devoted to the Works of
      Frederick Chopin.* Warszawa: PWN-Polish Scientific
      Publishers, 1963. 755 pp. ML 410.C54 I48

      Contains a number of papers related to Polish music,
      but not directly on Chopin and his works. Selected
      articles include:

      Barfuss, Franciszek. "Die polnische historische Oper
      in den Jugendjahren Chopins," pp. 503-6.
      Halski, Czesław R. "The Polish Origin of the Polka,"
      pp. 530-37.
      Prokopowicz, Maria. "Musique imprimée à Varsovie en
      1800-1830," pp. 593-597. See item 329.
      Rudziński, Witold. "Źródła stylu muzycznego Stanisława
      Moniuszki" [Sources of the musical style of Stanisław
      Moniuszko], pp. 598-600.

Sutkowski, Adam. "The Pelpin Organ Tablature (1620-1630):
A Valuable Musical Document of Polish Music Culture in
Late Renaissance," pp. 628-29.
Wilkowska-Chomińska, Krystyna. "Nicolas de Cracovie
et la musique de la Renaissance en Pologne," pp. 640-
45.

Reviews: Maurice Brown, *Music and Letters* 45, no. 3
(1964): 268-70; Peter J. Pirie, *Music Review* 25, no. 4
(1964): 365-66; *Ruch Muzyczny* 7, no. 24 (1963): 17;
Ewald Zimmermann, *Musikforschung* 19, no. 1 (1966): 96-
97; *Notes* 22, no. 1 (1965): 716-17; *Musica* 19, no. 6
(1965): 327; *Beiträge zur Musikwissenschaft* 9, no. 1
(1967): 71-74.

156. _____. *Polsko-rosyjskie miscellanea muzyczne* [Polish-
        Russian musical miscellany]. Kraków: Polskie
        Wydawnictwo Muzyczne, 1967. 469 pp. ML 300.L495 P6

A collection of articles written to explore the musical
contacts between Russians and Poles from as early as the
fifteenth century. The contributors examine the work
of specific composers, identify cross influences, and
provide details concerning the activities of Poles who
spent part of their careers in Russia. The bibliography
includes Polish literature on Russian music. All the
articles are in Polish.

Reviews: *Ruch Muzyczny* 12, no. 11 (1968): 17;
Sovetskaya Muzyka 32 (May 1968): 120-24; *Muzyka* 13,
no. 4 (1968): 98-101.

157. Łyjak, Wiktor Z. "Nowe informacje o zespołach
        muzycznych w Polsce" [New information about musical
        groups in Poland]. *Muzyka* 29, no. 3 (1984): 91-96.

Publishes short bits of information on specific chapels
of the eighteenth and nineteenth centuries taken from
ecclesiastical records. Most of the information
pertains to lists of musical instruments.

158. Maciejewski, Tadeusz. "Notatki z przeszłości
        muzycznej Łowicza" [Notes from old music of Łowicz].
        Muzyka 18, no. 3 (1973): 91-109; 19, no. 1 (1974):
        77-78.

A musical history of the city of Łowicz. Focuses on
music from the collegiate chapel of Łowicz now in the
collection of the Warsaw Music Society. Catalogs the
relevant sources on Łowicz contained in this library.

159. _____. "Polish Organ Music up to the End of the
        Nineteenth Century." *Polish Music* 13, no. 2 (1978):
        3-11.

Concentrates on the literature notated in Polish
tablatures and other early manuscript examples.
Describes the decline of organ composition in the
eighteenth and nineteenth centuries. With the nineteenth century a number of organ composers are quickly
mentioned, with the article continuing through the
romantic compositional style of M. Surzyński.

160. McCredie, Andrew D. "New Perspectives in European
        Music Historiography: A Bibliographical Survey of
        Current Research in Medieval and Renaissance Slavic
        and Byzantine Sources." *Miscellanea Musicologica:
        Adelaide Studies in Musicology* 4 (1969): 22-127.

"Poland," pp. 24-70. Reviews the historiography of
Polish music in research on the Middle Ages through
the eighteenth century. In assessing the literature,
McCredie pays close attention to contributions in
congress reports. The emphasis is maintained on the
main musicologists of the mid-twentieth century, such
as Feicht, Lissa, and Chomiński, and to a lesser
extent Szweykowski and Perz. Manuscript sources are
given special consideration. Many references to the
Polish literature were extracted from the articles in
Musik in Geschichte und Gegenwart. This coverage of
the musicological literature results in a good survey
of early Polish music, including different genres and
sources.

161. Morawski, Jerzy. "Les conditions du developpement de
        la culture musicale du passe en Pologne et en
        France (similitudes et différences)." *Muzyka* 17,
        no. 2 (1972): 18-28. Translation of "Warunki
        rozwoju kultury muzycznej w dawnych wiekach w Polsce
        i we Francji (podobieństwa i roznice)." *Muzyka* 17,
        no. 2 (1972): 5-17.

Compares the general cultural development of the two
countries during the Middle Ages, an unlikely approach
generated by the cultural exchange which was the aim
of this journal volume. Notes differences in the
development of music styles, considering both sacred
and secular music. Concludes that polyphony in Poland
was not as well developed as in France during the
period.

162. *New Oxford History of Music,* 10 vols. London: Oxford
University Press, 1954- . ML 160.N44

Through his editorship of several volumes in the series
and contribution of a number of specialized articles,
Gerald Abraham can be credited with the excellent
coverage of Polish and East European music in the *New
Oxford History of Music.* Each volume is well-documented
with generous footnotes and bibliographical citations.
See items 207, 225, 238, 292, 377.

163. Ochlewski, Tadeusz, ed. *An Outline History of Polish
Music.* Warsaw: Interpress Publishers, 1979.
194 pp.

Waldorff, Jerzy. "Introduction," pp. 8-23.
Obniska, Ewa. "Early Music," pp. 24-73.
Swolkień, Henry. "From Chopin to Szymanowski," pp. 74-
133.
Michalski, Grzegorz. "New Music," pp. 134-86.

An outline of composers and their works, and the most
important historical trends. Incorporates post-war
research. The introduction discusses musical life and
institutions in Poland. Presented without
documentation; does contain a name index. There are
about 80 pages of illustrations at the end of the
volume.

164. Perz, Mirosław. "Ancienne musique polonaise et sa
place dans la culture européene." *Ruch Muzyczny* 12,
no. 17 (September 1-15, 1968): 14-15.

This article is a condensed history of Polish music
to the nineteenth century. It relates Polish

achievements to the music of Western Europe, and
because of this aim tends to mention works that
specifically reveal this connection. This issue of
Ruch Muzyczny was published in French to coincide with
the arrival of foreigners for the Warsaw Autumn
Festival in that year.

165. Podejko, Paweł. "Na marginesie dotychczasowych
      wzmianek o życiu muzycznym na Jasnej Górze w
      Częstochowie" [Marginalia on the references to date
      concerning musical life at the Jasna Góra Monastery
      in Częstochowa]. *Muzyka* 12, no. 1 (1967): 37-42.

      Continued archival research required correction of
      previously published literature on musical activities
      at the monastery. Relates particularly to the
      author's study on unknown Polish musicians (item 166).

166. _____. *Nieznani muzycy Polscy: kompozytorzy,*
      dyrygenci, instrumentaliści, wokaliści (1572-1820)
      [Unknown Polish musicians: composers, conductors,
      instrumentalists, and vocalists (1572-1820)].
      Z dziejów muzyki polskiej, no. 11 Bydgoszcz:
      Bydgoskie Towarzystwo Naukowe, 1966. 132 pp.
      ML 306.P75n

      Presents some fragmentary information on 371 musicians
      (28 of them composers) of Polish or other origin who
      worked primarily at Poland's chapels. Podejko cites
      archival records at Jasna Góra in Częstochowa as the
      sources of most of his information. This biographical
      dictionary is supplemented with a list of specific
      sources cited, an index of places, and an English
      summary of the introduction.

167. Reiss, Józef. *Almanach muzyczny krakowa 1780-1914*
      [Musical almanac of Cracow, 1780-1914], 2 vols.
      Kraków: Nakładem Tow. Miłośników historii i zabytków
      Krakowa, 1939. ML 21.R42

      Volume 1 chronicles Cracow's opera presentations and
      concert events, including performances of military
      music. The book is organized by headings of composers,
      institutions, such as the Cracow Philharmonic, and

music societies. The second volume is organized more
by persons and includes a listing of concerts from
1780 to 1914. Provides an index of names for access
to information on specific musicians.

168. _____. *Mała historia muzyki, popularny podręcznik
dla uczniów i samouków* [A short history of music,
a popular handbook for students and self-learners].
Kraków: Polskie Wydawnictwo Muzyczne, 1960.

A general music history text which incorporates aspects
of Polish music. The short sections on the history of
Polish music include: Polish music of the seventeenth
century, Polish style in music of the eighteenth
century, Polish music before Chopin, the music of
Chopin, Polish music after Moniuszko, and the music of
Young Poland.

Review: *Ruch Muzyczny* 4 (September 15, 1960): 17-18.

169. Śledziński, Stefan. *Muzyka polska. Informator* [Polish
music. Guidebook]. Kraków: Polskie Wydawnictwo
Muzyczne, 1967. 505 pp. ML 306.S55

Part 1 of the book features essays on each period of
music history by recognized specialists. Twentieth-
century music, folklore, and the performance of music
in Poland are subjects also featured in individual
essays. Part 2 provides basic information (with
addresses) on music institutions and organizations,
publishers, schools, libraries and museums, music
stores, and festivals. Although the addresses are
potentially very useful, some of them may be outdated
at this time. A major section of the book is a catalog
of available orchestral, chamber, solo, choral, vocal,
and stage works with their respective instrumentations.
For a modest size book, a great deal of information
can be extracted.

170. Świętochowski, Robert. "Kapela oo. Dominikanów w
Gidlach" [The chapel of the Dominican Fathers in
Gidel]. *Muzyka* 18, no. 4 (1973): 58-74.

Archival documents deriving from the years 1615 to
1775 are employed to compile a local musical history.
Lists over 100 musicians active in Gidel.

171. Szamajewa, Kira. "Muzyka polska w Kijowie" [Polish
          music in Kiev]. *Muzyka* 17, no. 1 (1972): 59-73.

Presents the highlights of Polish-oriented concert
life, beginning with the mid-nineteenth century.
Concerts presented by Henryk Wieniawski and other
Poles on tour, and a production of Moniuszko's *Halka*
in 1874 are some of the major events. In the early
twentieth century, Jan Paderewski, Wanda Landowska,
and Artur Rubinstein visited Kiev, and they were
followed by other performers as twentieth-century
musical life unfolded.

172. Szczepanik, Teresa Janina. "Studies in the history of
          Polish music from the Middle Ages to the present
          day; an annotated translation of five essays."
          M.Mus. thesis, University of Miami, 1976.

Translates five selected studies from Polish into
English. Selections include: Feicht, "Music in medieval
Poland," *Studia nad muzyką polskiego średniowiecza*
(item 184); Reiss, "Leaders of Polish music during
the Golden Age" and "Master-builders of Polish musical
culture at the beginning of the 19th century" in
Najpiękniejsza ze wszystkich jest muzyka polska;
Strumiłło, "The origins of Polish opera," *Szkice z
polskiego życia muzycznego 19. wieku* (item 348); and
Chomiński, "Serial dodecaphony in Poland," *Kultura
muzyczna polski ludowej 1944-1955* (item 464).

173. Wawrzykowska-Wierciochowa, Dioniza. *Polska pieśń
          rewolucyjna. Monografia historyczna* [Polish
          revolutionary songs. Historical monograph].
          Warszawa: Wydawnictwo Związkowe CRZZ, 1970. 443 pp.

Covers patriotic songs from 1791 to World War II.
Discusses the origin of songs, their meaning in
historical context, and publications and performance
history. Some of the melodies are provided. Includes
a first line index, title list, and name index.

174. Węcowski, Jan. "Polish Religious Music." *Polish Music*
     15, no. 1-2 (1980): 3-21; 15, no. 3 (1980): 9-27;
     15, no. 4 (1980): 15-34; 16, no. 1-2 (1981): 14-32;
     16, no. 3-4 (1981): 29-47; 17, no. 1-2 (1982): 39-
     62; 17, no. 3-4 (1982): 22-42; 18, no. 1-2 (1983):
     21-33; 18, no. 3-4 (1983): 21-35.

     Religious music in Poland begins with the inception of
     Roman Catholicism in 966. The article covers centers
     of liturgical music and extant manuscripts. The
     overview continues through discussion of the specific
     characteristics of Polish religious music, the main
     composers, and prominent institutions. Tends to
     merely list names of the composers as the history of
     Polish church music approaches the twentieth century.

175. *Z dziejów polskiej kultury muzycznej* [From the history
     of Polish musical culture]. Vol. 1, Kultura
     staropolska [Old Polish Culture], ed. Stefani
     Łobaczewska, Tadeusz Strumiłło, and Zygmunt M.
     Szweykowski. Kraków: Polskie Wydawnictwo Muzyczne,
     1958. Vol. 2, Od Oświecenia do Młodej Polski [From
     the Enlightenment to Young Poland]. Kraków:
     Polskie Wydawnictwo Muzyczne, 1966. 358, 703 pp.
     ML 306.Z15

     The most comprehensive history of Polish music. The
     various chapters in each volume were written by leading
     Polish musicologists to cover the history of music in
     Poland from the Middle Ages through early twentieth
     century. The chapter structure of the second volume
     suffers from an orientation to only a few major
     composers. The well-documented writing concentrates on
     composers and their roles, but unfortunately the book
     is becoming increasingly out of date. Reproduces
     plates from various manuscript sources, but lacks
     musical examples to support the text. The appendixes
     include lists of composers' works, an extensive
     bibliography, and an index.

     Review: Ladislav Mokrý, *Musikforschung* 13, no. 1
     (1960): 70-72.

176. Zazulski, Kazimierz. "Życie muzyczne w szkole
       pijarskie w Łowiczu w XVII i XVIII wieku" [Musical
       life at the Piarist school in Łowicz in the
       seventeenth and eighteenth centuries]. *Muzyka* 18,
       no. 3 (1973): 110-21.

       After general information on the history of the Piarist
       order in Łowicz from the year 1668, documentary
       evidence is given of musical activities at the Piarist
       school and the city in general. Lists the contents
       of a register of instruments from the collegiate
       church.

177. Zientarski, Władysław. "Z dziejów parafialnej w
       Grodzisku Wielkopolskim" [From the parish history
       of Grodzisk Wielkopolski]. *Muzyka* 26, no. 1 (1981):
       45-54.

       Adds to information about the musical life of this
       town. Provides information gleaned from public records.

                              Middle Ages

178. Bąk, Fulgencjusz. "Średniowieczne Graduały
       Franciszkańskie" [Medieval Franciscan Graduals].
       Musica medii aevi 3 (1969): 91-112.

       Publishes comparative information on fourteen Polish
       Graduals. Finds that the books are consistent in the
       items included, although there are certain deviations
       in the Commune Sanctorum. The appendixes include an
       inventory of *Gradual G 205* and a list of sequences in
       all the manuscripts. The study includes an English
       summary.

179. Bernat, Zdzisław. "Pontyfikał wrocławski z XII wieku
       jako zabytek muzyczny" [The Wrocław Pontifical of
       the twelfth century as a musical historical
       monument]. *Musica medii aevi* 3 (1969): 7-29.

       Studies the manuscript Biblioteka Kapituła in Wrocław,
       Ms. 149. Determines that the cheironomic notation is
       in the manner of St. Gall, originating in the

Salzburg diocese. Rubrics in the manuscript give some
indication of the level of performance at Wrocław
Cathedral. The author compares this pontifical with
other Polish manuscripts and discusses variants in the
items present and their respective melodies. Includes
an English summary.

180. Biegański, Krzysztof. "Fragment jednego z najstarszych
     zabytków diastematycznych w Polsce (dodatek do ms.
     149 Biblioteka Kapituły Gnieznieńskiej - fr. 149)"
     [The fragment of one of the oldest diastematic
     monuments in Poland (supplement to ms. 149 of the
     Gniezno Chapterhouse Library)]. In *Studia Hieronymo
     Feicht septuagenario dedicata,* ed. Zofia Lissa,
     96-119. Kraków: Polskie Wydawnictwo Muzyczne, 1967.

     Reinterprets prior research on the *Missale plenarium*
     (see item 572, vol. 11) and fragment *Fr. 149.* Provides
     a description of the manuscript with photographs. The
     text is analyzed from a liturgical standpoint and
     compared to other manuscripts. The author determines
     from the notation and comparison of melodies that the
     fragment is of middle Italian provenance dating from
     the eleventh to twelfth centuries. He further
     speculates on why this manuscript is now held in Poland.

181. Brewer, Charles Everett. "The Introduction of the Ars
     nova into East Central Europe: A Study of Late
     Medieval Polish Sources," 2 vols. Ph.D. diss.,
     City University of New York, 1984. 633 pp.

     Discusses the spread of the Ars nova to Poland.
     Examines theoretical treatises and manuscripts in Ars
     nova notation. The medieval Polish sources are
     compared to those of Bohemia and Hungary.
     (Dissertation Abstracts 45 (1985): 2294-A)

182. Feicht, Hieronim. "Liturgical Music in Medieval
     Poland." *Polish Musicological Studies* 1 (1977): 58-
     124. See item 131.

     The chant tradition in Poland begins in 966 with the
     acceptance of Christianity in the Roman rite. Feicht
     discusses separately the Benedictine, Cistercian,

Dominican, and Franciscan versions of liturgical music, as well as Polish contributions to the chant repertory. The article concludes with a cursory examination of some of the music in Polish manuscripts. Represents a comprehensive introduction to chant in Poland. The study was previously published as "Muzyka liturgiczna w Polskim średniowieczu." *Musica medii aevi* 1 (1965): 9-52.

183. _____. "Mittelalterliche Choralprobleme in Polen." *Musik des Ostens* 2 (1963): 84-90.

The history of chant in Poland focuses on the relevant manuscripts and centers of activity. Discusses variants between Polish versions of the chant repertory and the Gregorian chant of Western Europe.

184. _____. *Studia nad muzyką polskiego średniowiecza* [Study on the music of the Polish Middle Ages]. Opera musicologica Hieronymi Feicht, no. 1. Kraków: Polskie Wydawnictwo Muzyczne, 1975. 400 pp. ML 306.2.F4

Contains twelve articles by Feicht on Polish music of the Middle Ages, including both general information on music in medieval Poland and specific studies. The subjects include Polish hymns and songs, the Bogurodzica song, the Polish chant repertory, and polyphonic music. Several articles are published in German, including "Mittelalterliche Choralprobleme in Polen" (see item 183) and "Quellen zur mehrstimmigen Musik in Polen vom späten Mittelalter bis 1600." All the Polish writings conclude with a summary in English. The book also has an extensive list of Feicht's musicological work and many examples and plates to support the ideas presented in the articles.

Reviews: Jan Stęszewski, *Muzyka* 14, no. 3 (1969): 109-13; Henri Musielak, *Revue de musicologie* 61, no. 2 (1975): 326-29; *Ruch Muzyczny* 19, no. 24 (1975): 18.

185. Göllner, Theodor. "Eine mehrstimmige tropierte
        Weinachtslektion in Polen." *Acta Musicologica* 37,
        no. 3-4 (1965): 165-178.

        Introduces the two-part piece "Jube domne benedicere"
        from the Stary Sącz, *Graduale D2*. Compares this to
        other sources. Provides three photographs of the
        manuscript and examples of the music copied in the
        original notation.

186. Lewański, Julian. "Dramat i dramatyzacje liturgiczne
        w średniowieczu polskim" [Drama and liturgical drama
        in medieval Poland]. *Musica medii aevi* 1 (1965):
        96-174.

        Organized by the subject matter of plays, including:
        Processio in Ramis Palmarum
        Mandatum
        Depositio Crucis
        Elevatio Crucis
        Visitatio Sepulchri
        Gives full Latin texts of liturgical dramas. Illustra-
        tions from manuscripts are found at the end of the
        volume.

187. Mälinowska, Maria. "Medieval Music in Poland."
        Archeology 26, no. 1 (1973): 38-42.

        Summarizes archaeological research that has increased
        our information about music in Poland during the sixth
        through thirteenth centuries. Describes instruments
        of that period from archaeological findings and
        iconography, providing plates and drawings of the
        instruments. These are mostly wind and string
        instruments, local versions of early musical instruments
        found throughout Europe.

188. Morawski, Jerzy. "De Accentibus epistolarum. Research
        on Liturgical Recitation in Poland." *Polish
        Musicological Studies* 2 (1986): 149-97. See item
        131.

        Studies Polish medieval sources with regard to
        recitation of epistles.

189. _____. *Polska liryka muzyczna w średniowieczu.*
      Repertuar sekwencyjny cystersów (XIII-XVI w.)
      [Polish musical poetry in the Middle Ages. The
      repertory of Cistercian sequences in the thirteenth
      to sixteenth centuries]. Warszawa: Polskie
      Wydawnictwo Naukowe, 1973. 338 pp. ML 3051.P64 M7

      Studies the Cistercian repertory in Poland as the
      beginning of a greater study on the Polish sequence.
      Presents the history of sequences and sources of
      sequences in Poland. Uncovers chant theory as applied
      to the sequence repertory and the performance practice
      of sequences. Characterizes the textual-musical
      relations in the Polish sequence and tries to place the
      Polish sequence in the context of a general European
      tradition. Includes a general index, index of textual
      incipits, and list of sources. Plates from various
      manuscripts are provided.

      Reviews: Tadeusz Maciejewski, *Muzyka* 19, no. 4 (1974):
      90-93; *Ruch Muzyczny* 17, no. 17 (1973): 9.

190. _____. "Uwagi o wielogłosowej praktyce wykonawczej na
      Śląsku" [Attention to the polyphonic performance
      practice in Silesia]. *Muzyka* 11, no. 2 (1966): 45-
      53, 150-51.

      The article concentrates on monasteries in Silesia
      beginning in the thirteenth century. Discusses the
      first examples of polyphony in Cistercian graduals and
      the incidence of alternatum practice in these
      manuscripts. It is not clear whether the latter pieces
      were intended as polyphony. The author describes the
      repertory of sacred music and suggests a possible
      performance practice. He interprets specific markings
      in sequences of the *Gradual of St. Vincent Norbertans*
      from Wrocław. An English summary is provided.

191. Perz, Mirosław. "The Oldest Source of Polyphonic Music
      in Poland--Fragments from Stary Sącz." *Polish
      Musicological Studies* 1 (1977): 9-57. See item 131.

      Presents information about a manuscript of organa,
      2-voice motets, and conductus from the Library of the

Convent of St. Clare at Stary Sącz. Perz reconstructs
the arrangement of the original manuscript, placing
the 42 pieces and 5 mirror impressions that remain.
The music is compatible with the repertory of F, W2,
and Ma.

192. _____. "Organum, Conductus und mittelalterliche
Motette in Polen: Quellen und Probleme." In
*International Musicological Society. Report of the
Eleventh Congress. Copenhagen 1972, 593-97.*
Copenhagen: Edition Wilhelm Hansen, 1979.
ISBN 8774550268   ML 26.I6 v. 11

See item 193.

193. _____. "Organum, conductus i średniowieczny motet w
Polsce. Źródła i problemy" [Organum, conductus, and
medieval motet in Poland; sources and problems].
Muzyka 18, no. 4 (1973): 3-11.

Considers the dissemination of Notre Dame polyphony to
Poland. Discusses examples from the *Magnus liber
organi* corpus in Polish manuscripts leading to the
hypothesis that by about 1300 a mannered form of the
Parisian school had reached Eastern Europe.

194. Pikulik, Jerzy. "Graduał płocki z XIV/XV wieku" [The
Płock Gradual from the fourteenth to fifteenth
centuries]. *Muzyka* 18, no. 2 (1973): 95-99.

Lists and discusses the sequences in this Gradual.

195. _____. "Sekwencje polskie" [The Polish sequences].
Musica medii aevi 4 (1973): 7-128; *Musica medii aevi*
5 (1976): 6-194.

There are several review articles related to this research
on the Polish sequence.

196. Kowalewicz, Henryk. "Uwagi filologa o pracy Jerzego
     Pikulika 'Sekwencje polskie'" [Philological cautions
     regarding the work of Jerzy Pikulik: "Polish
     Sequences"]. *Muzyka* 20, no. 4 (1975): 114-21.

197. Pikulik, Jerzy. "Henrykowi Kowalewiczowi w odpowiedzi"
     [In reply to Henryk Kowalewicz]. *Muzyka* 21, no. 3
     (1976): 91-97.

198. Pikulik, Jerzy. "Henrykowi Kowalewiczowi jeszcze raz
     w odpowiedzi" [Once more in answer to Henryk
     Kowalewicz]. *Muzyka* 23, no. 3 (1978): 110-12.

     Continues the discussion on the repertory of Polish
     sequences.

The differences of perspective on the medieval sequence in
Poland are further presented in the following pairs of
articles.

199. Kowalewicz, Henryk. "Najstarza sekwencja o św.
     Wojciechu: Annua recolamus--I. Tekst" [The oldest
     sequence on St. Adalbert--I. Text]. *Musica medii
     aevi* 3 (1969): 30-36.

200. Pikulik, Jerzy. "Najstarza sekwencja o św. Wojciechu:
     Annua recolamus--II. Melodia" [The oldest sequence
     on St. Adalbert--II. Melody]. *Musica medii aevi* 3
     (1969): 37-42.

201. Kowalewicz, Henryk. "Śląska sekwencja 'Presul sancte
     Fabiane'. Opracowanie filologiczne i tekst" [The
     Silesian sequence "Presul sancte Fabiane." A
     philological and textual study]. *Muzyka* 22, no. 2
     (1977): 89-97.

202. Maciejewski, Tadeusz. "Śląska sekwencja 'Presul sancte
     Fabiane'. Opracowanie muzykologiczne i melodia" [The
     Silesian sequence "Presul sancte Fabiane." A
     musicological and melodic study]. *Muzyka* 22, no. 2
     (1977): 97-100.

203. Reginek, Antoni. "Śpiewy pasji choralowej w Polsce w
      XV i XVI wieku" [The plainsong passion chant in
      Poland in the fifteenth and sixteenth centuries].
      Musica medii aevi 7 (1986): 55-116.

      Offers an analysis of melodic figures and variants
      among nine Polish sources of plainsong Passions. This
      results in the isolation of different monastic and
      diocesan traditions. The article begins with an early
      history of the Passion in European music. The
      manuscript sources studied are described in detail.
      Provides tables of variants and musical examples.
      Includes an English summary.

204. Węcowski, Jan. "Początki chorału benedyktyńskiego w
      Polsce (968-1150)" [The beginning of Benedictine
      chant in Poland (968-1150)]. *Muzyka medii aevi* 2
      (1968): 40-51.

      Reviews the introduction of the Benedictine order to
      Poland. The earliest Benedictine source, the *Codex
      Gertrudianus* was lost in the mid-nineteenth century.
      Węcowski discusses the *Sacramentarium tynieckie*
      (c. 1060) by considering the origin of the manuscript
      and its contents. This source is noteworthy for its
      illuminated initials and cheironomic notation. Lists
      four later Benedictine manuscripts.

205. Witkowska, Elżbieta. "Anonimowy trakat chorałowy ze
      zbiorów Biblioteki Ossolineum" [An anonymous chant
      treatise from the collections of the Ossolineum
      Library]. *Muzyka* 20, no. 2 (1975): 62-72.

      A study of Wrocław, Biblioteka Ossolineum *Ms. 2297/I*,
      listing its contents on the subject of chant theory.
      Provides a concordance with the *Opusculum monochordale*
      of Valendrim and discusses the anonymous author's
      classification of music compared to other theorists.

206. Witkowska-Zaremba, Elżbieta. "Źródła rękopiśmienne do
        teorii muzyki w Polsce w XIII-XVI wieku" [Manuscript
        sources for the theory of music in Poland in the
        thirteenth through sixteenth centuries]. *Musica
        medii aevi* 7 (1986): 250-68.

        Lists manuscript sources in Poland, following the RISM
        format. Provides an English summary of the
        introduction.

                              Renaissance

207. Abraham, Gerald, ed. *The Age of Humanism 1540-1630.*
        New Oxford History of Music, vol. 4. London: Oxford
        University Press, 1968. ISBN 0193163047
        ML 160.N44 See item 162.

        Polish composers of the Renaissance and early Baroque
        are mentioned with discussion of key musical
        compositions. The text is supported by musical
        examples. Polish instrumental style and its influence
        outside of Poland is contained in a separate section.
        Composers represented include: Leopolita, Wacław z
        Szamotuł, Zieleński, and Mielczewski. The volume begins
        with a plate of the "Ballet polonaise of 1573."

        Reviews: Howard Brown, *Notes* 26 (1969): 133-36; Paul
        Doe, *Music and Letters* 51 (1970): 66-69; Jeremy Noble,
        Musical Times 109 (1968): 539-40; Claude V. Palisca,
        Journal of the American Musicological Society 23 (1970):
        133-36.

208. Braun, Werner. "Altpolnische Tänze in nordwestdeutscher
        Überlieferung." *Musik des Ostens* 6 (1971): 33-47.

        Discusses five anonymous Polish dances found in
        Oldenburg, Niedersachseschen Staatsarchiv, *Bestand 20-
        6D II C2.* Provides concordances with other manuscripts
        and compares variants with these other sources.

209. Głuszcz-Zwolińska, Elżbieta. "Über die Untersuchungen
     zur Musikkultur der polnischen Renaissance im 16.
     Jahrhundert." In *Musica slavica; Beiträge zur
     Musikgeschichte Osteuropas*, ed. Elmer Arro, 312-24.
     Wiesbaden: Franz Steiner Verlag, 1977. 446 pp.
     ISBN 3514021574 ML 240.B35

     Discusses the historiography of sixteenth-century Polish
     music, beginning with the scholarly work of nineteenth-
     century scholars. Liberal footnotes point to Polish
     sources for further research. Covers the work of the
     present generation of mature scholars, so well
     represented in this research guide.

210. Halski, Czesław Raymond. "Murky: A Polish Musical
     Freak." *Music and Letters* 39, no. 1 (January 1958):
     35-37.

     An etymology of the term "Murky bass," signifying
     broken octaves in the bass part of a keyboard piece.
     The term evidently derives from the Silesian village
     of Murcki and may be related to the use of traditional
     instruments in this region.

211. Hławiczka, Karol. "Zur Geschichte der polnischen
     evangelischen Gesangbücher des 16. und 17.
     Jahrhunderts." *Jahrbuch für Hymnologie und Liturgik*
     15 (1970): 167-91.

     A comprehensive history of Protestant songbooks
     beginning in 1544. There is a short description of
     each edition with notes on the amount of music in the
     book. Covers Lutheran songbooks, books of the
     Bohemian Brothers, as well as products of the Polish
     Reformation and songbooks of the Antitrinitarians.

212. Insko, Wyatt Marion. "The Cracow Tablature." Ph.D.
     diss., Indiana University, 1964. 510 pp.

     The Tablature of the Monastery of the Holy Spirit in
     Cracow is dated 1548. It contains mostly sacred works,
     the repertory relating to the tablature of Jan of
     Lublin. The composers of some works are identified

in the manuscript; others are identified by the author.
The author finds three styles of intabulation. The
dissertation includes transcriptions of the music.
(Dissertation Abstracts 26 (1966): 5473)

213. Klobubowska, Jadwiga. "Muzyka francuskiego renesansu
      w Polsce" [Music of the French Renaissance in Poland].
      Muzyka 17, no. 2 (1972): 29-38.

      Discusses anonymous works identified as French
      compositions in Polish manuscripts, mostly instrumental
      versions of French vocal works. Also addresses the
      issue of French prints in Poland. Includes a summary
      in French.

214. Perz, Mirosław. *Mikołaj Gomółka: monografia,* 2nd ed.
      Warszawa: Polskie Wydawnictwo Naukowe, 1981. 366 pp.
      ISBN 8322401507 ML 410.G639 P5

      A well-documented biography of Gomółka, including a
      presentation of sources. Focuses on an heuristic
      analysis of the first edition of *Melodie na psałterz
      polski,* including a watermark study of the paper.
      Compares Gomółka's music in this psalm collection to
      the work of other composers of the period by directly
      comparing melodies to other sixteenth-century sources.
      Identifies chromatic conflict between voice parts of
      psalms. Concludes that Gomółka's *Melodie na psałterz
      polski* is important in Polish cultural history as an
      experiment in literature and music.

      Reviews: Henri Musielak, *Revue de musicologie* 62, no. 2
      (1976): 306-9; Jan Stęszewski, *Muzyka* 19, no. 2 (1974):
      98-100.

215. _____. "Motety Marcina Leopolity" [The motets of
      Marcin Leopolita]. In *Studia Hieronymo Feicht
      septuagenario dedicata,* ed. Zofia Lissa, 157-89.
      Kraków: Polskie Wydawnictwo Muzyczne, 1967.

      Discusses the following motets, known from versions in
      organ tablatures:
      1. Resurgente Christo Domino
      2. Cibavit eas ex adipe frumenti Alleluia

3. Mihi autem nimis honorati sunt amici tui Deus
4. Spiritus domini replevit orbem terrarum
Analyzes the music for compositional technique and
form, making comparisons to other motets. Perz
speculates on the chronology of Leopolita's motet
writing.

216. _____. "Nieznany polski trakat choralowy Marka z
Płocka (1518)" [An unknown Polish chant treatise
of Marek of Płock]. *Muzyka* 13, no. 4 (1968): 75-80.

Describes the manuscript of the Biblioteka Klasztoru
Franciszkanów we Wschowie *Hortulus Musices Choralis,*
which adds to our knowledge of Marek of Płock.

217. Perz, Mirosław and Elżbieta Zwolińska. "Do dziejów
kapeli rorantystów w XVI stuleciu oraz biografii
Krzysztofa Borka" [The history of the Rorantist
chapel in the sixteenth century as well as the
biography of Krzysztof Borek]. *Muzyka* 16, no. 2
(1971): 34-47.

New information was gleaned from receipts of the
Rorantist chapel dating 1548 to 1594. Thirteen of the
thirty-five receipts concern the composer Borek, and
additionally there was found a contract from 1547.
The authors fit this information into what is known
of Borek's career and activities.

218. Sparger, Avealoie Dennis. "The Sacred Music of Andrzej
Hakenberger." D.M.A. diss., University of Illinois,
1981.

Provides a biography of Hakenberger (c. 1574-1627)
which places him within the context of Polish music of
the sixteenth to seventeenth centuries. The most
important part of this Catholic composer's career was
spent at the Protestant Marienkirche in Gdańsk. His
music is found in the Pelpin Tablature, and two motet
collections, *Sacri modulorum concentus* (pub. 1615) and
Harmonia Sacra (pub. 1617). Hakenberger's music shows
the influence of the Venetian style of the period. The
author describes the Marienkirche building and provides

specifications of the organ. The dissertation includes
editions of motets. The music manuscript and text are
legible, but not the most carefully copied.
(Dissertation Abstracts 42 (1982): 4642-A)

219. Szweykowska, Anna. "Przeobrażenia w kapeli królewskiej
      na przełomie XVI i XVII wieku" [The transformation
      in the royal chapel at the turn of the seventeenth
      century]. *Muzyka* 13, no. 2 (1968): 3-21.

      Details activities of the chapel of Sigismund III
      through court records. Notes changes in personnel as
      the chapel grew through the addition of Italian
      musicians. Shows that musicians came to Cracow from
      Italy, especially Rome, but also from Graz, Austria.

220. _____. "Widowiski baletowe na dworze Zygmunta III
      (4 czerwca 1592, 13 oraz 18 grudnia 1605)" [Ballet
      performances at the court of Sigismund III (4 June
      1592, 13 and 18 December 1605)]. *Muzyka* 11, no. 1
      (1966): 27-36, 85.

      Documents three ballet performances for weddings.
      Extant descriptions allow for reconstruction of
      performances. Emphasizes magnificent costumes. Quotes
      from sixteenth-century accounts in Polish and German.

221. Szweykowska, Anna and Zygmunt M. Szweykowski. "Wacław
      z Szamotuł--Renesansowy muzyk i poeta" [Wacław z
      Szamotuł--Renaissance musician and poet]. *Muzyka* 9,
      no. 1-2 (1964): 3-28, 127.

      Revises the composer's biography based on considerations
      of new sources. Focuses on activities in music and as
      a humanist. A summary in French is provided.

222. Szweykowski, Zygmunt M. "Kilka uwag o twórczości
      mszalnej Giovanni Francesco Aneria związanej z
      Polską" [Some remarks about the masses of G.F.
      Anerio connected with Poland]. *Muzyka* 17, no. 4
      (1972): 53-64.

Remarks on Anerio's version of the Palestrina, *Missa Papae Marcelli* and provides revised information on the dates of Anerio's activities in Poland. Also discusses this composer's *Missa Constantia* and *Missa Pulchra es*.

223. White, John R. "The Tablature of Johannes of Lublin." *Musica Disciplina* 17 (1963): 137-62.

Serves as an introduction to the author's edition of the manuscript published in the *Corpus of Early Keyboard Music* (see item 583). Gives general comments about the music and kinds of pieces. Speculates on the sources of the music, citing perpetuation of mistakes. Prints a catalog of the tablature with the short pieces arranged by type. Cites placement in the original manuscript.

224. Wilkowska-Chomińska, Krystyna. "Szkoła krakowska od końca XV do połowy XVI wieku" [The Cracow school from the beginning of the fifteenth century to the middle of the sixteenth century]. *Muzyka* 11, no. 2 (1966): 54-67, 152.

Follows five composers active in Cracow during this period: Mikołaj z Krakowa, Mikołaj z Chrzanowa, Seweryn Koń, N.Z., and Heinrich Finck. Observes style changes in the music of Finck during his stay in Poland from 1492 to 1510. Evidence of changes in Finck's rhythmic, harmonic, and polyphonic and structural practices can be found in Polish tablatures. Study reinforces the conclusion that Cracow was subject to greater influence from Italy than from the Netherlands. An English summary is provided.

Baroque

225.   Abraham, Gerald, ed. *Concert Music (1630-1750)*. New
       Oxford History of Music, vol. 6. London: Oxford
       University Press, 1986. 786 pp. ISBN 0193163063
       ML 160.N44 v. 6 See item 162.

       Overlaps with information in earlier volumes of the
       New Oxford History of Music and focuses on Polish
       dances in the music of other European composers.

226.   Buba, Jan, Anna Szweykowska and Zygmunt Szweykowski.
       "Kultura muzyczna u pijarów w XVII i XVIII wieku"
       [The musical culture among the Piarists in the
       seventeenth and eighteenth centuries]. *Muzyka* 10,
       no. 2 (1965): 15-32; *Muzyka* 10, no. 3 (1965): 20-32,
       98-99.

       Based on information gleaned from the Piarist Archives
       in Cracow. Gives original Latin references and Polish
       translations of documentary material. The names of
       many musicians are learned from these sources. The
       order was active musically in nine locations. The
       article also examines an inventory of instruments and
       music from Wieluń. Summary provided in French.

227.   Chaniecki, Zbigniew. "Nieznane kapele polskie z XVII i
       XVIII wieku" [Unknown Polish chapels from the
       seventeenth and eighteenth centuries]. *Muzyka* 17,
       no. 4 (1972): 84-96.

       Suggests a new category of "military orchestras."
       Gives information on thirteen ensembles from expense
       records preserved in archives in Cracow, Poznań, Lublin,
       and Warsaw.

228.   _____. "Przyczynki do dziejów kapel w Polsce"
       [Footnotes to the history of chapels in Poland].
       Muzyka 17, no. 1 (1972): 94-97.

       Presents notes on the court of Tomasz Józef Zamoyski
       (1678-1725), determined from expense records which
       list the names of musicians.

229. _____. "W sprawie kapeli Stanisława Lubomirskiego i
     początków opery włoskiej w Polsce" [In the affair
     of Stanisław Lubomirski's chapel and the beginnings
     of Italian opera in Poland]. *Muzyka* 13, no. 3
     (1968): 58-65.

     Corrects information previously published on music at
     the Lubomirski court and offers a list of musicians
     active from 1645 to 1649. Revises thought on the
     introduction of Italian opera in Poland by showing that
     resources for opera production were assembled by the
     late 1640s.

230. Chrzanowski, Tadeusz and Tadeusz Maciejewski. *Graduał
     karmelitański z 1644 roku o. Stanisława ze Stolca*
     [The Carmelite Gradual from 1644 of Father Stanisław
     of Stolec]. Warszawa: Instytut Wydawniczy Pax,
     1976. 111 pp. ML 410.S81224 C5

     Discusses the chant and art work of this liturgical
     book. In terms of music, Maciejewski isolates elements
     of Polish non-liturgical song in some of the chant
     melodies. Includes an inventory of the contents and
     musical examples for some of the chants. The elaborate
     miniatures of the manuscript are reproduced in black
     and white or color plates. Summarizes the information
     in French.

231. Długosz, Józef. "Rachunki kapeli nadwornej księżia
     Władysława Dominika Ostrogskiego w latach 1635-
     1642" [Receipts of the court chapel of Prince
     Władysław Dominik Ostrogski in the years 1635 to
     1642]. *Muzyka* 15, no. 1 (1970): 58-85.

     Examines archival records of receipts for music expenses
     at this magnate's court. The records reveal the size
     of the chapel's musical resources. Prints a list of
     the receipts.

232. _____. "Źródła do dziejów kapeli nadwornej
     Lubomirskich w latach 1595-1644" [Sources of the
     history of the Lubomirski court chapel in the years
     1595-1644]. *Muzyka* 13, no. 4 (1968): 84-88.

Corrects information on this court as included in the
Słownik muzyków polskich (see item 21) and adds new
information gleaned from archival sources.

233.   Feicht, Hieronim. *Studia nad muzyką polskiego
       renesansu i baroku* [Study on music of the Polish
       Renaissance and Baroque]. Opery musicologica
       Hieronymi Feicht, no. 3. Kraków: Polskie
       Wydawnictwo Muzyczne, 1980. 562 pp.
       ISBN 8322401310 ML 3677.F43

       Contains articles on the Leopolita *Easter Mass* and
       general works of the composers Dębolecki, Scacchi,
       Pękiel, Mielczewski, and Gorczycki. Also presented are
       overviews of Polish Baroque music, Dresden chapel music,
       and eighteenth-century Polish music. Summaries of the
       studies are given in English.

234.   Gołos, Jerzy. "Italian Baroque Opera in Seventeenth-
       Century Poland." *Polish Review* 8, no. 2 (1963):
       67-75.

       Discusses all early dramatic music, but especially
       Italian opera under Władysław IV (1632-1648).
       Continues through the eighteenth century.

235.   _____. "Repertuar pieśniowy wieku XVII w świetle nowo
       odkrytego rękopisu 127/56 Biblioteki Jagiellońskiej
       w Krakowie" [The repertoire of Polish secular song
       of the seventeenth century in light of the newly
       discovered manuscript 127/56 of the Jagiellonian
       Library in Cracow]. *Muzyka* 10, no. 2 (1965): 3-14,
       73.

       Tries to pair secular poetic texts with keyboard
       arrangements of music in the manuscript. An English
       summary is provided.

236.   _____. "An Unknown Keyboard Notation for the Early
       Seventeenth Century." *Polish Review* 8, no. 4 (1963):
       97-100.

Information on the notation of a non-music manuscript,
Biblioteka Jagiellońska *Ms. 24*. The music is French
and Italian secular vocal music of the late sixteenth
to seventeenth centuries. Gołos differentiates the
notational system from examples in Johannes Wolf,
Handbuch der Notationskunde (1919).

237. Krzyżaniak, Barbara. *Kantyczki z rękopisów
karmelitańskich (XVII/XVIII w.)* [Carols from
Carmelite manuscripts of the seventeenth to
eighteenth centuries]. Kraków: Polskie Wydawnictwo
Muzyczne, 1977. 226 pp. ML 3687.K79

An historical study and musical analysis of Polish
carols (*kolędy*), concentrating on the manuscript
Biblioteka Główna Uniwersytetu im. A. Mickiewicza w
Poznaniu, *Ch 251*. The songs are classified by function
and the repertory is searched for national elements.
The book has an English summary, list of concordances,
and bibliography.

238. Lewis, Anthony and Nigel Fortune. *Opera and Church
Music 1630-1750*. New Oxford History of Music, no.
5. London: Oxford University Press, 1975. 869 pp.
ISBN 0193163055 ML 166.N44 v. 5 See item 162.

Continues the discussion of Polish composers begun in
volume 4 of the series (see item 207) with the composers
Pękiel, Rożycki, Szarzyński, and Gorczycki. This
volume includes a bibliography and list of works by
Polish composers of the period.

239. Maciejewski, Tadeusz. "Inwentarz muzykaliów kapeli
karmelickiej w Krakowie na Piasku z lat 1665-1684"
[An inventory of musicalia of the Carmelite chapel
in Cracow from the years 1665-1684]. *Muzyka* 21,
no. 2 (1976): 77-99.

Adds considerably to the information in the *Słownik
muzyków polskich* (item 21) on this chapel. Lists 545
musical pieces and provides a list of instruments of
the chapel. Serves as a source of genres in the
repertory. Includes an alphabetical list of composers
and musicians.

240. _____. "Przyczynek do biografii Andrzeja Wołoszki
      (ca. 1700-1757) i do historii kapel karmelickach"
      [Footnote to the biography of Andrzej Wołoszko and
      to the history of Carmelite chapels]. *Muzyka* 20,
      no. 2 (1975): 73-81.

      A manuscript necrology in the Biblioteka Klasztoru
      Karmelitów in Cracow reveals fifty names of Russian
      and Lithuanian musicians attached to this order around
      the year 1688. The new information corrects the entry
      on Wołoszko published in item 21. Eighteenth-century
      inventories provide further lists of musicians and the
      instruments in use during the period.

241. Pamuła, Maria. "Pojęcie tonów i śpiewu kościelnego w
      'Musicae practicae erotemata' Starowolskiego"
      [The concept of modes and church singing in *Musicae
      practicae erotemata* of Starowolski]. *Muzyka* 19, no.
      1 (1974): 54-68.

      Discusses the seventeenth-century treatise of Szymon
      Starowolski (1588-1656) with regard to solmization,
      modes, mensural theory, and counterpoint.

242. Perz, Mirosław. "Inwentarz przemyski (1677)" [The
      Przemyśl Inventory (1677)]. *Muzyka* 19, no. 4 (1974):
      44-69.

      Describes the Franciscan manuscript Wrocław Ossolineum
      Ms. 9615/II (Wn microfilm No. 8124) which contains
      many names (or initials) and a register of music.
      Discusses the significance of the information.

243. _____. "Notatki do dziejów kapeli zamoyskiej w XVII
      stuleciu" [Notes on the history of the Zamoyski
      chapel in the seventeenth century]. *Muzyka* 20,
      no. 1 (1975): 76-79.

      Notes about the residence of Tomasz and Jan "Sobiepan"
      Zamoyski with a list of musicians active at the court
      from 1636-1660.

244. Skrzypczak, Sabina. "Notes towards a biography of the
     Polish composer Grzegorz Gerwazy Gorczycki."
     Musicology Australia 8 (1985): 33-38.

     Reviews the Polish literature on this composer and
     subsequently criticizes the traditional documentation
     for his birthdate. Provides a bibliography
     incorporating current research.

245. Stęszewski, Jan. "Marcina Mielczewskiego 'Canzon prima
     a 2' na tle rękopisu Biblioteki Jagiellońskiej sygn.
     127/56" [The "canzon prima a 2" in the background
     of the manuscript Biblioteka Jagiellońska signature
     127/56]. *Muzyka* 12, no. 1 (1967): 27-36.

     Compares this canzona to concordances in the Biblioteka
     Jagiellońska manuscript. Analyzes the melodies from
     the context of folk tunes and dance melodies.
     Stęszewski sees the origin of the music in popular
     melody and confirms in more detail the general premise
     that national dance rhythms were incorporated in music
     of the period.

246. Świętochowski, Robert. "Kapela oo. Dominikanów w
     Gidlach" [The chapel of the Dominican Fathers in
     Gidle]. *Muzyka* 18, no. 4 (1973): 58-74.

     Compiles a history from archival documents deriving
     from the years 1615 to 1775. Lists over 100 musicians
     active in Gidle.

247. _____. "Kapela oo. Dominikanów w Podkamieniu" [The
     Dominican Fathers' chapel in Podkamień]. *Muzyka* 21,
     no. 3 (1976): 56-76.

     Pieces together a history of the chapel in the
     seventeenth and eighteenth centuries. Provides a list
     of about 150 musicians.

248. Szweykowska, Anna. "Dramma per music w teatrze
     Władysława IV" [The 'dramma per musica' in the
     theater of Władysław IV]. *Muzyka* 15, no. 3 (1970):
     35-46.

Reports that ten new operas were staged at the royal
court from 1635 to 1648. Discusses each of the operas
and concludes that the themes are similar to Italian
works of the period. There is some individual
treatment of plot and theme by the librettist Puccitelli,
the Polish king's secretary. The theme of chivalry
was popular in Poland at that time. Includes an
English summary.

249.   _____. "Imprezy baletowe na dworze Władysław IV"
        [The ballet enterprise at the manor of Władysław IV].
        Muzyka 12, no. 2 (1967): 11-23.

Draws on the diary of Stanisław Radziwiłł to establish
the production of at least 13 ballets between 1633 and
1648. Shows that these productions were in the
Italian ballet style, but descriptions of the ballets
are too general to determine details. Ballets were
popular in the time that Cecilia Renata was queen
(died in 1644), and the entertainments were separated
from the carnival season during this period. During
the reign of Jan Kazimierz (c. 1650) the association
with carnival was reestablished. Summary in French.

250.   _____. "Kapela królewska Jana Kazimierza w latach
        1649-1652" [The royal chapel of Jan Kazimierz in
        the years 1649-1652]. *Muzyka* 13, no. 4 (1968):
        40-48.

Updates knowledge on music at the royal court by
considering a new source, Archiwum Głównym Akt Dawnych
ASK I 305. Establishes through these court records
that the chapel was as large as 70 people. The records
also provide information on the structure of music
groups at court.

251.   _____. "Kapele magnackie i szlacheckie w Polsce w
        połowie XVIII wieku" [Chapels of the magnates and
        nobility in Poland in the middle of the eighteenth
        century]. *Muzyka* 8, no. 1-2 (1963): 75-104, 205-6.

New information found in the eighteenth-century
newspapers *Kurier Polski* and *Gazeta Polska*. The article
offers an alphabetical list of names at whose courts
music activities can be documented.

252. _____. "Musical Theater in Poland." In *International
     Musicological Society. Report of the Twelfth
     Congress. Berkeley 1977,* ed. Daniel Heartz and
     Bonnie Wade, 698-701. Kassel: Bärenreiter and
     American Musicological Society, 1981. 912 pp.
     ISBN 3761806493 ML 26.I6 v. 12

     Presents information on the seventeenth-century
     "dramma per musica" at the royal court between 1635 and
     1648. Describes general format and style, commenting
     on intermedii, recitative, chorus, and staging. In
     the second half of the seventeenth century stage works
     in French, ballet, and Italian opera were presented.
     Also mentions school dramas, religious plays,
     intermedii, and literary comedies in Polish.

253. Szweykowska, Anna and Zygmunt M. Szweykowski. "W kręgu
     mecenatu rodu Sobieskich" [The Sobieski family's
     circle of patronage]. *Muzyka* 29, no. 3 (1984):
     3-24.

     Discusses the 1733 manuscript Biblioteka Akademii Sztuk
     Pięknych w Krakowie *Ms. HD 1528/1-3* from the collegiate
     church in Żółkiew, ancestral estate of Jan Sobieski.
     Presents a history of the collegiate chapel and offers
     notes about 14 anonymous musical works in the
     manuscript. Includes thematic catalog.

254. Szweykowski, Zygmunt M. "Concertato Style in Polish
     Vocal-Instrumental Music of the Seventeenth Century."
     Polish Musicological Studies 1 (1977): 155-66. See
     item 131. Originally published as "Styl
     koncertujący w polskiej muzyce wokalno-
     instrumentalnej." *Muzyka* 15, no. 1 (1970): 3-14.

     Discusses the widespread utilization of concertato
     techniques in Polish religious music of the seventeenth
     century. Provides examples of both successive
     concertato and the simultaneous type of concertato,
     and illustrates further concertato techniques displayed
     within melodic lines.

255. _____. "A Concise Characterization of the Polish
     Musical Production in the Baroque Era." In *Musica
     slavica. Beiträge zur Musikgeschichte Osteuropas*,
     ed. Elmer Arro, 325-33. Wiesbaden: Franz Steiner
     Verlag, 1977. 446 pp. ISBN 3514021574 ML 240.B35

     Begins with information on Italian musicians working at
     Polish music centers in the Baroque period. The author
     then discusses his own theory for the formal division
     of Polish Baroque sacred music. He adopts textual
     considerations as the basic criteria for formal
     systemization of Polish vocal-instrumental sacred
     music.

256. _____. "Jan Brant (1554-1602) i jego nowo odkryta
     twórczość muzyczna. Z muzycznych poszukiwań w
     Szwecji (III)" [Jan Brant (1554-1602) and his newly
     discovered musical creation. From musical research
     in Sweden (3)]. *Muzyka* 18, no. 2 (1973): 43-72.

     A documentary biography of the composer and description
     of his music.

257. _____. "Sylwetka kompozytorska Damiana Stachowicza
     (1658-1699)" [A silhouette of the composer Damian
     Stachowicz (1658-1699)]. *Muzyka* 7, no. 1 (1962): 3-
     13, 59.

     Presents what is presently known about the composer's
     life. Stachowicz was a member of the Piarist order in
     Łowicz. Discusses style of specific compositions. The
     summary is in French.

258. _____. "Tradition and Popular Elements in Polish Music
     of the Baroque Era." *Musical Quarterly* 56, no. 1
     (1970): 99-115.

     Views the incorporation of Polish traditional elements
     in art music of the seventeenth century as reflecting
     Sarmatism. Szweykowski finds that the uses of Polish
     elements coexist between the forms of art music of the
     general European Baroque and "traditional popular music,"
     resulting in a local art that transcends social
     divisions.

259. _____. "Unikalne druki utworów Aspirilia Pacellego.
      Z muzycznych poszukiwań w Szwecji (II)" [Unique
      prints of works of Aspirilio Pacelli. From musical
      research in Sweden]. *Muzyka* 17, no. 1 (1972): 74-
      93.

      Catalogs the nine Masses of Pacelli from the two
      remaining partbooks, Royal Library in Stockholm *147E*,
      music for the parts Altus Primi Chori and Tenor Primi
      Chori. Szweykowski further finds that partbooks for
      the motets in Pacelli's *Sacrae Cantiones*, preserved
      in the University Library of Uppsala, complement the
      books of the University Library, Wrocław, thus forming
      a complete set.

260. _____. "Wenecki koncert rondowy w polskiej praktyce
      kompozytorskiej okresu baroku" [The Venetian rondo
      concerto in the practice of Polish composers of the
      Baroque period]. In *Studia Hieronymo Feicht
      septuagenario dedicata*, ed. Zofia Lissa, 220-26.
      Kraków: Polskie Wydawnictwo Muzyczne, 1967.

      Analyzes seventeenth-century Venetian compositional
      techniques in the works of Mielczewski, Charśnicki,
      Szarzyński, and Kreczmar (1631-1696).

261. Targosz-Kretowa, Karolina. *Teatr dworski Władysława
      IV (1635-1648)* [The court theater of Władysław IV
      (1635-1648)]. Kraków: Wydawnictwo Literackie, 1965.
      341 pp. PN 2859.P63 W33

      Opens by presenting the history of theater in Poland
      from the Middle Ages and providing background on Italian
      theater during the time of Władysław's travels to Italy
      as crown prince. The study draws on written records
      (no musical scores or drawings are extant) to document
      presentations of Italianate theater, opera, ballet, and
      commedia dell'arte at Władysław's royal court.
      Provides an outline of activities. Summaries are
      included in English and Italian.

      Reviews: Wiarosław Sandelewski, *Rivista italiana di
      musicologia* 4 (1969): 151-56; Anna Szweykowska,
      Muzyka 11, no. 2 (1966): 162-70.

Classic and Pre-Classic

262. Abraham, Gerald. "Some Eighteenth-Century Polish
     Symphonies." In *Studies in Eighteenth-Century Music:
     A Tribute to Karl Geiringer on His Seventieth
     Birthday,* ed. H.C. Robbins Landon, with Roger E.
     Chapman, 13-22. New York: Da Capo Press, 1979.
     425 pp. ML 55.G24 S8

     Abraham reviews how knowledge of the symphony in Poland
     has increased since the 1930s. He summarizes the
     material presented in Polish publications, adding his
     own insight and assessment of the music and trying to
     relate the Polish symphony to influences from the West.
     The article concentrates on works of A. Haczewski,
     Bazyli Bohdanowicz, Jakub Gołąbek, Namieyski, Pietrowski,
     and Józef Elsner.

263. Belza, Igor'. *Mikhal Kleofas Ogin'skiy.* Moskva:
     Izdatel'stvo Muzyka, 1965. 127 pp. ML 410.045 B4

     Covers Ogiński's political activities, as well as his
     musical interests and compositions. Includes a
     bibliography.

264. Ciechanowiecki, Andrzej. *Michał Kazimierz Ogiński und
     sein Musenhof zu Słonim.* Beiträge zur Geschichte
     Osteuropas, no. 2. Köln: Bohlau Verlag, 1961.
     212 pp. ML 410.045 C5

     A history of Polish music in the eighteenth century
     emphasizing the role of chapel orchestras and music in
     the life of the Polish nobility. Provides a biography
     of M.K. Ogiński and his experience as a musician.
     Describes the musical resources at the family estate in
     Słonim, Lithuania, concentrating on the court theater,
     musical instruments, and repertory in the second half
     of the eighteenth century. The study is well-documented,
     relying chiefly on the Ogiński papers in the Potocki
     Archives of the Polish Academy of Sciences (PAN) in
     Cracow. Appendixes provide a list of musicians at
     Słonim and expense records for the court ballet,
     published in the original Polish, as well as German
     translation.

Reviews: Günter Birkner, *Musikforschung* 17, no. 3
(1964): 325-26; Jerzy Gołos, *Musical Quarterly* 49,
no. 4 (1963): 531-33; Jerzy Gołos, *Muzyka* 8, no. 3
(1963): 81.

265. Freytag, Werner. *Musikgeschichte der Stadt Stettin im*
      18. Jahrhundert. Greifswald: Universitätsverlag
      Ratsbuchhandlung L. Bamberg, 1936. 171 pp.
      ML 279.P6 no. 2

Covers music from the city's German period in the
eighteenth century, with a concentration on churches,
organists, concerts, and theaters. Discusses the
compositions of local composers. Appendixes include
lists of church and town musicians and the stop lists
of city organs.

266. Glowacki, John M. "Early Polish Operas." In *Paul A.*
      Pisk: Essays in his Honor, ed. John M. Glowacki,
      131-140. Austin: University of Texas Press, 1966.
      294 pp. ML 55.P6 G6

Nędza Uszczęśliwiona [Misery made happy] is considered
to be the first Polish opera, but Glowacki suggests
that it is really a vaudeville. He discusses the music
of this work and especially influences from Western
sources. He next considers *Zoska, czyli Wiejskie*
Zaloty [Zosia or country courtship] by Kamieński and
notes similarities in plot among early Polish operas.
Translations from French and Italian were also popular
in this period. Glowacki also studies the national
spirit of Stefani's *Cud, czyli Krakowiacy i Górale* [The
Miracle, or the Cracovians and Mountaineers].

267. Gołos, Jerzy. "'Apollo Prawodawca' - Opera szkolna z
      czasów Oświecenia" ["Apollo the Lawgiver" - A school
      opera from the Enlightenment]. *Muzyka* 13, no. 2
      (1968): 22-33.

Discusses a school opera from part of a larger
manuscript from Vilna dating 1789. The work has both
sung and spoken texts, and includes instrumental
interludes and the polonaise. Gives examples to show

the didactic nature of the dialogue. Provides an
outline of the scenes which constitute the prologue
and four acts. An English summary is provided.

268. Idaszak, Danuta. "Wojciech Dankowski." *Hudebni vĕda*
      10, no. 3 (1973): 188-98.

      A summary of the author's research on Dankowski.
      Reviews the literature on the composer and manuscript
      sources. Information on Dankowski in Czech is
      incorporated into the composer's biography. Discusses
      the style characteristics of his music. A summary is
      supplied in German.

269. _____. "Źródła rękopiśmienne do mszy żałobnych
      Wojciecha Dankowskiego" [Manuscript sources of the
      requiem masses of Wojciech Dankowski]. *Muzyka* 12,
      no. 4 (1967): 16-28.

      Gives a history of requiems in Polish musical
      literature. At the end of the eighteenth century
      Dankowski composed three requiems utilizing vocal-
      instrumental forces. Concludes with a thematic
      catalog of Dankowski's requiem masses.

270. Łyjak, Wiktor Z. "Przyczynki do dziejów muzyki u
      panień benedyktynek w Sandomierzu" [Footnotes to
      music history of the Benedictine Sisters in
      Sandomierz]. *Ruch Muzyczny* 27, no. 16 (August 7,
      1983): 26-27.

      Discusses music at the convent in the eighteenth and
      early nineteenth centuries. The chief contributor to
      musical life was Jadwiga Dygulska, organist and
      copyist. The article also names other musicians and
      instruments at the cloister, and there is even evidence
      of there having been an orchestra.

271. Miazga, Tadeusz. "Alan Mach--skryptor i kompozytor
     choralny XVIII wieku" [Alan Mach--scribe and chant
     composer of the eighteenth century]. In *Studia
     Hieronymo Feicht septuagenario dedicata*, ed. Zofia
     Lissa, 284-97. Kraków: Polskie Wydawnictwo
     Muzyczne, 1967.

     Describes the work of a Dominican composer, active in
     Cracow, who wrote eight books of chants. The article
     discusses the notation, liturgical elements, and
     modality of these church melodies. Considers Mach's
     achievement in chant reform.

272. Mrowiec, Karol. "Niewykorzystane źródło do dziejów
     Kapeli Akademickiej w Krakowie" [An unused source
     for the history of the Academic Chapel in Cracow].
     Muzyka 12, no. 2 (1967): 32-45.

     Extracts information from Biblioteka Jagiellońska
     Ms. 915 (eighteenth century) on the responsibilities
     of singers, organist, and cantor, as well as their
     compensation. Reproduces two complete documents in
     Polish. This chapel is not listed in item 21.

273. _____. *Pasje wielogłosowe w muzyce polskiej XVIII
     wieku* [The polyphonic passion in Polish music of the
     eighteenth century]. Kraków: Polskie Wydawnictwo
     Muzyczne, 1972. 198 pp. ML 3051.P64 M77

     Begins by reviewing the history of Passion settings in
     Poland and then discusses twelve vocal-instrumental
     Passions from the years 1721-1815. The book emphasizes
     characteristics which seem to be peculiar to the
     Passion in Poland, different from Passion music
     originating in Germany. Musical examples are provided
     in a separate pamphlet. A summary in English is
     provided.

     Review: Jiři Sehnal, *Hudebni věda* 11, no. 3 (1974):
     297-98.

274. Mrygoń, Adam. "Działalność Bazylego Bohdanowicza w
     Wiedniu" [The activities of Bazyli Bohdanowicz in
     Vienna]. *Muzyka* 20, no. 4 (1975): 83-94.

     Increased information in the composer's biography
     concerning his Viennese period. Chronicles the concerts
     of Bohdanowicz and lists compositions held in Austrian
     collections. Also provides notes about other members
     of the family.

275. Muchenberg, Bohdan. "Engel--Zapomniany kompozytor
     polski XVIII wieku" [Engel--forgotten Polish composer
     of the eighteenth century]. *Muzyka* 10, no. 4 (1965):
     32-38.

     Assembles data on the composer Jan Engel, concentrating
     on symphonies and vocal-instrumental works. Notes the
     wide dissemination of Engel's music in Poland.

276. _____. "Z zagadnień dokumentacji symfonii polskiej
     drugiej połowy XVIII wieku" [The problems of
     documentation of Polish symphonies from the second
     half of the eighteenth century]. *Z dziejów muzyki
     polskiej* 14 (1969): 65-86.

     Utilizes the Breitkopf thematic catalogs as a source
     of information on the Polish symphony. The author
     notes that several composers in the catalog are
     labelled as having been active in Poland and he
     identifies anonymous works in Polish archives through
     the thematic incipits. Although the works of Jan
     Engel have received attention as early printed
     symphonies in Poland, the Breitkopf catalog reveals
     that a symphony by Marcin Józef Żebrowski was
     published earlier.

277. Pośpiech, Remigiusz. "Twórczość mszalna Marcina
     Józefa Żebrowskiego" [The Masses of Marcin Józef
     Żebrowski]. *Muzyka* 31, no. 1 (1986): 67-97.

     Studies four Masses by this composer from the second
     half of the eighteenth century. The complete text of
     the Mass ordinary was set in a variety of textures.
     Polish dance melodies and rhythms can be found in the

music and two of the compositions are Christmas
Masses. Compares the structural and textual layout
of the music. There are a number of musical examples.
Dates the Masses on the basis of stylistic assessment.
Includes an English summary.

278. Prosnak, Jan. *Kultura muzyczna Warszawy XVIII wieku*
      [The music culture of Warsaw in the eighteenth
      century]. Studia i materiały do dziejów muzyki
      polskiej, no. 2. Kraków: Polskie Wydawnictwo
      Muzyczne, 1955. 320 pp. ML 297.8.W42 P7

      Covers both the Saxon and Stanisław periods in
      eighteenth-century Polish history. Organized by genre,
      the book reveals that theater and opera form a great
      part of the musical activity in this century. Also
      covered are music schools, ballet, publishing, and
      music stores. Prosnak concentrates on presenting
      information regarding Polish music, rather than foreign
      music performed in Warsaw. Includes plates, musical
      examples, a thematic catalog of early Polish operas,
      list of sources, index of names, and bibliography.

279. Przybylski, Tadeusz. "Rodzina Kratzerów" [The Kratzer
      family]. *Muzyka* 14, no. 1 (1969): 34-53.

      Uses information from archival records in Cracow about
      members of this musical family, especially Franciszek
      Ksawery Kratzer and his eldest son, Kazimierz Kratzer.
      Other members of the family are followed into the
      nineteenth century.

280. _____. "Wacław Sierakowski--działacz muzyczny Krakowa
      czasów Oświecenia (1741-1806)" [Wacław Sierakowski--
      musical worker of Cracow in the time of the
      Enlightenment (1741-1806)]. *Muzyka* 16, no. 1 (1971):
      50-63.

      Sierakowski was a canon and prefect at Wawel Chapel in
      Cracow. Presents Sierakowski's life and activities
      that can be documented, primarily in the years between
      1780 and 1787. Activities stemmed around a singing
      school, children's music training, and performances of
      music in Cracow.

281. Reiss, Józef. "Dzieje symfonii w Polsce" [A history
      of the symphony in Poland]. In *Muzyka polska:
      monografia zbiorowa*, ed. Mateusz Gliński, 131-141.
      Warszawa: Muzyka, 1927.

      Outlines the history of the Polish symphony and other
      orchestral pieces of the eighteenth and nineteenth
      centuries by presenting works known at the time of
      publication. For example, the *Symphony in B-flat* of
      Antoni Milwid is given as the earliest Polish
      symphony. Outdated by subsequent research.

282. Stęszewska, Zofia. "Muzyka taneczna jako źródło badań
      międzynarodowych kontaktów kulturalnych na
      przykładzie Polski i Francji" [Dance music as a
      source of research on international cultural contact
      in the example of Poland and France]. *Muzyka* 17,
      no. 2 (1972): 39-56.

      Gauges the tremendous French influence on dance and
      opera in the second half of the seventeenth century.
      Mentions specific contacts between France and Poland.
      Discusses French dances in Poland, including examples
      by Polish composers found in tablatures, and traces
      dance types. Also considers Polish dances in France.
      The author concludes that the interest in French dance
      forms did not overtake the polonaise in Poland. Summary
      provided in French.

283. Strumiłło, Tadeusz. "Do dziejów symfonii polskiej"
      [Towards a history of the Polish symphony].
      Muzyka No. 5-6 (1953): 26-45.

      Describes the role of symphonic music in eighteenth-
      century Poland, reversing the emphasis in prior
      scholarship by placing the church as the most important
      center of orchestral writing. Symphonies were
      performed at church services and were especially
      prevalent in Wielkopolska [Great Poland]. Strumiłło
      discusses the use of the word "sinfonia" in Polish
      sources of the eighteenth century, listing each known
      work with the relevant historiography. The Polish
      symphonies are grouped chronologically by style, with

general conclusions drawn regarding Polish and German
works of the same period. Making a note of works by
Western composers in Polish archives, Strumiłło
revises the view that Józef Elsner introduced the
Classical style to Poland.

284. Szweykowska, Anna. "Mapa muzykowania w Rzeczypospolitej
     w połowie XVIII wieku" [A musical map of the Polish
     Commonwealth in the middle of the eighteenth
     century]. *Muzyka* 16, no. 2 (1971): 85-105.

Information on music in eighteenth-century Poland was
taken from the newspaper *Kurier Polski* [Polish Courier].
The article consists of an alphabetical list of place
names with attending references to musical activities
at each location in the years 1730 to 1750. These
locations are mostly private chapels, city chapels,
and churches. The result is a more comprehensive view
of music in mid-eighteenth-century Poland.

285. Węcowski, Jan. "La musique symphonique polonaise du
     XVIIIe siècle." In *Musica Antiqua Europae Orientalis*,
     ed. Zofia Lissa, 334-53. Warszawa: Państwowe
     Wydawnictwo Naukowe, 1966.

Discusses 20 known Polish symphonists, summarizing the
information gathered to date on each composer and his
works. The author maintains the view that churches
were the centers for the eighteenth-century Polish
symphony. He also provides a catalog of symphonies by
non-Polish composers found in Polish archives.

286. Wilkowska-Chomińska, Krystyna. "Muzyka polscy w
     Królewcu" [Polish music in Królewiec]. *Muzyka* 16,
     no. 4 (1971): 62-72.

Music in Królewiec was dominated by the Podbielski
family. The author provides a musical sketch of
several generations of the family, mentions other
Polish musicians in the region, and assesses the
general Polish cultural life of the town. Musical
considerations concentrate on the sonatas of Krystian
Wilhelm Podbielski, their adherance to sonata form, and
use of ornaments. Includes a number of musical
examples.

287. _____. "Polska sonata fortepianowa w XVIII w." [The
      Polish piano sonata in the eighteenth century].
      Rocznik chopinowski 8 (1969): 108-24.

      Primarily concerns two collections of sonatas by
      Krystian Wilhelm Podbielski. Discusses the influence
      of C.P.E. Bach exhibited by these twelve works, as well
      as the ornamentation and use of national elements.

288. Żórawska-Witkowska, Alina. "Kapela Antoniego
      Tyzenhauza w Grodnie" [The chapel of Antoni
      Tyzenhauz in Grodno]. *Muzyka* 22, no. 2 (1977): 3-
      35.

      Recounts the history of the Tyzenhauz court in
      Lithuania, which employed an orchestra of about 30
      musicians. Lists musicians from 1779-1780 and discusses
      the repertory of the orchestra. Foreign contact was
      maintained through the travels of Leon Sitański,
      violinist and conductor of the ensemble. Includes an
      English summary.

289. _____. "Kultura muzyczna w stanisławowskiego Warszawie"
      [The musical culture in Warsaw during the reign of
      Stanisław August]. *Ruch Muzyczny* 29, no. 14 (1985):
      13-16.

      Acknowledges that the period represents a regression in
      Warsaw's music activities because music was emphasized
      more at the courts in the countryside. Relates the
      general social conditions of eighteenth-century Poland
      which resulted in an emphasis on foreign composers and
      musicians. Discusses the emergence of Polish opera,
      theater and concert life, music education, instrument
      builders, and music societies.

290. _____. "Kultura muzyczna w stanisławowskiej Polsce"
      [The musical culture of Poland during the reign of
      Stanisław August]. *Ruch Muzyczny* 29, no. 16
      (August 4, 1985): 13-16.

Expands the discussion to consider the role of music
in the entire country. Presents population statistics
while addressing general cultural conditions. The
article discusses court life and music in the life of
the nobility, including the place of Polish dances.
Other topics include music at the residences of
different families, music in churches and religious
orders, and public theater in various cities.

291. _____. "Stanisław August i muzyka" [Stanisław August
       and music]. *Ruch Muzyczny* 29, no. 15 (July 21,
       1985): 13-16.

Presents information on the musical background and
interests of Poland's last king, Stanisław August
Poniatowski, who preferred opera and ballet. Discusses
music performed at the royal court and the popularity
of European composers.

Romantic (19th Century)

292. Abraham, Gerald, ed. *The Age of Beethoven, 1790-1830.*
       New Oxford History of Music, vol. 8. London:
       Oxford University Press, 1982. 747 pp.
       ISBN 019316308X ML 160.N44 v. 8 See item 162.

The Age of Beethoven, 1790-1830 focuses on two areas of
early nineteenth-century Polish music, opera and song.
Opera is covered on pp. 523-28 in a short survey
beginning with the first opera in Polish and the
achievements of Józef Elsner and Karol Kurpiński.
Abraham emphasizes national elements in Polish opera,
showing that folk rhythms and melodies are associated
with peasant characters, but not the nobility. He also
gives examples of Italian influence. In covering song
on pp. 574-78, Abraham includes only major composers
and collections from the beginning of the century, such
as the *Historical Songs* of Niemciewicz and works by
Elsner, Kurpiński, Maria Szymanowska, and Chopin.

Review: William S. Newman, *Notes* 40, no. 1 (1983):
47-49.

293. Berwaldt, Jacek. "Twórczość Feliksa Janiewicza" [The
        creative works of Feliks Janiewicz]. *Muzyka* 12,
        no. 1 (1967): 44-58.

      Janiewicz's music exhibits the gallant style and early
      Classical style. The author characterizes the composer's
      style by considering his approach to sonata and rondo
      forms. Provides a list of works.

294. _____. "Życie Feliksa Janiewicza (1762-1848)" [The
        life of Feliks Janiewicz (1762-1848)]. *Muzyka* 11,
        no. 3-4 (1966): 98-105.

      A chronicle of Janiewicz's activities. Concert
      activities are taken mostly from secondary sources
      rather than original newspaper announcements and
      reviews.

295. Bilińska, Jolanta. "Opery Mozarta na scenach polskich
        w latach 1783-1830" [The operas of Mozart on the
        Polish stage in the years 1783-1830]. *Muzyka* 22,
        no. 1 (1977): 79-102.

      Recounts the performance of Mozart operas in Poland
      beginning with a production of *Die Entführung* in 1783.
      The operas were presented in both Polish and the
      original language; the *Magic Flute* was perhaps the
      most popular in this period. Offers a selection of
      newspaper reviews of the *Magic Flute* and *Don Giovanni*.
      Includes a summary in English.

296. Chechlińska, Zofia, ed. *Szkice o kulturze muzycznej
        XIX wieku*, 5 vols. to date. Warszawa: Państwowe
        Wydawnictwo Naukowe, 1971- . ML 196.S95

      An irregular serial publishing articles on nineteenth-
      century Polish musical institutions accompanied by
      detailed chronicles and data. Volume 2 (1973) has
      summaries in English at the end of the volume. Volume
      3 continues the earlier tradition by providing
      articles on otherwise unaddressed aspects of
      nineteenth-century Polish music and supplying pages of
      documentation from nineteenth-century sources,
      especially music and general newspapers. English

summaries appear at the conclusion of most of the
articles. Each volume includes an index. Individual
articles include items 308, 310, 312, 313, 316, 320,
329, 330, 335, 336, 347, and 357.

Reviews: Alina Nowak-Romanowicz, *Muzyka* 19, no. 4
(1974): 86-90; *Muzyka* 17, no. 1 (1972): 106-9; *Ruch
Muzyczny* 17, no. 14 (1973): 16; *Muzyka* 24, no. 4
(1980): 96-100.

297. Chechlińska, Zofia. "Z problematyki badań nad muzyką
     polską XIX w." [Problems of research on Polish
     music of the nineteenth century]. *Muzyka* 24, no. 4
     (1979): 83-91.

The nineteenth-century was a weak period in Polish
music, causing fragmentary research, except in Chopin
studies. Musicological work has been mostly on the
actual music, in accordance with a stereotypical view
of nineteenth-century music. Chechlińska discusses the
national character in Polish music of this period and
identifies criteria for "Polishness." She summarizes
research conducted by the Instytut Sztuki, Polska
Akademia Nauk and presents the need for a synthesis of
Polish music in the nineteenth century using data on
musical life in a wider assortment of music centers.

298. Dziębowska, Elżbieta. "On the Polish National School."
     Polish Musicological Studies 2 (1986): 128-48. See
     item 131. Originally, "O polskiej szkole narodowej."
     Szkice o kulturze muzycznej XIX wieku 1 (1971): 13-
     32. See item 296.

Defines the term "national school" and evaluates the
use of the word "national" in music historiography.
Finding the essence of the Polish national school in
Chopin, Moniuszko, and Kolberg, the author isolates
folk music as the most important element in the
creation of a national consciousness in nineteenth-
century Polish music.

299. Frączyk, Tadeusz. *Warszawa młodości Chopina* [Warsaw
      in Chopin's youth]. Kraków: Polskie Wydawnictwo
      Muzyczne, 1961. 444 pp.

      Frączyk provides more information and insight into the
      growth of Warsaw as a city rather than a study of
      Chopin. He begins with a sociological overview of
      the city in the early nineteenth century and discusses
      such institutions as schools, from elementary through
      university study, the conservatory, and galleries.
      Other institutions that contributed to Warsaw's
      cultural life are print shops and bookstores. Also
      included is some discussion of social life in Warsaw
      and Chopin's place in this cultural life. Includes a
      name index.

      Review: *Muzyka* 9, no. 3-4 (1964): 142-44.

300. Gabryś, Jerzy and Janina Cybulska. *Z dziejów polskiej
      pieśni solowej* [From the history of Polish solo
      songs]. Kraków: Polskie Wydawnictwo Muzyczne, 1960.
      397 pp. ML 2851.P6 Z2

      Actually represents two books bound together: Gabryś,
      Początki polskiej pieśni solowej w latach 1800-1830
      [The beginnings of Polish solo songs in the years 1800
      to 1830], pp. 5-250 and Cybulska, *Romans wokalny w
      Polsce w latach 1800-1830* [The vocal romance in Poland
      in the years 1800 to 1830], pp. 251-398. Covers the
      structure and style of nineteenth-century songs. The
      pieces are categorized by genre, such as romance, duma,
      and ballad. There is a chapter on the *Śpiewy historyczne*
      of Niemciewicz. Composers represented include Elsner,
      Kurpiński, Maria Szymanowska and amateurs such as
      Michał Kleofas Ogiński and Antoni Radziwiłł. Probes
      into the structure of the songs through musical
      examples.

      Review: *Muzyka* 9, no. 3-4 (1964): 142-44.

301. Gołos, Jerzy. "Some Slavic Predecessors of Chopin."
      Musical Quarterly 46, no. 4 (1960): 437-47.

Illustrates with musical examples the similarities and possible influences that Bohemian and Polish composers of the prior generation had on Chopin's musical style.

302. Górski, Ryszard. *Oskar Kolberg: Zarys życia i działalności* [Oskar Kolberg: An outline of his life and activities]. Warszawa: Ludowa Spółdzielnia Wydawnicza, 1970. 279 pp. ISBN 3812693
      GN 21.K57

A biography of Kolberg and monograph on his musical activities. Covers the genesis of his writings on Polish folklore. Concentrates on his most significant work, *Lud w jego zwyczajach, obrzędach, zabawach, pieśniach, muzyce i tańcach*. Notes are placed at the end of the volume; there is no index.

303. Grigoriew, Wladymir. *Henryk Wieniawski: życie i twórczość* [Henryk Wieniawski: life and works]. Warszawa: Państwowe Wydawnictwo Naukowe, 1986.

A translation from the 1966 Russian edition. Develops Wieniawski's biography as the life of a national musician and portrays the composer as a Pole fated to travel and live away from his native country. Contains some detailed discussion of the music. Includes a list of works, repertoire, chronology, and bibliography, as well as many plates and illustrations. Short abstracts in Russian, English, French, and German.

304. Janta, Aleksander. *A History of Nineteenth Century American-Polish Music, with Annotated Bibliography and Illustrations*. New York: The Kościuszko Foundation, 1982. 186 pp. ML 120.V5 J26

Concentrates on the period before 1865. Contains annotated catalogs of compositions by composers of Polish origin, by American composers inspired by Polish subjects, and of American pieces based on Polish dances such as the krakowiak, mazurka, and polonaise. Also includes sections on the friends of Chopin, Paul Emil Johns and Julian Fontana, and the American opera of Edward Sobolewski, *Mohega, the Flower*

of the Forest. Contains an index of composers and
examples of frontispieces from prints of music. The
title page cites a bibliography, but the book provides
only footnotes.

305. Jachimecki, Zdzisław. "Stanislaus Moniuszko." *Musical
      Quarterly* 14 (1928): 54-62.

      Gives only a short biography of Moniuszko's life.
      Discusses the songs of the Home Song Books. Relates
      Moniuszko's development as an opera composer, but only
      concentrates on *Halka* and *Straszny Dwór.* Also
      discusses his dramatic cantatas and church music.

306. Kaczyński, Tadeusz and Jerzy Morawski. "L'oeuvre de
      Moniuszko." *La Musique en Pologne* 5 (September
      1969): 30-38.

      Begins with an assessment of the importance of
      Moniuszko. Discusses the classifications of this
      composer's songs, their folk elements, foreign
      characteristics, and Polish rhythms. The operas are
      grouped as comic, serious, and national works. Also
      mentions Moniuszko's cantatas, religious works, and
      instrumental music.

307. Kobylańska, Krystyna, ed. *Chopin w kraju: dokumenty i
      pamiątki.* Kraków: Polskie Wydawnictwo Muzyczne,
      1955. 296 pp.

      _____. *Chopin in his own land. Documents and
      souvenirs.* Kraków: Polskie Wydawnictwo Muzyczne,
      1955. 296 pp. ML 88.C46 K57

      This oversized album consists of reproductions and
      photographs of documents from the first half of the
      nineteenth century, pertaining not only to Chopin, but
      to other composers and general musical life. The book
      concludes with notes to supplement the short
      explanations printed with the plates. Indexes of music,
      letters, newspaper reports, and portraits are included,
      as is a bibliography.

308. Kosim, Jan. "Ernst Theodor Amadeus Hoffmann i
       Towarzystwo Muzyczne w Warszawie" [E.T.A. Hoffmann
       and the Music Society in Warsaw]. *Szkice o
       kulturze muzycznej XIX wieku* 2 (1973): 105-79.
       See item 296.

       Offers a history of Warsaw's first music club organized
       during the period of E.T.A. Hoffmann's stay in the
       city, 1804-1807. This organization had a minimal
       participation of Poles.

309. Kuzik, Aleksander. "Recepcja 'Śpiewów historycznych'
       J.U. Niemcewicza w kulturze muzycznej polski
       porozbiorowej" [The reception of the "Historical
       Songs" of J.U. Niemcewicz in post-partition Polish
       music culture]. *Poezja* 15, no. 3 (1980): 97-100.

       Explains the song collection's elite and popular role
       in Polish culture. Recounts early reception and
       educational role. Explains the role of the song
       collection after 1830. The songs had a special
       influence on the nobility and intelligentsia.

310. Kwiatkowska, Magdalena. "Życie muzyczne Warszawy w
       latach 1795-1806" [The musical life of Warsaw in the
       years 1795-1806]. *Szkice o kulturze muzycznej
       XIX wieku* 5 (1984): 9-91. See item 296.

       Considers music in theaters, foreign performers,
       ballets, concerts, church music, and private home
       concerts during the Prussian period. Devises a
       repertory of music from newspaper accounts. Makes
       note of publishing activities and catalogs the
       publications issued as a part of the collection
       Wybór pięknych dzieł muzycznych i pieśni polskich
       (1803-1805). An opera list adds significantly to
       item 44. Includes an English summary.

       Review: William Smialek, *Notes* 44, no. 4 (1988): 720-
       22.

311. Leiser, Clara. *Jean de Reszke and the Great Days of
         Opera*. New York: Minton, Balch, and Co., 1934.
         337 pp. ML 420.R36 L41

      Gives the Polish background of the family and the
      singer's early interest in opera. The book then
      follows the career of the opera star. This is a
      popular account, quoting letters and adding dialogue.
      Covers his travels around the world as a performer.

312. Lachowicz, Stanisław. "August Freyer--szkic
         biograficzny" [August Freyer--biographical essay].
         Szkice o kulturze muzycznej XIX wieku 3 (1976):
         324-39. See item 296.

313. Lubecka, Danuta. "Twórczość muzyczna Augusta Freyera"
         [The musical creations of August Freyer]. *Szkice
         o kulturze muzycznej XIX wieku* 3 (1976): 340-58.
         See item 296.

      These two articles present considerable information on
      Freyer (1803-1883), a lesser known Polish musician
      recognized in his own time as an organist. Corrections
      are made to the work of other scholars and a list of
      Freyer's works with source and publication details is
      included.

314. Lachowicz, Stanisław. "Uzupełnienia do artykułu o
         A. Freyerze w 'Szkicach o kulturze muzycznej XIX w.'"
         [A supplement to the article on A. Freyer in *Szkice
         o kulturze muzycznej XIX wieku*]. *Muzyka* 21, no. 4
         (1976): 70-72.

315. Lesure, François. "L'Histoire de Pologne dans la
         musique française de 1830 à 1865." *Muzyka* 17, no. 2
         (1972): 57-65.

      Presents the French reaction in music to Polish
      political events in the nineteenth century, principally
      the 1830 November Insurrection and the January
      Insurrection of 1863. Many compositions by Polish
      emigrés were published in France. Provides a list of
      publications related to the "Polish question."

316. Lisowska, Agnieszka. "Karol Kurpiński jako pisarz,
     działacz i organizator muzyczny w Warszawy" [Karol
     Kurpiński as a musical writer, worker, and organizer
     in Warsaw]. *Szkice o kulturze muzycznej XIX wieku* 2
     (1973): 181-231. See item 296.

     Publishes a magister thesis that fills some of the void
     in scholarship on an important figure in nineteenth-
     century Polish music. No discussion of Kurpiński's
     music is undertaken.

317. Lissa, Zofia. *Polonica Beethovenowskie.* Kraków:
     Polskie Wydawnictwo Muzyczne, 1970. 168 pp.
     ML 410.B4 L565

     Probes all the possible connections between Beethoven
     and Polish music, including Beethoven's Polish students,
     his use of folklore and the polonaise rhythm, the
     reception of Beethoven's music in Poland, and Beethoven
     documents in Polish archives.

     Reviews: J.G. Görlich, *Neue Zeitschrift für Musik* 131,
     no. 3 (March 1970): 158-59; Irene Poniatowska,
     Muzyka 15, no. 4 (1970): 118-21; *Ruch Muzyczny* 14,
     no. 9 (1970): 17.

318. Maciejewski, B.M. *Moniuszko: Father of Polish Opera.*
     London: Allegro Press, 1979. 154 pp. ML 410.M71 M3

     Presents Moniuszko's life and career, but with minimal
     discussion of Polish music in the period as a whole.
     Includes plot synopses of the operas and evaluates
     other genres of composition relying on the complete
     works edition published by Polskie Wydawnictwo
     Muzyczne. A list of works is appended.

319. Moniuszko, Stanisław. *Listy zebrane* [Collected letters],
     ed. Witold Rudziński. Kraków: Polskie Wydawnictwo
     Muzyczne, 1969. 679 pp.

     A collection of 820 letters with explanatory notes.
     The introduction, summarized in both English and
     German, discusses the character of the letters and
     language used by Moniuszko. Includes a bibliography

of published letters, glossary of regional words, and
indexes of compositions and names. Plates of selected
letters are interspersed with the text.

Review: Krzysztof Meyer, *Muzyka* 16, no. 2 (1971):
132-37.

320. Morawska, Katarzyna. "Badania nad muzyką dawną w
Polsce w XIX wieku" [Research on old Polish music in
the nineteenth century]. *Szkice o kulturze muzycznej
XIX wieku* 3 (1976): 7-129. See item 296.

Examines the historiography of studies completed in the
nineteenth century on Polish music before 1600. Divides
the scholarship into three periods: 1800-1850, the
collection of old Slavic materials; 1850-1870, the
leadership of Józef Sikorski in collecting archival
materials; the end of the nineteenth century, and the
intensification of writing on old Polish music which led
to the introduction of musicology as a university
discipline in 1911. Analyzes the greatest achievements
of Polish musical scholarship during the nineteenth
century.

321. Nowak-Romanowicz, Alina. *Józef Elsner. Monografia.*
Kraków: Polskie Wydawnictwo Muzyczne, 1957. 352 pp.
ML 410.E58 N6

A well-documented biography with discussion of musical
activities, educational importance, and compositions.
Chapter 8 assesses the place and significance of Elsner
in the history of Polish music, but needs revision in
light of newer research. The book includes a list of
Elsner's works, with indications of manuscripts, reviews
of performances, publications, and documentation. Also
includes an extensive bibliography.

Review: Jan Prosnak, *Muzyka* 4, no. 3 (1959): 93-96.

322. Nowak-Romanowicz, Alina. "Nauka teorii muzyki w
podręcznikach doby klasycyzmu polskiego (1750-1830)"
[The study of music theory in textbooks of the
time of Polish Classicism (1750-1830)]. *Muzyka* 25,
no. 3 (1980): 53-66.

Discusses 13 theory books, especially concentrating on
the writings of Sierakowski, Elsner, and Kurpiński.
Focuses on the development of Polish terminology about
music.

323.   _____. "Niektóre problemy opery polskiej między
        oświecenien a romantyzmem" [Some problems of Polish
        opera between the Enlightenment and Romanticism].
        In *Studia Hieronymo Feicht septuagenario dedicata,*
        ed. Zofia Lissa, 328-36. Kraków: Polskie Wydawnictwo
        Muzyczne, 1967.

Changes in Polish opera are discovered with the
repertory of public theater in Warsaw at the beginning
of the nineteenth century. The author observes that
there is more folklore in opera after 1815, and at
this time national elements increased and new genres
developed, such as melodrama and "komedioopera."
Differentiates genres and notes the changes in style
and theme until about 1830.

324.   Perkowska, Małgorzata. "Początki i rozkwit kariery
        pianistycznej Paderewskiego" [The beginning and
        prime of Paderewski's pianistic career]. *Muzyka* 22,
        no. 3 (1977): 39-59.

With the support of press reports discusses Paderewski's
first concerts, the foreign concerts, and his development as a virtuoso. Includes the repertory played
during his early period and its reception in the Polish
and foreign press. Assesses the reasons for his
success.

325.   Powroźniak, Józef. *Karol Lipiński.* Kraków: Polskie
        Wydawnictwo Muzyczne, 1970. 259 pp. ML 410.L56 P6

A biography and chronicle of activities with photographs
of the composer. Incorporates some discussion of
compositions and violin technique. Provides a list of
works and a short bibliography which includes only nine
items directly on Lipiński. Includes an index of names.

Review: *Ruch Muzyczny* 15, no. 16 (1971): 19.

326. Poźniak, Włodzimierz. "Polska muzyka kameralna XIX
      wieku" [Nineteenth-century Polish chamber music].
      Ruch Muzyczny 10, no. 17 (September 1-15, 1966): 6.

      Pursues the sociological reasons behind chamber music
      in nineteenth-century Poland. Names the main composers
      but only mentions a few compositions. No musical
      examples are given. Considers the place of instrumental
      music in general musical life.

327. Prokopowicz, Maria. "Musique imprimée à Varsovie en
      1800-1830." In *The Book of the First International
      Musicological Congress Devoted to the Works of
      Frederick Chopin,* ed. Zofia Lissa, 593-97. See
      item 155.

      Begins the discussion of music publishing in Warsaw at
      the end of the eighteenth century with the activities
      of Engel. Suggests social reasons for the development
      of music publishing in the nineteenth century.
      Considers the roles of Elsner, Cybulski, and Brzezina.

328. _____. "La musique imprimée de 1800 à 1831 comme
      source de la culture musicale polonaise de l'époque."
      Fontes artis musicae 14, no. 1-2 (1967): 16-22.

      Covers music of the same material as item 327. More
      attention is given to publications other than printed
      music, such as piano and instrumental methods,
      announcements in newspapers, and music stores.

329. _____. "Z działalności warszawskich księgarzy i
      wydawców muzycznych w latach 1800-1831" [From the
      activities of Warsaw booksellers and music
      publishers in the years 1800-1831]. *Szkice o
      kulturze XIX wieku* 1 (1971): 33-50. See item 296.

330. Mazur, Krzysztof. "Polskie edytorstwo muzyczne między
      powstaniem listopadowym a styczniowym" [Polish
      music publishing between the November and January
      insurrections]. *Szkice o kulturze muzyczny XIX
      wieku* 1 (1971): 51-90. See item 296.

Together these two articles cover Polish music
publishing from 1800-1863. Details given about the
printers, publishers, and music stores active in this
period.

331. Prosnak, Jan. "Pamiątki z powstania listopadowego"
        [Remembrances of the November Insurrection].
        Muzyka 14, no. 1 (1969): 93-

Illuminates pieces written specifically for the 1830
Insurrection, including a march by Damse and polonaise
of Sandmann. Gives plates of music.

332. _____. "Powstanie styczniowe w muzyce 1863-1963"
        [The January Insurrection in music 1863-1963].
        Muzyka 8, no. 1-2 (1963): 127-69, 206-7.

Reviews music inspired by the 1863 revolution, mostly
songs. The article considers the works of both Polish
composers and musicians abroad. Provides a thematic
catalog of songs. Also considers choral music, piano
music, and symphonic works. Includes plates of
printed music and a summary in French.

333. _____. *Stanisław Moniuszko*. Kraków: Polskie
        Wydawnictwo Muzyczne, 1964. 204 pp. ML 410.M71 P8

A short biography following the photographic format of
other albums in the series. Quotes from letters and
other primary source documents. Illustrations include
programs, manuscript pages, and scenes from musical
life of the period. Includes a list of important
works, discography, and a table listing the sources of
illustrations.

334. Przybylski, Tadeusz. "Fragmenty 'Dziennika Prywatnego'
        Karola Kurpińskiego" [Fragments from the private
        journal of Karol Kurpiński]. *Muzyka* 20, no. 4
        (1975): 104-113.

Reconstructs parts of the diary from sources which
utilized the manuscripts before their disappearance
in 1944. The resultant notes provide information on
musical life in Warsaw during 1829-1830.

335. Pukińska-Szepietowska, Hanna. "Muzyka w Dolinie
        Szwajcarska" [Music in the park "Swiss Valley"].
        Szkice o kulturze muzycznej XIX wieku 1 (1971): 91-
        162. See item 296.

    Presents a chronicle of the concerts held in the park
    Dolina Szwajcarska [the Swiss Valley], which in the
    nineteenth century was on the outskirts of the city of
    Warsaw.

336. _____. "Życie koncertowe w Warszawie (lata 1800-1830)"
        [Concert life in Warsaw (1800-1830)]. *Szkice o
        kulturze muzycznej XIX wieku* 1 (1971): 35-104.
        See item 296.

    Chronicles concert life utilizing newspaper evidence as
    the main source of information.

337. Raszewski, Zbigniew. *Bogusławski*, 2 vols. Warszawa:
        Polski Instytut Wydawniczy, 1972. 438, 365 pp.
        ISBN 8306006771

    A biography of the actor-director Wojciech Bogusławski
    which covers his stage works, including productions
    of Polish opera. Includes a name index.

338. Rudziński, Witold. *"Halka" S. Moniuszki* [Halka of S.
        Moniuszko]. Mała biblioteka operowa, no. 4.
        Kraków: Polskie Wydawnictwo Muzyczne, 1972. 101 pp.
        MT 100.M66 R8

    Relates the genesis of Moniuszko's most famous opera,
    his contact with the librettist Włodzimierz Wolski,
    and the attention given to the work as a national opera.
    Useful mostly for its outline of the plot with examples
    of the key musical items. Includes photographs from
    various productions.

339.   _____. *Moniuszko i jego muzyka* [Moniuszko and his
        music]. Warszawa: Państwowe Zakłady Wydawnictw
        Szkolnych, 1970.

        Limited to a short biography of the composer with
        illustrations of Moniuszko memorabilia and scenes of
        the nineteenth century. Discusses the music
        superficially. Includes a Moniuszko discography.

340.   _____. *Stanisław Moniuszko*, 2 vols. Kraków: Polskie
        Wydawnictwo Muzyczne, 1955. ML 410.M71 R83

        Extensively documents the life of the composer from his
        early years. Continues with later compositions and
        activities in volume 2. These two volumes offer the
        most complete biography of Moniuszko, but do not include
        detailed commentaries on his music. Concludes with an
        index of works, names, and illustrations.

        Reviews: Jan Prosnak, *Muzyka* 7, no. 3 (1962): 106-12;
        Ruch Muzyczny 8, no. 9 (1964): 16-17.

341.   Śledziński, Stefan. "Dzieje symfonii warszawskiej w
        pierwszej połowie XIX wieku" [History of the
        symphony in Warsaw in the first half of the nineteenth
        century]. *Rozprawy i notatki muzykologiczne* 1
        (1934): 60-66.

        Discusses the connections between Polish composers and
        the Viennese symphony. Reviews works from the early
        nineteenth century, including symphonies by Elsner,
        Lentz, Holland, Dobrzyński, Nowakowski, Lessel,
        Kurpiński, and Brzowski. This article is a
        condensation of the material in the author's 1932
        doctoral dissertation of the same title. Unfortunately,
        the dissertation was lost during World War II, as were
        the symphonic scores of Lentz, Holland, and Nowakowski,
        leaving this article to document the musical
        characteristics of these symphonies.

342.   _____. "Outline History of Polish Symphonic Music."
        Polish Music 15, no. 3 (1980): 35-41.

Discusses the change in our knowledge of the symphony
in Poland. Believes that social changes of the
eighteenth to nineteenth centuries affected the
development of the symphony. Eighteenth-century
composers are mentioned, but more attention is paid to
early nineteenth-century symphonic composers.
Concentrates on the work of Elsner, Lessel, and Holland.

343. _____. "Problemy rozwoju symfonii polskiej w XIX
          wieku" [Problems of the development of the Polish
          symphony in the nineteenth century]. Z dziejów
          muzyki polskiej 9 (1965): 32-43.

Notes that Polish composers only produced a modest
number of symphonies until the period of Young Poland
and concludes that the Polish symphony matured only in
the twentieth century. Reviews works produced in the
nineteenth century, including symphonies by Polish
composers working outside of Poland.

344. Smialek, William. "Ignacy Feliks Dobrzyński (1807-
          1867): His Life and Symphonies." Ph.D. diss.,
          University of North Texas, 1981.

Prepares the discussion of Dobrzyński's music and
activities with substantial information on the musical
life of nineteenth-century Warsaw. Presents an
overview of the Polish symphony which traces national
elements in this genre. Offers a biography of
Dobrzyński and discusses the style of his two
symphonies with a consideration of their place in the
history of Polish music. Includes a list of works,
bibliography, and edition of Symphony No. 2. See item
594. (Dissertation Abstracts 42 (1982): 2930-A)

345. _____. "Ignacy Feliks Dobrzyński i jego udział w
          wiedeńskim konkursie kompozytorskim w 1835 roku"
          [I.F. Dobrzyński and his part in a Viennese
          composition contest in 1835]. Muzyka 26, no. 2
          (1981): 95-98.

Presents the details of a contest in which Dobrzyński's
Second Symphony, incorporating Polish national elements

in each movement, was judged second to Franz Lachner's
Symphony No. 5, Op. 52. As a result of the contest,
Dobrzyński's symphony was performed on several occasions,
and this public attention seems to have generated an
opportunity for the composer to publish several of his
piano works in Germany.

346. Spóz, Andrzej. *Kultura muzyczna Warszawy drugiej
      połowy XIX wieku* [The music culture of Warsaw in the
      second half of the nineteenth century]. Warszawa:
      Państwowe Wydawnictwo Naukowe, 1980.

      Groups together individual essays on societies, music
      education, theaters, opera, ballet, song, symphonic
      and chamber music, publishing, journalism, and
      instrument manufacture. Includes an index of cited
      names.

347. _____. "Tradycje moniuszkowie w Warszawie Towarzystwie
      Muzycznym w latach 1871-1914" [The Moniuszko
      tradition in the Warsaw Music Society in the years
      1871 to 1914]. *Szkice o kulturze muzycznej XIX
      wieku* 2 (1973): 233-286. See item 296.

      Traces the early history of the society and its
      adoption of the Moniuszko dedication. The article
      is written by the present director of the society.

348. Strumiłło, Tadeusz. *Szkice z polskiego życia muzycznego
      XIX w.* [Essays on Polish musical life of the
      nineteenth century]. Małe monografie muzyczne,
      no. 5. Kraków: Polskie Wydawnictwo Muzyczne, 1954.
      243 pp. ML 306.S768

      Includes narrative studies on music and musical life.
      The nature of the book as a topical study results in
      an in-depth treatment of some areas without broad
      considerations. Does not only include the city of
      Warsaw. Although the detail is interesting and
      treatment full of insight, the book is weakened by a
      lack of documentation and no index. Some photographs
      and a few musical examples are included. More
      attention seems to be paid to the first part of the
      century.

Review: *Muzyka* 10, no. 1 (1965): 113.

349. _____. *Źródła i początki romantyzmu w muzyce polskiej.
     Studia i materiały* [Sources and beginnings of
     romanticism in Polish music. Studies and materials].
     Kraków: Polskie Wydawnictwo Muzyczne, 1956. 207 pp.

This book discusses the transition to Polish Romantic
music in the period before the 1830 Insurrection,
termed by the author the "sentimental" period from
Enlightenment to Romanticism. Strumiłło concentrates
on opera as the source of a national style, but
incorporates all genres of composition. Incorporates
many musical examples and provides more extensive
examples in an additional volume. Provides an index
of names and list of examples which might be useful for
finding representative works that have not been
published.

350. Swierzewski, Stefan. "Józef Ignacy Kraszewski o
     kompozytorach epoki romantyzmu" [J.I. Kraszewski
     about Romantic composers]. *Muzyka* 18, no. 2 (1973):
     73-94.

Presents a biography of Kraszewski emphasizing his music
criticism. Summarizes his writing on Beethoven, Gounod,
Liszt, Chopin, Wagner, and Berlioz.

351. Szczepańska-Malinowska, Elżbieta. "Sikorski, mały
     romantyzm, historia" [Sikorski, a little romanticism
     and history]. *Muzyka* 26, no. 2 (1981): 87-94.

Studies the music criticism of Józef Sikorski within the
context of the period between the nineteenth-century
insurrections. Offers a sketch of political and social
life in Warsaw, with the interpretation that musical
Romanticism is characterized by short pieces and
arrangements, much of it with patriotic gestures, as a
result of this climate. The author proposes that
Sikorski's work during this period required him to
struggle with absolute and relative values in music.

352. Szymański, Stanisław. "Krajobraz muzyczny Częstochowy
w połowie XIX wieku w świetle szkolnych archiwaliów
miejskich" [A musical landscape of Częstochowa in
the first half of the nineteenth century in light
of the school archives of the city]. *Muzyka* 21,
no. 1 (1976): 118-33.

Documents musical activity through city records rather
than the Jasna Góra monastery. Reviews the general
history of the city and provides a list of 31 musicians
active in the nineteenth century. Addresses the
activities of professional and amateur musicians, and
mentions Jewish musicians. Isolates lacunae in the
available information.

353. Vogel, Beniamin. "Muzycy, muzykańci i muzykusy Księstwa
Warszawskiego: szkic geografii muzycznej księstwa"
[Musicians of the Duchy of Warsaw: a sketch of the
Duchy's musical geography]. *Muzyka* 20, no. 2 (1975):
82-107.

Presents a statistical study of Poland in the
Napoleonic period focused on musicians and other music
professionals. Addresses the role of foreigners in
Warsaw. Lists musicians by name in tabular form.

354. _____. "Przemysł muzyczny Warszawy w dwudziestoleciu
międzywojennym" [The music industry in Warsaw between
the wars]. *Muzyka* 30, no. 3-4 (1985): 57-94.

Describes the decline of Warsaw as a center for musical
instrument manufacturing and the phonograph trade after
World War I. Supplements the narrative with an
alphabetical listing of names associated with the music
industry from 1918 to 1939, which includes detailed
activities of about 150 references. Also lists names
associated with the phonograph industry. Includes an
English summary.

355. _____. "Zagromadzenie organmistrzów i fortepianmistrów
w Królestwie Polskim 1815-1918" [A corporation of
organ-masters and piano-masters in the Kingdom of
Poland in the Polish provinces of Russia 1815-1918].
Muzyka 21, no. 4 (1976): 73-75.

Explains the origin of this assembly of instrument
makers. Provides a list of the leadership through the
nineteenth century. Includes an English summary.

356. Wawrzykowska-Wierciochowa, Dioniza. *Mazurek
      Dąbrowskiego* [The Dąbrowski mazurka]. Warszawa:
      Wydawnictwo Ministerstwa Obrony Narodowej, 1974.
      545 pp. ISBN 831106766X ML 3677.W38

      Provides detailed information on General Dąbrowski,
      the history of the mazurka, and its influence and
      significance through the decades. The appendix
      includes a list of printed versions from Poland and
      other countries, 1799-1969. Provides a bibliography.

357. Woźna, Małgorzata. "Jan Kleczyński--pisarz, pedagog,
      kompozytor" [Jan Kleczyński--writer, teacher,
      composer]. *Szkice o kulturze muzycznej XIX wieku* 3
      (1976): 130-323. See item 296.

      Activities of the editor of *Echo Muzyczne, Teatralne i
      Artystyczne*. Considerable supporting detail appended
      to the narrative with the bibliography of Kleczyński's
      writings, 1867-1895; list of musical works; and
      chronology of the composer's activities.

358. Zakrzewska-Nikiporczyk, Barbara. "Działalność
      wielkopolskich chórów kościelnych w latach 1870-
      1918" [The activities of church choirs of Great
      Poland during the years 1870-1918]. *Muzyka* 22,
      no. 3 (1977): 61-73.

      Relates the Polish activities of both amateur and
      professional choirs which served as a defense against
      Germanization in Wielkopolska [Great Poland]. The
      choirs performed works in Latin and Polish non-
      liturgical songs. The background for these musical
      activities can be found in the Cecilian movement.
      Includes an English summary.

359. _____. "Z dziejów polskiego świeckiego ruchu
        śpiewaczego w Wielkim Księtwie Poznańskim (lata
        1870-1892)" [The history of the Polish secular choir
        movement in the Grand Duchy of Poznań (1870-1892)].
        Muzyka 24, no. 2 (1979): 95-112.

        Publishes a good deal of information on secular choirs,
        such as the number of choirs, their activities, and
        repertory. Reports on choral congresses and their role
        in maintaining Polish culture. Includes an English
        summary.

360. Zduniak, Maria. "W sprawie utworów Józefa Elsnera"
        [On Józef Elsner's works]. *Muzyka* 22, no. 2 (1977):
        79-88.

        Presents works preserved in the Chapter Library and
        University Library in Wrocław. Adds new information to
        the catalog of Elsner's works by Nowak-Romanowicz in
        item 321. All these are sacred works given by the
        composer in 1830 to the Wrocław cathedral. Includes
        an English summary.

361. Żurawicka, Janina. *Inteligencja warszawska w końca
        XIX wieku* [The Warsaw intelligentsia at the end of
        the nineteenth century]. Warszawa: Państwowe
        Wydawnictwo Naukowe, 1978. 282 pp. HT 690.P6 Z8

        Incorporates a little scattered information on the
        number and role of musicians active in Warsaw.

Twentieth Century, History

362. Albers, Bradley Gene. "De Natura Sonoris I and II by
        Krzysztof Penderecki: A Comparative Analysis."
        D.M.A. diss., University of Illinois, 1978.

      Prepares the analysis with a discussion of Polish music
      from Szymanowski to Penderecki. Includes a biography
      of Penderecki, and continues with a comparative
      discussion of the two compositions. (*Dissertation
      Abstracts* 39 (1978): 2605-A)

363. Armytuś, Leszek. "Polska muzyka filmowa 1943-1960"
        [Polish film music, 1943-1960]. *Kwartalnik Filmowy*
        11, no. 2 (1961): 73-79.

      Offers a "filmography" listing composers alphabetically.
      Includes the filmwork, date of production, and film
      director. Summary in French.

364. Boehm, Jan. *Feliks Nowowiejski 1877-1946. Zarys
        biograficzny* [Feliks Nowiejski (1877-1946):
        Biographical outline], 2nd ed. Olsztyn: Wydawnictwo
        Pojezierze, 1977. 158 pp. ISBN 8205091269

      A biography of this composer and church musician, but
      one that does not give detailed study to his
      compositions. Provides photographs of the composer
      and selected pages of manuscript music. Short
      summaries are provided in English and German. Includes
      a bibliography and place-name index.

365. Bogdany, Wanda. "Spuścizna rękopiśmienna Antoniego
        Szaławskiego. Opis źródel" [The manuscript legacy
        of Antoni Szaławski. A description of the sources].
        Muzyka 22, no. 1 (1977): 103-16.

      Describes the manuscripts of Szaławski (d. 1973) now
      in the Biblioteka Narodowa (Wn). Provides a catalog
      of the collection and a chronological list of the
      composer's works. Includes an English summary.

366. Bristiger, Michał, Roger Scruton, Petra Weber-Bockholdt,
      eds. *Karol Szymanowski in seiner Zeit.* München:
      Wilhelm Fink Verlag, 1984. 212 pp. ISBN 3770522346
      ML 410.S99 K29

      A collection of essays. The first group relates
      Szymanowski to the early twentieth century and other
      cultural events of the time. Other essays directly
      concern Szymanowski's music. Musical examples accompany
      some contributions. Some of the material has been
      published elsewhere. (See items 399, 442). Several
      of the essays are in English, including the short
      biography by Chylińska.

      Reviews: Kenneth Campbell, *Tempo* no. 159 (December
      1986): 35-36; Isolde Vetter, *Musikforschung* 40, no. 1
      (1987): 68-70.

367. Carper, Jeremy Lee. "The Interplay of Musical and
      Dramatic Structures in *Jutro,* an Opera by Tadeusz
      Baird." Ph.D. diss., Washington University, 1983.
      129 pp.

      Analyzes the opera's music and libretto. The appendix
      provides a translation of the libretto and transcription
      of an interview with Baird. (*Dissertation Abstracts* 44
      (1984): 3198-A)

368. Cegiełła, Janusz. *Dziecko szczęścia: Aleksander
      Tansman i jego czasy* [Child of fortune: Aleksander
      Tansman and his times]. Warszawa: Państwowy
      Instytut Wydawniczy, 1986. 518 pp. ISBN 8306012569

      A biography incorporating many newspaper reviews.
      Relies on the composer's reminiscences as a source of
      anecdotal information. Covers Tansman's career to
      1938. Includes a list of works and index.

      Review: William Smialek, *Slavic Review* 47, no. 2
      (1988): 379-80.

369. _____. *Szkice do autoportretu polskiej muzyki
      współczesnej* [Essays for a self-portrait of
      contemporary Polish music]. Kraków: Polskie
      Wydawnictwo Muzyczne, 1976. 197 pp.

      A record of free dialogues conducted with a series of
      Polish composers from 1970 to 1975. Composers
      represented include: Witold Lutosławski, Tadeusz Baird,
      Kazimierz Sikorski, Krzystof Meyer, Bogusław Schäffer,
      Alexander Tansman, Wojciech Kilar, Włodzimierz Kotoński,
      Piotr Perkowski, Witold Frieman, Romould Twardowski,
      Augustyn Bloch, Konstanty Regamey, Roman Maciejewski,
      Zbigniew Turski, Bolesław Szabelski.

370. Chłopicka, Regina. "'Polish Requiem' by Krzysztof
      Penderecki." *Polish Music* 21, no. 1-2 (1986): 3-10.

      Places Penderecki's music within the aesthetics and
      philosophy of sacred music, and the Polish Requiem
      within the composer's oeuvre. Discusses the selection
      of text and significance of the work, but only provides
      a general description of the music.

371. Chomiński, Józef. "The Contribution of Polish Composers
      to the Shaping of a Modern Language in Music."
      Polish Musicological Studies 1 (1977): 167-215.

      Cites specific examples of twentieth-century techniques
      from the works of Polish composers, including the
      interest in tape music; increased use of percussion
      instruments; experiments in articulation, timbre,
      rhythm, and meter; focus on tone clusters; and the use
      of aleatory and new formal principles.

372. _____. *Studia na twórczościa Karola Szymanowskiego*
      [Studies on the creations of Karol Szymanowski].
      Kraków: Polskie Wydawnictwo Muzyczne, 1969. 351 pp.

      Contains essays on Szymanowski's work. Begins with
      general issues of the placement of Szymanowski in
      European music in relation to other composers of the
      early twentieth century. Continues with studies of
      specific pieces, such as *Słopiewnie,* the piano works,
      and Kurpian songs. Includes a list of Szymanowski's

works, index of names and compositions. Also includes
musical examples and analytical diagrams.

Reviews: Zofia Helman, *Muzyka* 16, no. 3 (1971): 126-
30; *Ruch Muzyczny* 13, no. 13 (1969): 18.

373. Chylińska, Teresa, ed. *Karol Szymanowski: Briefwechsel
      mit den Universal Edition 1912-1937.* Wien: Universal
      Edition, 1981. 123 pp. ISBN 370240161X
      ML 410.S99 A415

      _____. *Korespondencja Karola Szymanowskiego z Universal
      Edition.* Kraków: Polskie Wydawnictwo Muzyczne, 1978.

      Begins with an introductory essay. The letters are
      printed with footnotes.

      Reviews: Michael Stegemann, *Neue Zeitschrift für
      Musik* 144, no. 1 (January 1983): 40; *Musik und
      Gesellschaft* 32 (October 1982): 627-28.

374. _____. *Karol Szymanowski: Korespondencja* [Karol
      Szymanowski: Correspondence], vol. 1 1903-1919.
      Kraków: Polskie Wydawnictwo Muzyczne, 1982. 669 pp.
      ISBN 822240185X ML 410.S99 A4

      A documented collection of letters in a chronological
      arrangement. The introduction is provided both in
      Polish and English. Interspersed are photographs from
      Szymanowski's life. Biographical notes are provided
      for the names cited. There are indexes of names, works,
      and titles.

375. _____. *Szymanowski*, trans. A.T. Jordan. New York:
      Twayne Publishers and the Kościuszko Foundation,
      1973. Originally published as Teresa Bronowicz-
      Chylińska. *Karol Szymanowski.* Kraków: Polskie
      Wydawnictwo Muzyczne, 1961. 224 pp.
      ML 410.S9913 C561

      Conceived as a photograph album for a Polskie
      Wydawnictwo Muzyczne series and not as a discussion of
      music or definitive biography. There are small
      differences between the photographic content of the

Polish and English versions. The discography was
revised for the later English edition. Offers a more
complete discography and more detailed list of works
than item 419.

Reviews: Peter J. Pirie, *Music and Musicians* 22
(January 1974): 46-47; Michael Stegemann, *Neue
Zeitschrift* 145, no. 11 (November 1984): 56; *Ruch
Muzyczny* 6, no. 8 (1962): 21.

376.   _____. *Zakopiańskie dni Karola Szymanowskiego 1894-
        1936* [The Zakopane days of Karol Szymanowski, 1894-
        1936], 3rd ed. Kraków: Polskie Wydawnictwo
        Muzyczne, 1981. 98 pp. ISBN 8322401728
        ML 410.S99 Z3

A chronicle of Szymanowski's activities in the Zakopane
years. Quotes people that knew Szymanowski and the
composer's correspondence from the period. Reprints
Szymanowski's writings from these years. Much of this
book has been superceded by later publications of the
author.

377.   Cooper, Martin, ed. *The Modern Age 1890-1960.* New
        Oxford History of Music, vol. 10. London: Oxford
        University Press, 1974. See item 162.

Does not present broad coverage of twentieth-century
Polish composers. Several pages of text and examples
are devoted to Szymanowski, but the members of Młoda
Polska [Young Poland] and more contemporary composers
are only mentioned.

378.   Couchoud, Jean-Paul. *La musique polonaise et Witold
        Lutosławski.* Paris: Stock Plus, 1981. 238 pp.

Begins with a sketchy history of Polish music from the
Middle Ages. This expands into more substantial
information on Polish music after World War II, making
note of composers, performing ensembles, festivals, and
other key aspects of musical life. The main part of
the book derives from the author's interview with
Lutosławski about his music and ideas. Added to this
are a list of Lutosławski's musical works, chronology

of his activities, translations of several articles,
and a discography of contemporary Polish music.

Reviews: Jadwiga Paja, *Muzyka* 27, no. 3-4 (1982): 117-
21; *Ruch Muzyczny* 25, no. 12 (1981): 14-15.

379. Cox, Joseph Lee. "The Solo Trombone Works of Kazimierz
      Serocki." D.M.A. diss., North Texas State University,
      1981. 56 pp.

      Considers solo trombone works from Serocki's early
      neo-classical period. The paper discusses Polish
      neo-classicists, especially Grażyna Bacewicz and Michał
      Spisak. Analyzes the *Concerto* and *Sonatina for
      trombone*. (*Dissertation Abstracts* 42 (1982): 4967-A)

380. Dąbek, Stanisław. "Pieśni Karola Szymanowskiego do
      słów Jamesa Joyce'a" [Songs of Karol Szymanowski to
      texts of James Joyce]. *Muzyka* 24, no. 1 (1979):
      51-85.

      Analyzes the four songs opus 54, settings of the Joyce
      collection *Chamber Music*. Concentrates on the modality
      of the vocal part, and vertical and horizontal structures
      in the piano part. Also gives some attention to the
      formal structure of these songs. Provides a table of
      other composers' settings of these texts. Musical
      examples support the analysis.

381. Dibelius, Ulrich. "Polnische Avantgarde." *Melos* 34,
      no. 1 (January 1967): 7-16.

      Identifies the major trends in post-war Polish music,
      but mostly concentrates on the use of serial techniques.
      Includes musical examples.

382. _____. "Der Beitrag Polens." *Musica* 17, no. 3 (1963):
      105-8.

      Traces the twentieth-century Polish tradition which has
      led to the composers of the post-war generations.

383.   Dickinson, Peter.   "Polish Music Today." *Musical Times*
       108 (June 1967): 596-98.

       Discusses post-war Polish music by presenting the major
       composers and important pieces.

384.   Dobrowolski, Janusz.   "Katalog utworów fortepianowych
       Apolinarego Szeluty" [A catalog of the piano works
       of Apolinary Szeluto]. *Muzyka* 18, no. 4 (1973):
       75-82.

       Lists 205 piano works with the opus number, title, date
       of composition, and publication information.

385.   Droba, Krzysztof.   "The Music of Henryk Mikołaj Górecki."
       Music in Poland, 1984, no. 1:27-33.

       A sketch of the career of Górecki, with discussion of
       his style in different periods. Refers to specific
       pieces, especially religious music of the 1970s.
       Includes a list of works.

386.   Dulęba, Władysław and Zofia Sokołowska. *Paderewski,*
       2nd ed. Kraków: Polskie Wydawnictwo Muzyczne, 1976.
       181 pp. ML 410.P114 D8

       Follows a popular album format with many photographs.
       Covers Paderewski's life from infancy, considering the
       musical life of the period and his relationship with
       other musicians, as well as musical and political
       activities. Quotes from the composer's diaries as a
       source of insight. Does not discuss music nor provide
       any musical examples. Includes a list of compositions,
       list of repertory, discography, and list of sources for
       illustrations.

387.   Dziębowska, Elżbieta.   "Mieczysław Karłowicz jako krytyk
       muzyczny" [Mieczysław Karłowicz as a music critic].
       In *Studia Hieronymo Feicht septuagenario dedicata,*
       ed. Zofia Lissa, 425-38. Kraków: Polskie Wydawnictwo
       Muzyczne, 1967.

Discusses the emphasis in Karłowicz's criticism sent
from Germany to Polish publications. He had an interest
in conductors and violinists, frequently commented on
harmony and orchestration, and had definite opinions
on major works.

388. Ehrenkreutz, Stefan Maria. "The Fundamental Underlying
Determinants of Bogusław Schäffer's Musical Practice
and 20th-Century Musical Function." Ph.D. diss.,
University of Michigan, 1984. 312 pp.

A detailed analysis of *Four Pieces for String Trio*
(1962), examining the underlying determinants of the
music. (*Dissertation Abstracts* 45 (1985): 1907-A)

389. Erhardt, Ludwik. *Spotkania z Krzysztofem Pendereckim*
[A Meeting with Krzysztof Penderecki]. Kraków:
Polskie Wydawnictwo Muzyczne, 1975. 239 pp.
ML 410.P2673 E7

Derived from interview sessions with Penderecki and
gives impressions of the man and his music. Provides
a chronology of the composer's activities and photographs of him, but only a few musical examples of key
thematic material are given to heighten the discussion
of the music. Includes an index and discography.

Reviews: Krzysztof Bilica, *Muzyka* 21, no. 2 (1976):
103-5; Oldřich Pukl, *Hudebni věda* 17, no. 1 (1980):
89-90; *Sovetskaya Muzyka* 39 (November 1975): 126-27.

390. Fletcher, Marylynn Louise. "Pitch Constructions in the
Masques, op. 34 of Karol Szymanowski." D.M.A.
diss., University of Texas at Austin, 1984. 85 pp.

Provides a biography of Szymanowski and background
information on *Masques*. Examines the pitch structure
in each movement and then compares characteristics of
pitch in the entire piece. (*Dissertation Abstracts* 45
(1985): 1907-A)

391.   Folga, Zygmunt. "Dodekafonia Józefa Kofflera" [The
       dodecaphony of Józef Koffler]. *Muzyka* 17, no. 4
       (1972): 65-83.

       Confirms that Koffler, the first 12-tone composer in
       Poland, was not a student of Schoenberg. Analyzes the
       Variations on a Waltz of Johann Strauss, Op. 23 (1936)
       and discusses reviews of this work. Koffler had no
       immediate influence even in Poland.

392.   French, Peter. "The Music of Andrzej Panufnik."
       Tempo No. 84 (Spring 1968): 6-14.

       This short biography explains Panufnik's emigration to
       England. Groups Panufnik's compositions into those
       based on themes of sixteenth-century Polish composers,
       those inspired by Polish folklore, and finally composi-
       tions independent of Polish identity. Talks about
       major works and characteristics of the composer's music,
       including methods of construction.

393.   Gawrońska, Bożena. "Utwory na tasmę Bogusława
       Schäffera" [Works on tape of Bogusław Schäffer].
       Muzyka 20, no. 1 (1975): 57-75.

       A number of works were composed in the Experimental
       Studio of Polish Radio: *Symfonia elektroniczna,*
       Assemblages I-III, Hommage à Strzemiński, Monodram na
       tasmę, Konzert na tasmę, and *Temat: muzyka elektroniczna.*
       Discusses the technical means of sound production for
       each piece and relationships between the work and
       performance of electronic music.

394.   Godes, Catherine Anne. "Stylistic Evolution in
       Szymanowski's Three Piano Sonatas." D.M.A. diss.,
       University of Cincinnati, 1984.

       Examines Szymanowski's sonatas to show evolution of the
       composer's style from romantic ideals to modernism.
       Discusses the influences on these works. (*Dissertation*
       Abstracts 46 (1985): 550-A)

395. Hebda, Paul Thomas. "Spółka Nakładowa Młodych
     Kompozytorów Polskich (1905-1912) and the Myth of
     Young Poland in Music." Ph.D. diss., North Texas
     State University, 1987. 287 pp.

     Deals with the group of composers known collectively as
     Young Poland in music and the details of the Young
     Polish Composer's Publishing Company. Gives facts of
     the publishing company and examines historical
     misinterpretations of the enterprise. Considers the
     interrelationships among the four composers, Szymanowski,
     Szeluto, Fitelberg, and Różycki. Three concerts were
     sponsored by the company. The dissertation assesses
     the compositions performed and their reception.
     (*Dissertation Abstracts* 49 (1988): 10-A)

396. Helman, Zofia. "Koncepcja modalna w twórczości
     Szymanowskiego" [Modal conception in the creations
     of Szymanowski]. *Muzyka* 14, no. 4 (1969): 36-63.

     Begins by presenting an overview of the use of modal
     scales in twentieth-century music. Considers modal
     elements of Szymanowski's melodies, citing specific
     examples. Relates Szymanowski's melodic treatment to
     the works of other composers. Observes that in
     Szymanowski's music polymodality can be found in the
     same melody through transposition or can be the result
     of layered treatment.

397. _____. "Muzyczy i muzyka polska w Paryzu w okresie
     międzywojennym" [Musicians and Polish music in Paris
     in the interwar period]. *Muzyka* 23, no. 3 (1978): 80-
     105.

     Isolates the place of Polish music in the Franco-Russian
     "antiromantic" style of the interwar years, especially
     the young composers following Szymanowski. Focuses on
     the Society of Young Polish Musicians in Paris,
     consisting of 140 members active from 1926. Considers
     concerts in Paris by Polish performers, presentations
     of early music by Polish ensembles, the performance of
     works by Polish composers, and the assessment of
     French critics. Provides a table of Polish works
     performed in Paris from 1922-1939. Summary in French.

398. _____. "Muzyka polska między dwiema wojnami" [Polish
      music between the two wars]. *Muzyka* 23, no. 3
      (1978): 17-34.

      Explains that the period 1918 to 1939 is neglected due
      to lost source materials. Discusses several trends
      in music of the first half of the twentieth century:
      anti-romanticism after Szymanowski, a national style
      developed through incorporation of folk melodies from
      different regions of Poland or texts with old Polish
      references, and the neoclassicism of Polish composers
      in Paris under the influence of Nadia Boulanger.
      Discusses the individual style of Ludomir Rogowski and
      Józef Koffler.

399. _____. *Neoklasycyzm w muzyce polskiej XX wieku*
      [Neoclassicism in Polish music of the twentieth
      century]. Kraków: Polskie Wydawnictwo Muzyczne,
      1985. 251 pp. ISBN 8322402643 ML 27.P7 HB

      Begins with a general overview of neoclassicism in
      music and the music of Eastern Europe. Probes
      neoclassicism, the aesthetics of the movement in Polish
      music, and the related compositional techniques by
      considering each musical element in turn. Selects and
      compares musical examples from a variety of Polish
      composers, even considering the work of some Polish
      composers who lived outside of Poland.

400. Horowicz, Bronisław. *Le théâtre d'opera: histoire,
      realisations sceniques, possibilités.* Paris:
      Éditions d'aujourd'hui, 1976. 270 pp. ML 1700.H75

      Refers to the theatrical work of Wyspiański in passing.
      Several Polish works are cited in the bibliography.

401. Hoskins, Janina. *Ignacy Jan Paderewski (1860-1941):
      A Biographical Sketch and a Selective List of Reading
      Materials.* Washington: Library of Congress, 1984.
      32 pp. ISBN 0844404403 ML 134.P18 H7

This pamphlet includes several photographs of the
composer. The annotated bibliography is divided into
works by Paderewski and works about Paderewski.
Citations include call numbers and locations. Also
provides a list of works in chronological order.

402. Iwaszkiewicz, Jarosław. *Spotkania z Szymanowskim*
     [Meeting with Szymanowski], 3rd ed. Kraków:
     Polskie Wydawnictwo Muzyczne, 1981. 108 pp.
     ML 410.S99 I9

The famous writer's reminiscences of contact with
Szymanowski. (Iwaszkiewicz wrote several essays on
music.) Serves as a memoir of the period, to include
connections with other composers. Relates Iwaszkiewicz's
perception of events in Szymanowski's life.

403. Jadacki, Jacek Juliusz. "O Stanisławie Szpinalskim
     (1901-1957)" [About Stanisław Szpinalski].
     Muzyka 22, no. 1 (1977): 14-39.

Szpinalski was a piano student of Paderewski. Describes
Szpinalski's pianistic art, discusses his repertoire,
and analyzes recorded performances. Includes a list
of repertoire, discography, list of edited works,
bibliography, and an English summary of the text.

404. Jarociński, Stefan. "Polish Music after World War II."
     Musical Quarterly 51, no. 1 (1965): 244-258.

Proceeds from the premise that the music of Szymanowski,
and also neoclassicism, were important influences on
post-war composers. Considers Kazimierz Sikorski's
role as a teacher and notes that many of his students
later went to study in Paris. Some of the composers
discussed include: Józef Koffler, Roman Palester,
Panufnik, Spisak, Lutosławski, Baird, Schäffer, and
Penderecki. The historical overview acknowledges the
role of Warsaw Autumn.

405. _____. *Witold Lutosławski: materiały do monografii*
        [Witold Lutosławski: materials toward a monograph].
        Kraków: Polskie Wydawnictwo Muzyczne, 1967. 91 pp.
        ML 410.L965 A3

      Begins with a biographical sketch on Lutosławski.
      Reprints Lutosławski's writings on aesthetics, other
      composers, and his thoughts on several major compositions.
      Includes photographs of the composer, a list of works,
      list of writings and music reviews, and a bibliography.

406. Jasińska, Danuta. "Geneza i rys historyczny opery
        radiowej" [The genesis and historical features of
        radio opera]. *Muzyka* 18, no. 1 (1973): 66-77.

      Discusses the general concepts and history of radio
      opera. Includes a catalog of 17 Polish works in this
      genre.

407. _____. "Polskie opery radiowe" [Polish radio operas].
        Muzyka 19, no. 2 (1974): 31-44.

      Generalizes about opera for radio by analyzing specific
      Polish works.

408. Jasińska-Jędrosz, Elżbieta. *Rękopisy utworów
        muzycznych Karola Szymanowskiego. Katalog 1*
        [Manuscripts of musical works by Karol Szymanowski.
        Catalog 1]. Warszawa: Wydawnictwo Uniwersytetu
        Warszawskiego, 1983. 111 pp. ISBN 8300011234
        ML 134.S994 J3

      Describes Szymanowski manuscripts and their contents.
      The information includes title, shelf number, nature
      of manuscript (autograph or copy), and origin.

409. Jazwinski, Barbara Maria. "Four Compositions by
        Tadeusz Baird: Analytic Essay." Ph.D. diss., City
        University of New York, 1984.

      Discusses the development of Baird's compositional
      technique from 1957 to 1963. Selected works include:
      String Quartet No. 1 (1957), *Four Essays* (1958),

Exhertatai (1958-1960), and *Elegeia* (1973). Follows
Baird's evolution from twelve-tone writing to the use
of free atonal structures. (*Dissertation Abstracts* 45
(1984)

410. Kaczyński, Tadeusz. "Polish Composer in Paris:
      Aleksander Tansman's 80th Birthday." *Polish Music*
      12, no. 4 (1977): 20-23.

A short biographical sketch of the composer, which
especially probes into the Polish character of
Tansman's music.

411. _____. *Rozmowy z Witoldem Lutosławskim*. Kraków:
      Polskie Wydawnictwo Muzyczne, 1972. 173 pp.

      _____. *Conversations with Witold Lutosławski*, trans.
      Yolanta May. London: Chester Music, 1984. 152 pp.
      ISBN 0906594014 ML 410.L965 K23

Conversations with Lutosławski about some of his works
and contemporary music in general. Works receiving
attention include:

Trois poèmes d'Henri Michaux
String Quartet
Paroles tissées
Second Symphony
Livre pour orchestre
Les espaces du sommeil (English version only)
Violin concerto (Polish version only)

The questions of the interviewer probe the contruction
of the pieces. Musical examples are presented to
explain text. The Polish version has examples in a
separate pamphlet, and also a short recording.

Review: John Casken, *Musical Times* 127 (April 1986):
208-9.

412. Kałużny, Jan A. "Krzysztof Penderecki and his
      Contribution to Modern Musical Notation." *Polish
      Review* 8, no. 3 (1963): 86-95.

Begins by discussing the need for notational revision
in modern music. Penderecki utilizes diagrammatic and
real time notation, and graphic symbols to represent
clusters. Proceeds to analyze the notation of specific
instrumental and choral pieces.

413. Kański, Józef. "Apolinary Szeluto, 1884-1966." *Ruch
Muzyczny* 11, no. 2 (January 15-31, 1967): 16-17.

Provides a list of Szeluto's works. The biography
makes an assessment of his achievements. Includes
photographs of the composer.

414. Kosakowski, Ann Louise. "Karol Szymanowski's Mazurkas:
Cyclic Structure and Harmonic Language." Ph.D.
diss., Yale University, 1980. 329 pp.

Studies the *Mazurkas,* Op. 50 and 62. Develops a theory
of structure based on a directed cyclic motion of
perfect fifths. Uses sketch materials to support this
interpretation. (*Dissertation Abstracts* 43 (1983):
2488-A)

415. Lisicki, Krzysztof. *Szkice o Krzysztofie Pendereckim*
[Essays on Krzysztof Penderecki]. Kraków: Polskie
Wydawnictwo Muzyczne, 1975. 209 pp. ML 410.P2673 L6

Claims to be on Penderecki's life and music, but is not
in depth on either subject. Written for a popular
audience. The book does provide twentieth-century
background on Polish music and presents the composer's
major works. Includes a discography and list of
premieres of compositions.

Review: *Ruch Muzyczny* 18, no. 13 (1974): 15-16.

416. Lissa, Zofia. "Muzyka w polskich filmach
eksperymentalnych" [Music in Polish experimental
films]. *Kwartalnik Filmowy* 11, no. 2 (1961): 3-24.

Discusses the film music of the Polish composers H.
Gruel, W. Kotoński, A. Markowski, and Z. Turski as well
as general tendencies of music in Polish avant-garde
films. Summary in French.

417. Łobaczewska, Stefania. *Karol Szymanowski. Życie i
twórczość (1882-1937)* [Karol Szymanowski: life and
works]. Kraków: Polskie Wydawnictwo Muzyczne, 1950.
667 pp. ML 410.S99 L6

Pays great attention to methodology and makes a strong
effort to set the background for study of Szymanowski.
The psychological and sociological concerns are
representative of early post-war musicological writing
in Eastern Europe. Szymanowski's compositions are
related to each other, but there is not great depth to
the musical analysis. Musical examples are printed
at the end of the book. Includes photographs of the
composer, a list of works, and a bibliography.

418. McCoy, Molly Jane. "The Polish Songs of Szymon Laks."
D.M.A. diss., University of Texas at Austin, 1987.

Starts with a biography of Laks, including the early
Polish period, his activities in Paris, detention and
activities in Auschwitz, and musical accomplishments
after World War II. Considers the poets and poetry
selected by Laks for his Polish songs. Outlines the
general compositional techniques found in the songs and
offers detailed discussion of "Przymierze,"
"Staruszkowie," and "Erratum." Includes a bibliography.
(*Dissertation Abstracts* 48 (1987): 1051-A)

419. Maciejewski, B.M. *Karol Szymanowski: His Life and
Music.* London: Poets' and Painters' Press, 1967.
147 pp. ML 410.S99 M3

Recreates the story of Szymanowski's life and career,
trying to incorporate influences and events around the
composer. Quotes letters, reviews, and memoirs, but
lacks detailed discussion of Szymanowski's music. The
book provides some good background to benefit readers

without expertise in Polish language and culture. The
bibliography contains titles of Polish publications only
in English translation. Provides photographs, a
chronology of events, a discography, and an index.

Reviews: David Cox, *Tempo* no. 83 (Winter 1967-68): 32;
Robert Henderson, *Musical Times* 109 (January 1965): 37-
38; *Musical Opinion* 91 (February 1968): 275; *Ruch
Muzyczny* 12, no. 8 (1968): 17.

420. _____. *Twelve Polish Composers*. London: Allegro Press,
1976. 229 pp. ML 390.M176 T9

Presents insights from the author's personal contact
with contemporary composers and includes notes of
conversations, biographical sketches, photographs, lists
of works, and an index. The composers included are:
Antoni Szałowski, Roman Maciejewski, Witold Lutosławski,
Grażyna Bacewicz, Andrzej Panufnik, Kazimierz Serocki,
Tadeusz Baird, Augustyn Bloch, Romould Twardowski,
Krzysztof Penderecki, Zbigniew Rudziński, and Krzysztof
Meyer.

Review: Paul Griffiths, *Musical Times* 117 (June 1976):
493.

421. Maciejewski, B.M. and Felix Aprahamian, ed. *Karol
Szymanowski and Jan Smeterlin: Correspondence and
Essays*. London: Allegro Press, 1969. 160 pp.
ML 410.599M2

Publishes 58 letters written between 1924 and 1937 and
translates several of Szymanowski's writings into
English.

Review: Max Harrison, *Composer* (London) no. 36
(Summer 1970): 32.

422. Maciejewski, Tadeusz. "Contemporary Polish Organ Music."
Polish Music 13, no. 3 (1978): 3-8.

Begins with a note concerning recent research on the
organ manuscript of the Warsaw Music Society. Traces
the late Romantic style of church pieces in the first
decades of the twentieth century. Assesses the work
of Feliks Nowowiejski as an organ composer. New
compositional techniques were developed in the 1960s
and many composers created concert pieces in the
second half of the century.

423. Malinowski, Władysław. "La musique en Pologne au
        cours des années 1956-1966." *La Musique en Pologne*
        1 (May 1966): 5-11.

Describes the effects of post-World War II social
changes on music after 1956, emphasizing the
significance of contact abroad. Presents the background
of neoclassical style with folklore elements found in
the music of Szymanowski and others. A new period
began with the works of Bacewicz. Cites an interest in
the organization of sonority and structure, and later
pointalism as style characteristics of music in the
decade after 1956. Lutosławski contributed a synthesis
of techniques. Mentions many composers and compositions
of the period.

424. Markiewicz, Leon. "II Symfonia Witolda Lutosławskiego"
        [The Second Symphony of Witold Lutosławski]. *Muzyka*
        13, no. 2 (1968): 67-76.

Lutosławski's form and aleatoric style. In considering
the structure of the *Second Symphony*, the author
isolates meter, orchestration, and chord aggregates as
these elements contribute to form. Notes the role of
the conductor in presenting the work.

425. Minear, Paul S. "Krzysztof Penderecki: An Interpretation
        of the Lucan Passion." In *Death Set to Music:*
        Masterworks by Bach, Brahms, Penderecki, Bernstein.
        Atlanta: John Knox Press, 1987. 173 pp.
        ISBN 0804218749 ML 2900.M5

Concentrates on the choice of texts for this choral
work and the implications of the words. Discusses
music only in general terms.

426.   Orga, Atęs. "Electronic Music in Poland." *Composer*
       (London) No. 32 (Summer 1969): 22-27.

       Discusses the musical experimentation of Polish
       composers after 1956, under the influence of post-
       Webern composition concepts. Presents a relatively
       detailed history of electronic music to place in
       context the opening of the studio at Polish Radio in
       1957-1958. Leading composers of electronic music
       mentioned are: Dobrowolski, Kotoński, Markowski,
       Penderecki, Sokorski, and Wiszniewski.

427.   Panufnik, Andrzej. *Composing Myself*. London: Methuen,
       1987. 369 pp. ISBN 0413588807 ML 410.P1615 C6

       In this autobiography, the composer covers his
       education in Poland and describes the mounting tension
       which precipitated his leaving the country. The book
       is particularly enlightening with regard to the
       government's use of artists for its own means. Talks
       about the difficulties in leaving Poland and his
       subsequent life in Great Britain. Also covers the
       composition of his music. Includes a chronological
       list of works with information about commissions,
       dedications, premieres, and recordings. Includes an
       index.

Materials from a seminar devoted to the creations of
Krzysztof Penderecki. Publishes two articles and the text
of discussion from a seminar at the Higher School of Music
in Cracow.

428.   Rychlik, Józef. "Punktualism we wczesnej twórczości
       Krzysztofa Pendereckiego" [Pointalism in the early
       compositions of K. Penderecki]. *Muzyka* 21, no. 2
       (1976): 5-21.

429.   Droba, Krzysztof. "Hierarchia czynników formalnych w
       twórczości Krzysztofa Pendereckiego (na przykładzie
       Polimorfii)" [The hierarchy of formal elements in
       the compositions of K. Penderecki (seen in
       Polimorfia)]. *Muzyka* 21, no. 2 (1976): 22-28.

430.   Pisarenko, Olgierd. "Contemporary Polish Chamber Opera."
        Music in Poland 38 (1983): 44-50.

        Explains that opera is not at the forefront of
        contemporary Polish music and that efforts at chamber
        opera followed an emphasis in radio opera at Polish
        Radio. Discusses specific works to draw generalizations
        about chamber opera. Performances of chamber opera have
        been staged mostly at the Opera Kameralna in Warsaw and
        occasionally at other opera houses in Poland.

431.   Pituch, David A. "Polskie 'Echo' w Ameryce" [A Polish
        Echo in America]. *Ruch Muzyczny* no. 19 (September
        1979): 7-9.

        Relates information about a music periodical published
        from 1929-1933 in Chicago and edited by Bolesław
        Józef Zalewski. Describes the aim of the serial as
        being to uphold and cultivate Polish culture among the
        Polish emigration. Focuses on the editor and his
        publishing house and analyzes the periodical's content
        as centering on the activities of the singing society
        Związek Spiewaków Polskich w Ameryce. Each issue
        contained some popular music. A list of Polish music
        periodicals published in the United States is more
        complete than the information found in the *New Grove*
        article "Periodicals." (see item 23)

432.   Pociej, Bohdan. *Lutosławski a wartość muzyki* [Lutosławski
        and the value of music]. Kraków: Polskie Wydawnictwo
        Muzyczne, 1976. 132 pp. 132 pp. ML 410.L965 P6

        A philosophical and aesthetic overview of Lutosławski's
        music. One section is an interview originally
        published in *Poezja* (November 1973). There are many
        references to specific Lutosławski works.

433.   _____. "Symphonicism redivivus." *Polish Perspectives*
        20, no. 5 (May 1977): 44-51.

        Discusses Lutosławski's *Mi-parti* from the point of view
        of a symphonic work. Offers a description of the music
        and aesthetic interpretation, but not an in-depth study
        of the score.

434. Polony, Leszek. "O harmonice Mieczysława Karłowicza"
        [About Mieczysław Karłowicz's harmony]. *Muzyka* 24,
        no. 1 (1979): 29-49.

        A study of Karłowicz's harmonic style, relying on
        three symphonic poems: *Rapsodia litewska, Stanisław i
        Anna Oświecimowie,* and *Smutna opowieść.* Discusses the
        dichotomy of functional versus coloristic harmony in
        these orchestral works. The author finds functional
        harmony as the basis of the compositions. Uses
        harmonic diagrams and includes an English summary.

435. Prosnak, Antoni. "'Cztery Eseje' Bairda i perspektywy
        techniki serialnej" [*Four Essays* of Baird and the
        perspectives of serial technique]. *Muzyka* 9, no. 3-4
        (1964): 26-42, 134-37.

        Analyzes the composition and discusses its serial
        technique in light of the various possibilities.
        Musical examples enhance the text. An extended summary
        in German is supplied.

436. Rappoport, Lidia. "Sonorism: Problems of Style and
        Form in Modern Polish Music." *Journal of
        Musicological Research* 4, no. 3-4 (1983): 399-416.

        The term "sonorism" was coined by Józef Chomiński in
        1956 to refer to a focus on coloristic techniques in
        new music. Polish composers found different means of
        enriching sonorous textures. Probes the works of
        Serocki, Górecki, and Penderecki. Gives examples of
        notation of new sounds.

437. _____. "Symfonie Krzysztofa Meyera" [The symphonies
        of Krzysztof Meyer]. *Muzyka* 20, no. 1 (1975):
        37-56.

        Prepares a background for Meyer's style by discussing
        other works, then compares Meyer's works to those of
        other composers. Identifies changes in style after the
        First Symphony. Highlights and presents a formal
        overview of each movement of the three symphonies.
        Supports the text with musical examples.

438. _____. *Vitol'd Lyutoslavskiy*. Moskva: Muzyka, 1976.
       136 pp.

Discusses Lutosławski's compositions through the 1960s.
Gives greater attention to the *First Symphony* and
Concerto for orchestra.

439. Robinson, Ray. *Krzysztof Penderecki: A Guide to His
       Works*. Princeton: Prestige Publications, 1983.
       35 pp. ML 134.P45 R6

Gives a biographical sketch of the composer and a short
discussion of his style. The list of works is
classified by genre and incorporates performance times,
commissions, dedications, and publishers. There is a
separate list of premiere performances. A discography
lists over 60 recordings of Penderecki's works. The
Polish Muza label is given as "Polish Gramophone."
The bibliography has about 30 citations, mostly writings
in English.

440. Robinson, Ray and Allen Winold. *A Study of the
       Penderecki St. Luke Passion*. Celle: Moeck Verlag,
       1983. ISBN 3875490169 MT 115.P42 R6

Begins with brief surveys of Penderecki's career and
the history of the Passion as a musical setting.
Studies the text selected by Penderecki and provides an
overall description of the music. The book then
proceeds to more detailed discussion of the musical
materials and structure of the music. Includes a
bibliography and discography.

441. Samson, Jim. *The Music of Szymanowski*. New York:
       Taplinger Publishing Co., 1981. 220 pp.
       ISBN 0800875397 ML 410.S99 S25

A critical analysis and evaluation of Szymanowski's
music. The discussion of the composer's compositions
with musical examples proceeds chronologically and
incorporates pertinent background and biographical
information. An introductory chapter on the Polish
inheritance concentrates on late nineteenth-century

orchestral music. The author provides a list of
Szymanowski's works and a bibliography.

Reviews: Dika Newlin, *Library Journal* 106 (May 1, 1981):
977; Richard Koprowski, *Notes* 38 (1981): 69.

442.   _____. "Przegląd modeli analitycznych i próba ich
        zastosowania do analizy języka harmonicznego Karola
        Szymanowskiego" [The use of analytical models in
        the analysis of Szymanowski's harmonic language].
        Muzyka 28, no. 2 (1983): 27-36.

Generally places Szymanowski's musical style between
impressionism and atonality. Suggests models by which
to explore tonal elements in non-diatonic contexts by
examining the methods of Ernö Lendvai, Heinrich
Schenker, Rudolph Reti, and Edmond Costère. Provides
short examples of the application of these analytical
systems.

443.   Schäffer, Bogusław, ed. *Artur Malawski. Życie i
        twórczość* [Artur Malawski: life and works]. Kraków:
        Polskie Wydawnictwo Muzyczne, 1969. 417 pp.
        ML 410.M246 S3

The collected contributions of several scholars
provide comprehensive coverage of the composer.
Comprised of a biography of the composer, analyses of
specific works and genres, and a general essay on his
compositional technique. Chronicles Malawski's
musical activities and compositions. Includes
reproductions of photographs, scores, and correspondence.
Appended are a list of works and the indexes.

Review: Zofia Helman, *Muzyka* 26, no. 1 (1976): 99-102.

444.   _____. *Leksykon kompozytorów XX wieku* [Lexicon of
        twentieth-century composers], 2 vols. Kraków:
        Polskie Wydawnictwo Muzyczne, 1963. ML 390.S2615 L4

Intended as a general biographical dictionary, but
contains a great number of entries on Polish and East
European composers. The entries for each composer
consist of short biographical sketches with a list

of major works. Volume 2 concludes with an essay on
jazz that does not give attention to the Polish jazz
scene.

Reviews: Henryk Schiller, *Muzyka* 11, no. 3-4 (1966):
127-30; *Ruch Muzyczny* 8, no. 6 (1964): 17; *Ruch
Muzyczny* 12, no. 13 (1968): 19.

445. _____. "Twórczość Romana Haubenstocka" [The creations
of Roman Haubenstock]. *Muzyka* 20, no. 1 (1975):
11-36.

Biographical material on Haubenstock's activities,
including events in Poland and Israel. Traces the
composer's concern for form from the time of his
earliest works. Cites the most original works, such
as *Mobile* and *Tableaux,* to discuss style changes over
the course of Haubenstock's career. Contains no
musical examples.

446. Schiller, Henryk. "Kazimierz Sikorski au 85-ème
anniversaire de sa naissance." *La Musique en
Pologne*, 1980, no. 1-4:8-18.

Sikorski followed Szymanowski as Director of the
Conservatory in Warsaw. This biographical article
considers Sikorski as a composer and pedagog in the
tradition of Nadia Boulanger. Also mentions his other
musical activities and awards.

447. Schwinger, Wolfram. "Magische Klanglandschaften:
Krzysztof Penderecki und die polnische Avantegarde."
Musica 22, no. 1 (January-February, 1968): 4-7.

A general discussion of Penderecki's work and place in
Polish music.

448. Scott, Richard James. "Piano Music of Karol Szymanowski:
Metopes, Opus 29, and Masques, Op. 34." D.M.A.
diss., University of Wisconsin at Madison, 1985.

A detailed discussion of the music placed within the
historical and stylistic context. (*Dissertation
Abstracts* 46 (1986): 3188-A)

449. Śledziński, Stefan. "Polish Music Composition in the
Period of the Second Republic 1918-1939." *Polish
Music* 14, no. 1-2 (1979): 5-7.

Explains the conservative, anachronistic style of most
Polish composers after World War I and describes
changes in this style with the advent of new music
institutions. Mentions the composers of Young Poland
and especially concentrates on Szymanowski, discussing
his music and role in Polish musical life. Śledziński
relates the loss of many manuscripts from the interwar
period during World War II.

450. Stanilewicz, Maria. "Problemy formy w 'Muzyce żałobnej'
Witolda Lutosławskiego" [The problems of form in the
Funeral Music of Witold Lutosławski]. *Muzyka* 23,
no. 1 (1978): 33-44.

Analyses the formal structure of individual movements
and the relationship between movements. Finds the
movements of Lutosławski's *Funeral Music* to be
interdependent. Includes an English summary.

451. Stucky, Steven. *Lutosławski and His Music*. Cambridge:
Cambridge University Press, 1981. 252 pp.
ML 410.L965 S8

Begins with a biography of Lutosławski's creative life.
His early works are analyzed in the course of the
biography. Contains detailed discussion of the music
with musical examples. The book continues with
characterization of Lutosławski's late style. Separate
sections are devoted to *Jeux vénitiens, Trois poèmes
d'Henri Michaux, String Quartet, Paroles tissées,
Second Symphony, Livre pour orchestra, Cello Concerto,
Preludes and Fugue, Les espaces,* and *Mi-parti.*
Includes a catalog of the composer's works, discography,
bibliography, and index.

Reviews: Tadeusz Zieliński, *Muzyka* 30, no. 1 (1985):
97-103; *Music Review* 43, no. 3-4 (1982): 280; *Notes*
38, no. 4 (1982): 844-45.

452. Świerczek, Leon. *Bolesław Wallek Walewski.* Kraków:
      Polskie Wydawnictwo Muzyczne, 1975. 72 pp.

      A short biography and chronicle of the composer's
      activities. Discusses musical works and sources;
      provides a catalog of music. The book reproduces 11
      letters to and from Walewski, and 6 remembrances of the
      composer. The bibliography includes about 80
      references; there are no indexes.

      Review: *Ruch Muzyczny* 20, no. 19 (1976): 17-18.

453. Thomas, Adrian. *Grażyna Bacewicz: Chamber and
      Orchestra Music.* Los Angeles: Friends of Polish
      Music, University of Southern California, 1985.
      128 pp. ISBN 0916545032 ML 410.B08 T5

      Places Bacewicz's work in historical perspective and
      discusses the development of her compositional style.
      Selects 11 works for detailed examination. Concludes
      that there is an inconsistency of style and merit in
      Bacewicz's compositions and contends that the music
      presents both stylistic subtleties and contradictions.

454. Varga, Bálint András. *Lutosławski Profile.* London:
      Chester Music, 1976. 58 pp. ML 410.L967 A3

      Lutosławski talks about a variety of subjects, including
      his life, philosophy of music, influences on his
      composition, the Polish music scene, conducting, and
      teaching.

455. Vinton, John, ed. *Dictionary of Contemporary Music.*
      New York: E.P. Dutton and Co., 1974. 834 pp.
      ISBN 0525091254 ML 100.V55

      Includes the biographies of approximately 20 Polish
      composers. Also devotes an entry to "Poland." Composer
      entries contain biographical data, a list of principal
      compositions, and bibliography.

Review: Bogusław Schäffer, *Muzyka* 20, no. 2 (1975): 116-20.

456.   Wenk, Arthur. *Analyses of Twentieth-Century Music.*
       Supplement, 2nd ed.   MLA Index and Bibliography
       Series, no. 14.   Boston: Music Library Association,
       1984.   132 pp.   ISBN 0914954288   ML 118.W462

Organizes references to published analyses of musical
compositions alphabetically by composer.   Only well-
known Polish composers are represented.   Does not
consider Polish journals for indexing, which requires
a researcher to consult other reference works for the
complete analytical literature.   Includes an index of
authors.

457.   Wightman, Alistair.   "Szymanowski a kraj i kultura
       angielska" [Szymanowski, England, and English
       culture]. *Muzyka* 28, no. 2 (1983): 3-26.

Reviews Szymanowski's contact with England and the use
of English literature for texts in his music.   Emphasizes
the influence of the aesthetic ideas of Oscar Wilde and
Walter Pater on Szymanowski's artistic thought.
Includes an English summary.

458.   _____. "Szymanowski and Joyce." *Musical Times* 123
       (October 1982): 679-83.

Characterizes the Joyce songs as private songs.   Gives
an assessment of the poems of Joyce's *Chamber Music*
and a stylistic analysis of the song cycle with
relationship to other works.   Wightman advocates
rearrangement of the song order from the order of the
poems.

459.   Wilk, Wanda. *Szymanowski.* Polish Music History Series,
       no. 1.   Los Angeles: Friends of Polish Music,
       University of Southern California, 1982.   16 pp.
       ML 410.S99 W56

Provides only a short sketch introducing the work of
Szymanowski.   Includes a list of the composer's works,

available scores, bibliography, and a discography.
The bibliography concentrates on the literature in
English.

460. Zamoyski, Adam. *Paderewski.* New York: Atheneum, 1982.
ISBN 0689112483 ML 410.P11423

Attempts to find the real Paderewski, covering both the
musical and political careers. The author underscores
what he feels are the important events in Paderewski's
political-diplomatic life and chronicles his
compositional activities. Zamoyski finds the compositions defective in the sense that Paderewski was
obligated to write works with a nationalistic
statement. There are no musical examples nor detailed
analytical discussions. The book includes a list of
works, repertory, recordings, index, and bibliography.

Twentieth Century, Musical Life

461. Belanger, J. Richard. "Wiktor Labunski: Polish-American
Musician in Kansas City, 1937-1974: A Case Study."
Ed.D. diss., Columbia University Teachers' College,
1982.

Labuński (1895-1974) was a Polish immigrant who
experienced the challenges of adaptation to the United
States. He made numerous contributions to the Kansas
City Conservatory and city as a whole. The dissertation
was prepared from interviews and the Labuński papers
at the University of Missouri at Kansas City. Contains
a thematic catalog of 31 compositions. (*Dissertation
Abstracts* 43 (1982): 1461-A)

462. Brennecke, Wilfried. "Chopin and Polish Music:
Impressions of a Visit to Warsaw." *World of Music*
2 (April 1960): 26-29.

Reports on the International Chopin Conference of 1960.

463. _____. "International musikwissenschaftlicher
      Chopin-Kongress in Warshau." *Musikforschung* 14
      (1961): 68-72.

      Reports on the International Chopin Congress and
      provides the program of events and topics of discussion.

464. Chomiński, Józef M. and Zofia Lissa. *Kultura Muzyczna*
      Polski Ludowej 1944-1955 [The musical culture of
      Peoples' Poland, 1944-1955]. Kraków: Polskie
      Wydawnictwo Muzyczne, 1957. 317 pp. ML 297.5.K86

      Contributions by a variety of authors. The subjects
      addressed include the organization of musical life,
      musical compositions by genre, and the scholarly study
      of music. Provides information on concerts, music
      education, Polish radio, music publishing, film music,
      musicological and theoretical studies, ethnomusicology,
      and criticism. Includes photographs of the main music
      scholars of the early post-war period.

465. Dobrowolski, Andrzej. "The Effect of 'Warsaw Autumn'
      on the Development of Music Life in Poland." *Polish*
      Music 10, no. 1 (1975): 5-9.

      Evaluates the Warsaw Autumn festival from its
      beginnings in 1956. Outside works influenced Polish
      composers, especially those compositions structured in
      serial technique. Also mentions the influence of
      Polish Radio on contemporary music and its audience.

466. _____. "Wpływ festiwali 'Warszawska Jesień' na rozwój
      życia muzycznego w Polsce" [The influence of the
      Warsaw Autumn festival on the development of
      musical life in Poland]. *Muzyka* 20, no. 3 (1975):
      58-63.

      The original concept of the Warsaw Autumn Festival of
      Contemporary Music was to attract new music to Poland
      and bring Polish composers into contact with the West.
      Presents the history of the festival from 1956 and the
      influence the annual series of concerts has had in the
      development of the reputation of Polish orchestras for

performing new music. Also discusses the influence
of the festival on the programming of Polish Radio and
Television.

467. Dyzbardis, Stanisław. "Le Grand Theatre de Łódź."
   La Musique en Pologne 6/7 (1970-1971): 19-23.

   Focuses on the opera troupe since 1954, after considering
   the cultural assets of the city. Describes the opera
   building and facility, as well as the repertory of the
   theater. Presents information on the highly acclaimed
   foreign appearances of the group and spotlights
   specific artists.

468. Dziębowska, Elżbieta, ed. *Polska współczesna kultura
   muzyczna 1944-1964* [Polish contemporary music culture
   1944-1964]. Kraków: Polskie Wydawnictwo Muzyczne,
   1968. 457 pp. ML 306.5 D98

   Contributions by different authors on composition,
   music research, ethnomusicology, music education, radio,
   publishing, concert life, amateur music activities, and
   music societies in Poland. There is a diary of events
   during this twenty-year period and an extensive
   bibliography. Separate sections of the bibliography
   are devoted to work on folklore, and a discography is
   organized by composer.

   Reviews: Maria Piotrowska, *Muzyka* 14, no. 3 (1969):
   105-9; *Ruch Muzyczny* 12, no. 19 (1968): 16.

469. Fénelon, Fania, with Marcelle Routier. *Playing for
   Time,* trans. Judith Landry. New York: Atheneum,
   1977; originally published as *Sursis pour
   l'orchestre,* 1976. 262 pp. ML 429.F436 A33

   Relates the experience of musicians in the orchestra
   at the women's camp at Birkenau. Chronicles the
   musical activities in the Nazi concentration camps.

470. Fuks, Marian. "Muzyka w Gettach" [Music in the ghettos].
   Muzyka 16, no. 1 (1971): 64-76.

Separately considers the Jewish ghettos of Warsaw,
Cracow, and Łódź. Newspapers were utilized to
document street concerts, recitals, chamber music
performances, and even symphony concerts.

471. Golańska, Stefania. "La Société Frédéric Chopin à
        Varsovie." *La Musique en Pologne* 5 (September 1969):
        11-21.

Chronicles the history of the Society from its
conception at the end of the nineteenth century. Notes
key activities of the Society, such as the editing of
Chopin's works and the building of an archive. The
history continues with the reactivation of the Society
after World War II and change to the present name in
1950. Describes the facilities in the Ostrogski
Palace, the museum, and library. Mentions current
activities, such as editing of Chopin works, the
International Piano Competition, and other concerts.

472. Gołębiowski, Marian. *Filharmonia w Warszawie 1901-
        1976* [The Warsaw Philharmonic, 1901-1976]. Kraków:
        Polskie Wydawnictwo Muzyczne, 1976. 358 pp.
        ML 306.8.W4 F521

Collates photographs, concert calendars, and programs
of international tours and special events of the
orchestra from its creation at the beginning of this
century. Includes indexes of artists, guest artists,
and outside musical groups and orchestras that have
appeared under the Philharmonic's auspices. A
separately bound appendix translates the photograph
captions into English.

473. Görlich, Joachim Georg. "Kirchenmusik im heutigen
        Polen." *Musik des Ostens* 6 (1971): 48-56.

Reviews the state of church music in Poland,
concentrating on the activities of specific composers
and performers. Also notes the accomplishments of
choirs, summarizes research activities on sacred
music, the employment outlook for organists, and
famous organs.

474.   Grzybowski, Jan. "Le Studio experimental de la Radio
        diffusion polonaise à Varsovie. Entretien avec
        Józef Patkowski, directeur du Studio." *La Musique
        en Pologne* 8 (1972): 3-12.

        Discusses the fifteen-year history of the studio at
        Polish Radio from its genesis through its development
        as a pioneer in the field of electronic music.
        Mentions specifically the roles of the composers
        Dobrowolski, Kotoński, and Schäffer. Presents the
        current activities of the studio in the areas of
        composition and teaching, and compares these activities
        with foreign studios. Lists works issued on foreign
        record labels and foreign composers who have worked
        in the Warsaw facility. Tries to predict new trends
        in electronic music.

475.   _____. "Teatr Wielki II" [The Great Theater in Łódź].
        Ruch Muzyczny 11, no. 5 (March 1-15, 1967): 3-6.

        An exposé of plans for an opera theater in Łódź. Offers
        blueprints of the building complex. Relates the genesis
        of the building and description. (Many people feel
        that the opera and opera theater in Łódź compete
        successfully with the Teatr Wielki in Warsaw.)

476.   Helman, Alicja. *Na ścieżce dźwiękowej: O muzyce w
        filmie* [On the sound track: about music in film].
        Kraków: Polskie Wydawnictwo Muzyczne, 1968.

        Conceived as a general work on film music, but several
        Polish composers are highlighted, especially Tadeusz
        Baird, Andrzej Markowski, and Adam Walaciński.

477.   Jasiński, Roman. *Na przełomie epok: Muzyka w Warszawie
        (1910-1927)* [At the turn of epochs: music in Warsaw
        (1910-1927)]. Warszawa: Państwowy Instytut
        Wydawniczy, 1979. 654 pp. ISBN 8306000595
        ML 297.8.W4 J4

        Taken from a column in *Ruch Muzyczny* entitled "Przegląd
        prasy sprzed 50 lat," [Review of the press from 50
        years ago] which has been published from about 1960.
        Chronicles musical life in Warsaw by reprinting

selected reviews and announcements for each month
of the years covered by the book. Covers foreign
artists in Warsaw and Polish artists abroad as
reported in the Warsaw newspapers. Especially focuses
on the National Philharmonic and Warsaw opera during
this period.

478. Jazwińska, Zofia. "Les concerts en Pologne." *La*
         Musique en Pologne 3 (March 1968): 19-30.

Presents an overview of the increasing and diverse
concert life of Poland, mentioning specific ensembles,
organ recitals, festivals, contests, and societies.
Considers the impact of rural concerts for the large
audience they reach and discusses the repertory of
general and Polish works presented at all levels.

479. *Jazz Forum* No. 44/6 (1976): 19.

Reports on the evolution of the Polish Jazz Society
from the Federation of Polish Jazz Clubs founded in
1956. Presents some statistics of the Polish Jazz
Society.

480. Kaczyński, Tadeusz. "Polish Music and Musicians in
         Paris Fifty Years Ago." *Polish Music* 12, no. 2
         (1977): 11-16.

Focuses on the Society of Young Polish Musicians which
functioned in Paris in the first half of this century.
Covers the Polish composers involved and the influence
the association had on individual members.

481. Kopeczek-Michałska, Krystyna. "Jawne i tajne życie
         koncertowe w Warszawie w latach okupacji
         hitlerowskiej" [The open and secret concert life in
         Warsaw in the years of the Nazi occupation].
         Muzyka 15, no. 3 (1970): 47-64.

Describes the activities of music organizations, music
in coffee houses, official and secret activities of
orchestras, theater groups, and chamber ensembles.
Mentions many specific musicians and performers.

482. Kotoński, Włodzimierz. "La musique à la Radio
      Polonaise." *La Musique en Pologne*, 1974, no. 2:
      3-15.

      Describes broadcasting innovations, such as the
      chronicle of musical activities preceding the evening
      news, weekly reports on music in Warsaw, the emphasis
      on Polish music, children's programming, and efforts
      to reach the entire population.

483. Laks, Szymon. *Gry oświęcimskie* [Auschwitz melodies].
      London: Oficyna Poetów i Malarzy, 1979. 107 pp.
      D 805.P7 L34

      Recounts the author's experience in Auschwitz as a
      musician and director of music. Represents a reworking
      of his *Musiques d'un autre monde* published in 1948.

      Review: *Instrumentenbau* 33 (September 1979): 632.

484. Lee, Jan Patrick. "Musical Life and Socio-Political
      Change in Warsaw, Poland: 1944-1960." Ph.D. diss.,
      University of North Carolina at Chapel Hill, 1979.

      Considers the reconstruction of musical life within a
      national consciousness after World War II and
      reestablishment of Polish music on the international
      scene. Music festivals had a great role in the
      growth of musical life in this period. Composers
      discussed include: Tadeusz Baird, Witold Lutosławski,
      Zygmunt Mycielski, and Andrzej Panufnik. (*Dissertation
      Abstracts* 41 (1980): 14-A)

485. Lewis, Nigel. *Paperchase: Mozart, Beethoven, Bach . . .
      The Search for Their Lost Music.* London: Hamish
      Hamilton, 1981. 246 pp. ISBN 0241102359
      ML 93.L48

      Explains the story, much of it pieced together by
      speculation, of manuscripts missing from Berlin since
      World War II. Outlines the controversy and search for
      the manuscripts and the Polish state secret of their
      storage in the Jagiellonian Library, unknown until the
      late 1970s. Mentions the measures used to preserve

Polish musical manuscripts during war years. Presents
a popular account of the search for the missing
manuscripts, not well documented.

Reviews: Gerald Abraham, *Times Literary Supplement*
(December 25, 1981): 1490; *Economist* 281 (December 5,
1981): 112.

486. Marek, Tadeusz. "Grand Theatre of Warsaw. The History
          and the Jubilee." *Polish Music* 11, no. 2 (1976):
          3-9.

An historical overview of the operatic tradition in
Warsaw and especially the history of the Teatr Wielki.
Dwells on post-war activities. Gives a description
of the building and the Theater Museum.

487. _____. "Seventy-five Years of the Warsaw Philharmonic."
          Polish Music 11, no. 3 (1976): 3-11.

A history of Warsaw's orchestra from the nineteenth
century. Outlines the financing problems which were
overcome to create the orchestra. Describes the first
concert seasons, beginning in 1901. The article
continues with the history of the post-war orchestra,
reconstructions of music organizations and buildings.
Gives some idea of the orchestra's repertory.

488. _____. "75 ans d'existence de la Philharmonie de
          Varsovie." *La Musique en Pologne* 1975, no. 4:10-17.

Begins with the circumstances of the orchestra's
organization in 1901. At first there were many foreign
musicians. Mentions early financial trouble and
reconstruction after World War II with Witold Rowicki
as music director. No details are given on the
conductors or repertory of the orchestra.

489. Mattingly, Gabrielle. "Polish Classical Recordings
          Stage a Boomlet." *High Fidelity* 26, no. 3 (March
          1976): 70-72.

Reports on the success of the Polish Record Center of
America in Chicago. Most of the firm's business is
with retailers who wish to supply their respective
buyers' requests for classical recordings, especially
of twentieth-century Polish composers.

490.   Michalska, Krystyna. "Music During the Nazi Occupation
1935-1945." *Polish Music* 14, no. 1-2 (1979): 8-15.

Describes the work of the secret Musicians' Union with
the Home Army and efforts to circumvent the prohibition
of Polish and Jewish music during 1939-1940. Mentions
specific instrumental ensembles active in Warsaw and
Cracow, and the importance of home concerts in later
years of the war. Emphasizes the role of concerts in
supporting the ill-fated Warsaw Uprising.

491.   "Musical Life in Poland." *Southwestern Musician* 16,
no. 7 (March 1950): 6, 22-23.

Reports on musical life in post-war Poland, with
special focus on orchestras, music education, and folk
music groups.

492.   Ochlewski, Tadeusz. "Muzyka w Warszawie podczas
okupacji" [Music in Warsaw during the German
occupation]. *Ruch Muzyczny* 14, no. 11 (June 1-15,
1970): 16-17.

Outlines musical activities in a variety of areas,
especially concerts, appearances of performing artists,
continued teaching in music schools, and limited
publishing efforts.

493.   Osostowicz-Sutkowska, Alina. "Polish Music in the
Polish Radio-Records." *Polish Music* 10, no. 4
(1975): 17-29.

Considers the importance of Polish Radio in Polish
musical life. Recordings of leading Polish artists
and composers have been made for broadcast. Music
ensembles instituted as part of Polish Radio give
public concerts and foreign tours. Lists major
composers and their recorded works.

494. Paulu, Burton. *Radio and Television Broadcasting in
        Eastern Europe.* Minneapolis: University of
        Minnesota Press, 1974. 592 pp. ISBN 0816607214
        HE 8689.9.E22 P38

      "Polish Peoples' Republic," pp. 270-312.

      After presenting facts and statistics on Poland as a
      country, covers technical characteristics of
      broadcasting networks. Discusses news and children's
      programming, adult education, drama and entertainment,
      and documentaries. A major goal is to raise the
      cultural level of the population through the music
      programming. Mentions the orchestras of Polish Radio
      and Television and the broadcasting of both classical
      and lighter music, including jazz.

495. Piwkowska, Leonia. "Polish Music in Australia."
        Polish Music 16, no. 3-4 (1981): 70-72.

      Describes the increased programming of Polish works
      that came about in the 1970s with cultural contacts
      between Australia and Poland. Mentions specific
      performances and broadcasts.

496. Poniatowska, Irena. "Fifty Years of the Frederic Chopin
        Society 1934-1984." *Music in Poland* 39 (1984):
        9-26.

      Presents the goals of the organization at its founding
      and an overview of its subsequent development.
      Mentions the Society's library collections, publications,
      and conferences.

497. Prokopowicz, Maria. "Traditions and Achievements of
        Music Libraries and Library Science in the Polish
        People's Republic." *Fontis artis musicae* 26, no. 1
        (1979): 36-43.

      The reconstruction after World War II marks the
      creation of music libraries in Poland and separate
      collections. Traces privately supported collections
      from the nineteenth century. Describes the
      restructuring and rebuilding in the second half of the

twentieth century, considering especially the training
of staff and addition of university graduates after
1955, the establishment of cataloging policies, and
organization of conferences. Selects next priority as
the cataloging of manuscripts. Describes research on
the history of music publishing. The bibliography of
34 items includes 11 catalogs of Polish collections.

498. Rubinstein, Arthur. *My Young Years*. New York: Alfred
      A. Knopf, 1973. 478 pp. ML 417.R79 A3

499. _____. *My Many Years*. New York: Alfred A. Knopf,
      1980. 626 pp. ML 417.R79 A28 ISBN 0394422538

      The first book chronicles the pianist's life and his
      contact with Polish musicians and artists of the early
      twentieth century, especially Szymanowski. The chapter
      on "Childhood in Poland" describes musical life at the
      turn of the century. *My Many Years* continues the
      memoirs from World War I. The index in each volume
      provides quick access to the author's impressions of
      Polish artists who were in his acquaintance.

500. Waldorff, Jerzy, ed. *Opera poznańska 1919-1969* [Poznań
      opera 1919-1969]. Poznań: Wydawnictwo Poznańskie,
      1970. 219 pp. ML 1736.8.P68 P36

      Includes an historical study of the Poznań opera by
      Bogdan Ciszewski and Tadeusz Świtała. The book also
      has a chronology of performance activities and 12
      reminiscences of opera activities. 111 photographs
      are provided.

501. Whitehead, P.J.P. "The Lost Berlin Manuscripts."
      Notes 33, no. 1 (September 1976): 7-15.

      A summary of the post-war intrigue as presented in
      item 485. Reprints a list of musical manuscripts that
      are considered part of this group of musical sources.

502. Wodnicka, Helena. "Les théâtres musicaux en République
      Populaire de Pologne." *La Musique en Pologne* 6/7
      (1970-1971): 3-13.

The author claims that low ticket prices, in spite of
the high cost of opera production, have created an
annual attendance of 3,200,000 people in the many
Polish theaters opened since World War II. Mentions
the regional theaters, outdoor spectacles, and
foreign tours. Discusses demographics of the audience
and the varied repertory that even includes American
musicals.

Musica Antiqua Europae Orientalis

503. La Rue, Jan. "The Bydgoszcz Festival Celebrating
          Poland's Thousand Years." *Notes* 23, no. 3 (1967):
          455-61.

      Reviews the 1966 early music festival and the resultant
      collection of papers. Discusses the choice of music
      performed as part of the festival. Reproduces the
      table of contents of *Musica Antiqua Europae Orientalis,*
      vol. 1, with short comments on the content of the
      articles.

504. Brennecke, Wilfried. "Alte Musik Osteuropas." *Musica*
          20, no. 6 (1966): 288-289.

      Reports on the first Musica Antiqua Europae Orientalis
      festival devoted to the performance of early East
      European music and the presentation of scholarly
      papers.

505. Feil, Arnold. "VI. Kongress und Festival Musica
          Antiqua Europae Orientalis." *Musikforschung* 36,
          no. 3 (1983): 147.

      A short report on the 1982 Congress. The general
      theme of the meeting was Byzantine music and the
      folkmusic of southeastern Europe.

506. Węcowski, Jan. "Musica Antiqua Europae Orientalis,
          Sixth International Festival of Early Music, Sixth
          International Festival of Musicologists, Bydgoszcz
          1982." *Polish Music* 17, no. 3-4 (1982): 48-51.

Reports on participating performers and lists the 47
musicologists present. Remarks on the themes of
musicological discussion, especially the issue of
East-West contacts in music history.

Warsaw Autumn

507. Kaczyński, Tadeusz and Andrzej Zborski. *Warszawska
      jesień* [Warsaw Autumn]. Kraków: Polskie Wydawnictwo
      Muzyczne, 1983. 357 pp. ISBN 8322400020
      ML 297.8.W4 K2

      Explains the beginning of the annual Warsaw Autumn
      Festival of Contemporary Music and presents short
      synopses of the concerts for each of the years from
      1956 to 1981. Most of the album consists of
      photographs from each festival and calendars of programs
      presented. English translations are provided for the
      introduction and photo captions. Includes an index
      of composers and works.

508. Kaczyński, Tadeusz. "Twenty-five Years of the 'Warsaw
      Autumn' Festival." *Music in Poland* 38, no. 1-2
      (1983): 20-43.

      Presents an English translation of the introduction to
      Warszawska jesień (see item 507).

509. Helm, Everett. "Current Chronicle: Poland." *Musical
      Quarterly* 39, no. 1 (1959): 111-14.

      Reports on the second Warsaw Autumn festival in 1958.
      Comments on music in Polish society and provides short
      reviews of specific pieces performed.

510. _____. "Autumn Music." *Musical America* 81, no. 11
      (November 1961): 23-24.

      Reports on the Warsaw Autumn festival of 1961.

511. Carter, Elliott. "Letter from Europe." *Perspectives of New Music* 1, no. 2 (1963): 195-210.

      Discusses the Warsaw Autumn festival and general music culture of Poland on pages 201-205. Reports specifically on the events of the 1962 series of concerts.

512. Helm, Everett. "Warsaw. Adventure in Poland." *High Fidelity/Musical America* 15, no. 12 (December 1965): 185.

      Includes a history of the Warsaw Autumn festival and mentions works performed during 1965.

513. Kruttge, Eigel. "Das 42. Weltmusikfest der IGNM im Warschauer Herbst 1968." *NZ; Neue Zeitschrift für Musik* 129, no. 11 (November 1968): 474-75.

      Mentions the works of Polish composers performed.

514. Murray, Bain. "Adventures in Poland." *High Fidelity/ Musical America* 19, no. 12 (December 1969): MA 26-27.

      Mentions the performance of Lutosławski's *Livre pour orchestre* during the 1969 festival.

515. Jack, Adrian. "The Autumn in Warsaw." *Music and Musicians* 21, no. 4 (December 1972): 30-34.

516. Murray, Bain. "Warsaw Autumn: A Lab for New Sounds." *High Fidelity/Musical America* 26, no. 2 (February 1976): MA 38-39.

517. Markowski, Liesel. "Warschauer Herbst 1976: Zum 20. Mal Festival zeitgenossischer Musik." *Musik und Gesellschaft* 27 (January 1977): 31-35.

518. Shepherd, John. "Warsaw (International Festival of
         Contemporary Music)." *Music and Letters* 25, no. 5
         (January 1977): 46-48.

      Reports on the Warsaw Autumn Festival of 1976, which
      featured works by Penderecki, Lutosławski, Serocki,
      Zygmunt Krausse, and Augustyn Bloch.

519. Murray, Bain. "Warsaw Autumn No. 22." *High Fidelity/
         Musical America* 29, no. 2 (February 1979): MA 36-38.

520. de la Motte, Diether. "Warschauer Herbst 25 Jahre
         jung." *Musica* 36, no. 1 (January-February 1982):
         52-53.

      Reviews the concert series of 1981.

521. Samson, Jim. "Warsaw (Autumn)." *Musical Times* 122
         (December 1981): 842.

      Reports on low budget of the 1981 Warsaw Autumn
      Festival. Cites compositions by Lutosławski,
      Penderecki, Górecki, Schäffer, and Bohdan Mazurek.

522. Bielawski, Ludwig. "Etnografia muzyczna w XXV-leciu PRL" [Musical ethnography in the twenty-five years of the Polish People's Republic]. *Muzyka* 15, no. 2 (1970): 3-10.

   A summary of ethnomusicological activities from 1945 to 1970. Describes the rise of centers for the study of folklore and the achievements of specific scholars. A major effort was made to record folk melodies during this period and the publication of the complete works of Oskar Kolberg was a major project. Discusses the evolution of methodology and expansion of interest in ethnographic studies beyond Poland.

523. Czekanowska, Anna. "The Application of Polish Statistical Methods to the Classification of Folk Melodies." *Polish Musicological Studies* 2 (1986): 94-110. See item 131. Originally entitled "Zastowowanie polskich metod statystycznych do klasyfikacji melodii ludowych." *Muzyka* 14 (1969): 1.

   Reports on the author's application of the Wrocław taxonomy to Polish folk music using computer coding.

524. _____. "The Teaching of Ethnomusicology in Poland: Experience and Prospects." *Acta Musicologica* 58, no. 1 (1986): 24-34.

   Presents a history of ethnomusicology in Poland and its establishment as an independent discipline. Notes changes of emphasis in research from work on Polish traditional music to more general Slavic considerations, and in the last two decades, increasing interest in non-European research. Explains developments in

methodology and problems of preparation. Describes
the university curriculum for students of ethnomusicology and lists Polish dissertations in the
discipline.

525. Lange, Roderyk. "Historia badań nad tańcem ludowym w
     Polsce" [The history of research on the folk dance
     in Poland]. *Lud* 51 (1963): 415-49.

     Defines different folk dances; categorizes and
     discusses works separately in categories such as
     methodology, documentary studies, and regional studies.
     A bibliography lists 379 items.

526. Stęszewski, Jan. "A Review of Polish Ethnomusicological
     Research after 1945." *Polish Music* 8, no. 3-4
     (1973): 29-36.

     Begins with nineteenth-century antecedents. Notes the
     contribution of the Sobieskis in the collection of
     music and publication of material by region. Relates
     the state of ethnomusicology as a university discipline
     and summarizes the achievements of major scholars,
     discussing the types of studies completed and approach
     taken. An important institution in ethnomusicological
     research is the Folklore Archive of the Instytut
     Sztuki, Polish Academy of Sciences in Warsaw.

Polish Folk Music

527. Benet, Sula. *Song, Dance, and Customs of Peasant
     Poland.* New York: Roy Publishers, [1951]. 247 pp.
     DK 4110.B4

     Incorporates some scattered references to the singing
     of carols and dancing, especially the mazurka and
     polonaise.

     Review: Kathleen Frobel, *Ethnomusicology* 25, no. 2
     (May 1981): 330-31.

528. Grajewska-Harasiuk, Anna. "Przemiany stylistyczne
      tradycyjnego folkloru opoczyńskiego w procesie
      popularyzacji" [Stylistic transformations of
      traditional Opoczyń folklore in the process of
      popularization]. *Muzyka* 19, no. 3 (1974): 34-48.

      Focuses on the repertory of the folk performance group
      "Opocznianka." Discusses the sources of the repertory
      and compares tunes used by these modern performers with
      authentic melodies. Draws conclusions on the general
      directions to be found in the stylization of folk
      material.

529. International Commission on Folk Arts and Folklore.
      Collection phonothèque nationale (Paris). Paris:
      UNESCO, 1952. 254 pp. ML 156.4.F5 I5

      Lists in its holdings a collection of Polish folksongs
      recorded in 1941.

530. Majchrzak, Józef. *Polska pieśń ludowa na Dolnym Śląsku*
      [Polish folk songs from Dolny Śląsk]. Warszawa:
      Polskie Wydawnictwo Naukowe, 1983. 315 pp.
      ISBN 8301045019 ML 3627.M34

      The book explains the traditions of the region.
      Analyzes musical and textual characteristics of folk-
      songs. Uses many examples of texts and melodies to
      support the presentation.

531. Przerembski, Zbigniew Jerzy. "Regionale zróżnicowanie
      kulminacji melodycznej w polskich pieśniach
      ludowych" [Regional variations in the melodic climax
      in Polish folk songs]. *Muzyka* 31, no. 2 (1986):
      33-43.

      A general assessment of Polish folksong from 43
      published collections. Analyzes the melodic climax
      using Czekanowski statistical methods. Draws
      conclusions on regional variations in Polish folk
      melodies. Includes an English summary.

532. Sadownik, Jan, general ed. *Pieśni podhala. Antologia*
     [Songs of Podhala. Anthology]. Kraków: Polskie
     Wydawnictwo Muzyczne, 1971. 363 pp. M 1763.S

     The texts and music are presented separately, with the
     songs classified in general categories such as
     shepherd songs, love songs, etc. Offers commentaries
     on texts, music, and regional pronunciation of Polish.
     The book contains many photographs of country scenes,
     in addition to including a glossary and subject index.

533. Stęszewski, Jan. "Polish Folk Music." *Polish Music* 5,
     no. 2 (1970): 5-11.

     Gives an historical explanation of Polish dances and
     the success of stage groups such as Mazowsze and Śląsk.
     Underscores the importance of Oskar Kolberg and later,
     the work of the Sobieskis. Gives the musical
     characteristics of Polish folk music, especially the
     element of rhythm, and spells out regional
     differences.

534. _____. "Problems of the Theory and Method in Polish
     Research on Folklore in Music (the situation and
     tendencies since 1945)." *Polish Musicological
     Studies* 1 (1977): 237-60. See item 131.

     Focuses on the definition of folk music, sources of
     information, problems in transcription from sound
     recordings, and categorizations of folk melodies.

535. Swartz, Anne. "The Polish Folk Mazurka." *Studia
     musicologica* 17 (1975): 249-255.

     Differentiates the mazur, kujawiak, and oberek, noting
     that examples often do not fit labels. Discusses the
     stress patterns according to Aleksander Poliński and
     compares his definitions with melodies in Kolberg's
     Lud. Also refers to lutebooks from surrounding
     countries where Polish rhythms appear as Bauerntanz or
     Nachtanz.

536. Tomaszewski, Mieczysław. "PWM Publishers: Editions of
      Polish Folk Music." *Polish Music* 5, no. 2 (1970):
      12-18.

      Covers collections published by Polskie Wydawnictwo
      Muzyczne, the state music publishing house. Anthologies
      of folk music seem to have been stressed, and the
      publication of the complete works of Oskar Kolberg has
      been a major project. Mentions other scholarly studies
      issued by the publishing house.

537. Vetterl, Karl, ed. *A Select Bibliography of European
      Folk Music.* Prague: Czechoslovak Academy of
      Sciences, 1966. 144 pp. ML 128.F75 V48

      "Poland," pp. 76-81, contributed by Jadwiga Sobieska.

      Lists 50 references on Polish folk music, with English
      translations of the titles. Only short annotations
      are included.

      Review: Ann Briegleb, *Ethnomusicology* 12, no. 1 (1968):
      161-62.

538. Wieczorkiewicz, Bronisław. *Warszawskie ballady
      podwórzowe. Pieśni i piosenki warszawskiej ulicy*
      [Warsaw courtyard ballads. Songs and ditties from
      the streets of Warsaw]. Warszawa: Państwowy
      Instytut Wydawniczy, 1971. 453 pp. M 1762.W62 W3

      Arranges the street songs chronologically from about
      1900. Melodies are provided, as well as full stanzas
      of text. There are more lyrics printed than tunes
      because some were sung to well-known melodies.
      Concludes with an alphabetical list of songs and
      glossary of unusual and dialectal Polish words.

539. Wojcicki, Kazimierz Władysław. *Pieśni ludu
      Białochrobatów, Mazurów i Rusi znad Bugu* [Folksongs
      of Bialochorbats, Mazurs, and Ruthenians from above
      the Bug River], 2 vols., ed. Helena Kapełuś.
      Wrocław: Zakład Narodowy im. Ossolińskich Wydawnictwo,
      1976. M 1762.W6

A facsimile of the 1836 edition. Consists mostly of
text, but there is some music. The commentary and
indexes appear in volume 2.

540. Zakrzewski, Bogdan. *Pieśni ludu śląskiego za zbiorów
      rękopiśmiennych Józefa Lompy* [Folksongs of Silesia
      from the manuscript collections of Józef Lompa].
      Wrocław: Państwowe Wydawnictwo Naukowe, 1970.
      468 pp. ML 3687.L6

The introduction explains the work of Józef Lompa
conducted in the early nineteenth century and his
manuscripts of folksongs. Prints songs and texts,
grouped by function. Adds a glossary of archaic and
dialectic words and expressions. Includes a title and
incipit index.

Polish Jazz

541. Carl Gregor, Duke of Mecklenburg. *International Jazz
      Bibliography: Jazz Books from 1919 to 1968.*
      Sammlung musikwissenschaftlicher Abhandlungen, no.
      49. Baden-Baden: Verlag Hertz GmbH, 1969. 198 pp.
      ML 3561.J655

Includes seven items on Poland, some of which are
Polish translations of books originally in English.
Indexes of collections and series, persons, authors,
subjects, editions, and represented countries are
included.

542. _____. *1970 Supplement to International Jazz
      Bibliography and International Drum and Percussion
      Bibliography.* Graz: Universal Edition, 1971.
      ML 3561.J6 I51

Follows item 541.

Reviews: Frank J. Gillis, *Ethnomusicology* 18, no. 3
(1974): 460-61; Ekkehart Jost, *Musikforschung* 28, no. 1
(1975): 113-14.

543. Panek, Wacław, ed. *Z polskiej krytyki jazzowej.*
      Eseje, dyskusje, reportaże, recenzje, felietony,
      wywiady 1956-1976 [From Polish jazz criticism:
      essays, discussions, commentaries, reviews, columns,
      interviews, 1956-1976]. Kraków: Polskie Wydawnictwo
      Muzyczne, 1978. 275 pp. ML 3677.Z2

      Of the essays by different authors, some are reprints
      of articles published in other sources. Approximately
      half of the book is specifically on jazz in Poland.
      Concludes with a short bibliography.

                            North America

544. Glofcheskie, John Michael. *Folk Music of Canada's*
      Oldest Polish Community. Ottawa: National Museums
      of Canada, 1980.

      Reports on the music traditions found among Polish-
      Canadians of Kashubian origin in Renfrew County,
      Ontario. Polish songs were found to have been
      particularly important at weddings, funerals, and
      religious festivities. Attention is also given to the
      instrumental music practiced by the immigrant
      community.

      Reviews: Robert B. Klymasz, *Journal of American*
      Folklore 95 (1982): 491-92; Bruno Nettl, *Western*
      Folklore 40, no. 4 (1982): 344.

545. Kleeman, Janice Ellen. "The Origins and Stylistic
      Development of Polish-American Polka Music." Ph.D.
      diss., University of California at Berkeley, 1982.
      370 pp.

      Polish immigrants brought rural and urban styles of the
      polka to the United States between 1900 and 1920.
      Discusses the advent of polka recordings and regional
      styles of the United States. (*Dissertation Abstracts*
      43 (1983): 2488-A)

546. Kamiński, Włodzimierz. *Instrumenty muzyczne na ziemiach polskich i zarys problematyki rozwojowej* [Musical instruments in Polish territory and an outline of the problems of development]. Kraków: Polskie Wydawnictwo Muzyczne, 1971. 170 pp. ML 460.K33

Presents research on instruments from ancient times through the Renaissance, and the production of instruments to the nineteenth century. Contains many photographs of extant instruments and some of iconographic sources. Reprints a number of historical documents.

Review article:

547. Chaniecki, Zbigniew. "Uwagi o pracy Włodzimierz Kamińskiego 'Instrumenty muzyczne na ziemiach polskich--zarys problematyki rozwojowej'" [Remarks on the work of Włodzimierz Kamiński, "Musical instruments in Polish territory and an outline of the problems of development"]. *Muzyka* 22, no. 2 (1977): 100-103.

548. Gołos, Jerzy. *Polskie organy i muzyka organowa* [Polish organs and organ music]. Warszawa: Instytut Wydawniczy PAX, 1972. 511 pp. ML 592.P6 G6

The first part of the book presents a short history of organ building in Europe with an explanation of Polish organ building within that context. Part 2 is a survey of Polish organ compositions. Appended material includes lists of stops on Polish organs, a glossary of organ terms, a list of organists throughout Polish musical

history, and a list of source material. A register of
places sometimes provides stop lists for specific
instruments. Over 70 plates of Polish organs are
provided. Diagrams throughout the volume explain
technical features; some examples of Polish organ music
are given. Includes a bibliography.

Reviews: *Ruch Muzyczny* 18, no. 10 (1974): 18; *Organ
Yearbook* 5 (1974): 133-34; *Hudební věda* 13, no. 2
(1976): 189-91.

549. _____. "Portable Organs in Poland." *Organ Yearbook*
     3 (1972): 36-47.

Describes positive-in-chest organs. Discusses specific
examples of instruments and Polish characteristics.
Offers plates of instruments.

550. _____. "Some rare technical features found in the
     historic organs of Poland." *Organ Yearbook* 10
     (1979): 34-47.

Observes peculiarities of Polish organs in the areas
of windchest and action; stops, pipes and pipe metal;
air supply and bellows; and tuning and temperament.
Photographs of specific instruments are supplied to
illustrate these characteristics.

551. Kamiński, Włodzimierz. *Skrzypce polskie* [Polish violins].
     Kraków: Polskie Wydawnictwo Muzyczne, 1969. 96 pp.
     ML 510.K29

A popular account of the history of violins in Poland
from the Middle Ages through the nineteenth century.
Many photographs of historical instruments, including
folk instruments, are provided. The text refers to
specific museum examples. Includes a catalog of
instruments presented in the plates.

Reviews: Alicja Jarzębska, *Muzyka* 28, no. 4 (1973):
87-90; *Ruch Muzyczny* 14, no. 5 (1970): 19.

552. Krzyżaniak, Barbara. "Informacje o ludowych
          instrumentach muzycznych w tekstach kolęd"
          [Information about folk musical instruments in carol
          texts]. *Muzyka* 17, no. 4 (1972): 116-21.

      Relies on Biblioteka Uniwersytecka w Poznaniu *Ch. 251*
      (1721) as source of carols. Classifies references to
      instruments, which consist mostly of dudy, skrzypce,
      and multanki. Also notes instruments used in ensembles,
      as related to the song texts.

553. Olędzki, Stanisław. *Polskie instrumenty ludowe* [Polish
          folk instruments]. Kraków: Polskie Wydawnictwo
          Muzyczne, 1978. 113 pp. ML 522.P6 04

      A photograph album of folk instruments with short
      explanations. The instruments are from Polish museums,
      mostly chordophones and aerophones, such as bagpipes
      (dudy). An English summary of the introduction and
      list of instruments is provided but not bound into the
      book.

554. Sąsiadek, Eugeniusz. "Les problems actuels de l'art
          vocal et la culture générale du chant en Pologne."
          La Musique en Pologne, 1979, no. 1-4:31-43.

      In spite of the presence of soloists on the world opera
      and concert stages, the author finds several problems
      in the training of Polish vocalists. Improvement
      should be made in vocal pedagogy in the general and
      music schools, and greater assistance might be given
      to young singers. There is no mention of specific
      teachers or performers.

555. Simon, Alicia. "Polish Instruments and Constructors of
          Instruments in Poland." *Hinrichsen's Musical Year
          Book* 7 (1952): 220-26.

      General comments on the history of instrument making in
      Poland. Includes information on bagpipes, violins,
      cittern and guitar, organs, and pianos. Gives names
      of makers and some indication of foreign influences.

556. Szydłowska-Ceglowa, Barbara. *Staropolskie nazewnictwo
      instrumentów muzycznych* [Old Polish nomenclature of
      musical instruments]. Wrocław-Warszawa-Kraków-
      Gdańsk: Zakład Narodowy im. Ossolińskich--
      Wydawnictwo PAN, 1977. 288 pp. ML 522.P6 S9

      Contains lexicological analyses of 55 Polish names for
      musical instruments. Organized by groups of instruments.
      Includes a bibliography.

      Review: Zbigniew Chaniecki, *Muzyka* 23, no. 2 (1978):
      98-103.

557. Zwolska, Barbara. "Instruments folkloriques dans les
      musées polonaise." *La Musique en Pologne,* 1975,
      no. 2:19-23.

      Begins with the history of instrument collecting from
      the nineteenth century. There was a consolidation of
      collections at Szydłowiec in 1975. Presents the
      principles used in the disposition of this Museum of
      Folk Instruments. Gives the addresses of three
      instrument museums.

PEDAGOGY

558. Aliferis, James. "A U.S. - Poland Comparison of Scores on the Aliferis College Entrance Test." *Council for Research in Music Education Bulletin* No. 75 (Summer 1983): 14-22.

This achievement test was given in the United States in the 1950s and also administered in Poland, but a report of the Polish test results was not issued until 1972. The article compares gender in music schools and chosen instruments of students. A comparison of the test results leads to the conclusion that music achievement is higher in Poland, probably because students are placed in special music schools before college.

559. Bojus, Julia E. "Music Education in Poland." Ph.D. diss., University of Miami, 1972.

Much of the study is based on observation in the state schools of Poland. A history of music education in Poland was constructed from secondary sources. A great deal of the dissertation is devoted to contemporary music education. Bojus explains the hierarchy of music schools in Poland, with an explanation of their objectives, curriculum, and evaluative tests. A number of statistical tables support the commentary. The author concludes that music schools in Poland provide a strong program of instruction, but music in general education is neglected and held in low esteem. The bibliography includes general materials on Polish music, as well as music education. (*Dissertation Abstracts* 33 (1972): 2966-A)

560. Chaniecki, Zbigniew. "Z dziejów wychowania muzycznego
      w Polsce" [From the history of music education in
      Poland]. *Muzyka* 26, no. 2 (1981): 47-86.

      A history of music education before the nineteenth
      century, with a concentration on the education of the
      nobility with regard to music.

561. Gabryś, Jerzy. "L'enseignement musical en Pologne."
      La Musique en Pologne 2 (July 1967): 7-16.

      Considers the multilateral goals of Polish music
      education and describes the reorganization of schools
      in People's Poland. Describes the studies at each
      of the three levels of music schools. Presents the
      division of the faculties into subject area in the
      seven music schools at the highest level, the superior
      schools, and credits these institutions with having a
      great role in the cultural life of contemporary Poland.

562. Hermach, Edward. "Polska koncepcja wychowaniu
      muzycznego" [The Polish concept of music education].
      Ruch Muzyczny 13, no. 10 (May 15-31, 1969): 5-6.

      Primarily concerns music education for school children.
      Gives examples of musical activities which especially
      concentrate on rhythmic movement.

563. Mushalko, Donald Francis. "Preparation of Music
      Teachers in Poland." Ph.D. diss., University of
      Pittsburgh, 1982. 112 pp.

      Uses a descriptive approach to studying Polish music
      programs from kindergarten through institutions of
      higher education. Also considers aesthetic education
      in Polish schools. (*Dissertation Abstracts* 44 (1983):
      1016-A)

564. Piasek-Wanski, Michael I. "Karol Szymanowski's
      Philosophy of Music Education." Ed.D. diss.,
      University of the Pacific, 1981.

The greater part of this dissertation sets a framework
for Szymanowski's philosophy. The author refers to
Szymanowski's writings on music education and the
evolution of his views. Szymanowski believed in the
social value of music and that composers should promote
culture through their musical activities. The study
includes a bibliography. (*Dissertation Abstracts* 42
(1981): 2016-A)

565. Wierszyłowski, Jan. "Problemy wychowania muzycznego w
     Polsce" [The problems of music education in Poland].
     Muzyka 12, no. 4 (1967): 61-66.

     This essay identifies the aims of music education in
     Poland to be consistent with general cultural education
     at all levels of the school system. The author offers
     twelve considerations for the successful functioning
     of the music education curriculum.

MUSIC AND RELATED DISCIPLINES

566. Dąbkowski, Grzegorz. "Słownictwo zawodowe środowiska
      muzyków warszawskich" [Professional vocabulary of
      the environment of Warsaw musicians]. *Przegląd
      Humanistyczny* 6 (1971): 97-106.

      A study of the special vocabulary of musicians.
      Discusses the real Polish names for instruments and
      popular terms, some adopted from foreign musical
      terms. Discusses selected musical terms and phrases,
      but does not provide a glossary.

567. Jankowska, Mirosława. "The first step in a music
      profession." *Council of Research in Music Education
      Bulletin* No. 66-67 (Spring-Summer 1981): 30-32.

      Analyzes data assembled from interviews with 59
      instrumentalists who graduated from the Warsaw
      Akademia Muzyczna between 1968 and 1970. The survey
      revealed that 95 percent of the musicians had some
      professional experience before receiving their
      diplomas, and that after graduation, 93 percent entered
      full-time employment, mostly with orchestras.

568. Polakowski, Krzysztof Z. "Polish Research on the
      Psychology of Music." *Journal of Research in Music
      Education* 20, no. 2 (1972): 286-88.

      Summarizes Polish studies of the 1960s, especially the
      development of tests to predict student success in
      instrumental music, research on the psychological
      conditions of pianistic achievement, and work by the
      author on music memory.

MUSIC AND LITURGY

569. Hławiczka, Karol. "Melodie Wacława z Szamotuł,
     Cypriana Bazylika i Mikołaja Gomółki w kancjonale
     brzeskim" [Melodies of Wacław of Szamotuł, Cyprian
     Bazylik, and Mikołaj Gomółka in the Brzeski
     Cantional]. *Muzyka* 13, no. 1 (1968): 95-100; 13,
     no. 2 (1968): 83-92.

     Views the publishing of cantionals as a reflection of
     the Polish Reformation. Shows how melodies in a
     songbook from Brzeski (1723) were used in cantionals of
     the sixteenth through nineteenth centuries. Traces
     melodic outlines in the nineteenth-century publication
     of E.C. Julius Horn, *300 polnische Choral-Melodien zum
     evangelisch-polnischen Gesangbüche.*

570. Mrowiec, Karol. "Kolędy w osiemnastowiecznych
     rękopisach Biblioteki Klasztoru św. Andrzeja w
     Krakowie" [Carols in eighteenth-century manuscripts
     in the library of St. Andrew's Monastery, Cracow].
     Muzyka 18, no. 3 (1973): 51.

     Considers seven cantionals and songbooks of the
     eighteenth century and constructs a table of
     concordances. Discusses the characteristics, style,
     and function of the music.

571. Wawrzykowska-Wierciochowa, Dioniza. "O melodiach
     pieśni 'Boże coś Polskę'" [About the melody of the
     song "Boże coś Polskę"]. *Muzyka* 31, no. 3 (1986):
     57-81.

     Traces this well-known text of Alojze Feliński through
     different musical versions and misattributions from the
     time that the text was first used in 1816. Provides

plates of printed versions of the song. Some of the
versions were published outside of Poland. See the
follow-up article by Alina Nowak-Romanowicz, "Uwagi do
artykulu Dionizy Wawrzykowskiej-Wierciochowej" [Remarks
on the article of Dioniza Wawrzykowska-Wierciochowa],
Muzyka 32, no. 1 (1987): 80.

EDITIONS OF POLISH MUSIC

572. *Antiquitates Musicae in Polonia,* ed. Hieronim Feicht
and Mirosław Perz. Graz: Akademische Druck- U.
Verlagsanstalt; Warsaw: Polish Scientific Publishers,
1963- . M2.A533

Vol. 1. Pelpin Tablature, thematic catalog.

Vols. 2-7. Pelpin Tablature, facsimile.

Vol. 8. Pelpin Tablature, transcriptions.

Vols. 9-10. Pelpin Tablature, choral compositions,
transcriptions.

Vol. 11. Missale plenarium, Bibl. Capit. Gnesniensis
Ms. 149, analyses.
Contains detailed explanations of the music in English.

Vol. 12. Missale plenarium, Bibl. Capit. Gnesniensis
Ms. 149, facsimile.

Vol. 13. Sources of polyphony up to c. 1500, facsimiles.
Presents music from 25 Polish manuscript sources with
comments on the music.

Vol. 14. Sources of polyphony up to c. 1500,
transcriptions.
The editorial comments and discussion of variant
transcriptions are extensive.

Vol. 15. The Organ Tablature of the Warsaw Music
Society.
Contains critical notes and transcriptions of the
music.

Information to accompany the music in each volume is
only in English.

165

Reviews: *Antiquitates musicae in Polonia*, vol. 1:
George S. Golos, *Musical Quarterly* 50, no. 4 (1964):
537-39; *AMP*, 2-7: George S. Golos, *Musical Quarterly*
56, no. 2 (1970): 294-95; *AMP*, 11-12: Benjamin Rajeczký,
Muzyka 21, no. 2 (1976): 100; *AMP*, 13: Martin Staehelin,
Musikforschung 30, no. 2 (1977): 259-61; *AMP*, 13-14:
Piotr Poźniak, *Muzyka* 24, no. 2 (1979): 115-29; *AMP*,
14: Martin Staehelin, *Musikforschung* 36, no. 3 (1983):
169-72; *Muzyka* 34, no. 2 (1979): 120-29.

573.   Barański, Franciszek. *Jeszcze polska nie zginęła!*
       Pieśni patriotyczne i narodowe [Poland has not yet
       perished. Patriotic and national songs], 2 vols.
       New York: Polish Book Importing Co., 1944. 158,
       103 pp.

       Contains 137 songs in a simple piano arrangement with
       melody in right hand. Additional texts are compiled in
       volume 2. A table of contents is in volume 2.

574.   Contoski, Joseph. *Treasured Polish Christmas Customs*
       and Traditions: Carols, Decorations, and a Christmas
       Play. Minneapolis: Polanie Publishing Co., 1972.
       198 pp.

       The Christmas play includes music. There are 46 Polish
       Christmas songs with easy piano accompaniments. Texts
       are provided in both Polish and English.

575.   _____. *Treasured Polish Songs with English Translations*.
       Minneapolis: Polanie Publishing Co., 1953. 352 pp.
       M 1762.P56 T7

       Collects 220 familiar Polish songs in piano-vocal
       arrangements set to both English and Polish texts.
       Represented are Christmas carols (*kolędy*), religious
       songs, art songs, and ballads.

576.   *Dawna polska muzyka organowa/Musique d'orgue polonaise*
       ancienne, ed. Joachim Grübich. Kraków: Polskie
       Wydawnictwo Muzyczne, 1968. 58 pp. M6.G78 D3

Includes 21 pieces from 1530-1650, mostly pieces already published in other collections. (See items 577, 591, 595.) Music is edited with fingerings and registrations.

577. Feicht, Hieronim, ed. *Muzyka staropolska* [Old Polish Music]. Kraków: Polskie Wydawnictwo Muzyczne, 1966. 404 pp. M2.F29

Provides scores of selected pieces from the Middle Ages through eighteenth century. Information about the music is provided in both Polish and English. The pages of music are interspersed with relevant illustrations. Critical notes are in Polish.

Review: Jan Stęszewski, *Muzyka* 14, no. 3 (1969): 109-13.

578. *Florilegium musicae antiquae.* Kraków: Polskie Wydawnictwo Muzyczne, 1962- .

Some of the volumes are the works of Polish composers.

579. Harasowski, Adam. *Polish Christmas Carols. Najpiękniejsze polskie kolendy* [sic] [The most beautiful Polish carols]. Glasgow: Książnica Polska, 1947. 27 pp. M 1762.H373P6

A piano-vocal score with English and Polish texts. Includes 21 songs. The list of contents is in both Polish and English, and there is a short pronunciation guide.

Hymnals

580. Adamuś, Ludwik, ed. *Śpiewnik pieśni religijnych kościoła wyznania Baptyskiego w Ameryce* [Religious songbook for the Baptist denomination in America]. Philadelphia: American Baptist Publication Society, 1917. 235, 43 pp.

247 hymns are grouped by theme. The music is in
typical four-part hymn arrangements, all with Polish
texts only. An alphabetical list of hymns is included.

581. Siedlecki, Jan. *Śpiewniczek zawierający pieśni
      kościelne z melodyami dla użytku wiernych* [Songbook
      containing church songs with melodies for faithful
      use]. Kraków: Nakład i własność XX. Misyonarz na
      Kleparzu; Główny skład, Warszawa: Gebethner i Wolff,
      1901. 526 pp. M 2142.P5 S58

      Notates hymn melodies with an accompaniment line on the
      same staff in arrangement for two treble voices.
      Arranges the hymns by liturgical season. Includes some
      prayers and service music, such as mass settings in
      Polish and Latin. Provides a first line index.

582. *Śpiewnik Polsko-Narodowego Katolickiego Kościoła*
      [Hymnal of the Polish National Catholic Church],
      2nd ed. [Scranton:] Zjednoczone Chóry PNKK [United
      Choirs of the PNCC], 1960.

      Presents hymns in four-part piano vocal score arranged
      in the hymnal by liturgical season. Includes some
      service music and mass settings. Supplemented with a
      first line index.

583. Jan z Lublina. *Tablature of Keyboard Music,* 6 vols.,
      ed. John Reeves White. Corpus of Early Keyboard
      Music, no. 6. American Institute of Musicology,
      1964-1967. M 2.J26T2

      See item 223.

      Review: Józef M. Chomiński, *Muzyka* 10, no. 4 (1965):
      52-55.

584. *Moniuszko, Stanisław: Dzieła,* ed. Witold Rudziński.
     Kraków: Polskie Wydawnictwo Muzyczne, 1965- .
     M 3.M75

     Series A, vol. 1. Songs 1. Śpiewnik domowy I,
     Śpiewnik domowy II, Other songs 1837-1844.
     Review: Krzysztof Mazur, *Muzyka* 11, no. 2 (1966): 170-
     75.

     Series A, vol. 2. Songs 2. Śpiewnik domowy III,
     Śpiewnik domowy IV, Other songs 1844-1855.

     Series A, vol. 3. Songs 3. Śpiewnik domowy V,
     Śpiewnik domowy VI, Other songs 1856-1859.

     Series A, vol. 4. Songs 4. Songs from 1860-1872.

     Series A, vol. 5. Songs 5. Various other songs, songs
     with orchestra, song fragments.

     Series A, vol. 6. Choral music. Ostrobramski litanies.

     Series E, vol. 33. Instrumental music 2. 1st String
     Quartet in D minor, 2nd String Quartet in F major.

     Series E. vol. 34. Instrumental music 3. Piano works,
     including works for piano-four hands.

     Preface to each volume is presented in both Polish and
     German. Some of the songs in this complete works
     edition have texts in different languages--French or
     Russian. Critical notes are only printed in Polish.

585. *Monumenta Musicae in Polonia,* Józef M. Chomiński.
     Kraków: Polskie Wydawnictwo Muzyczne, 1966- .

586.   Nicolas Zieleński, Opera omnia, v. 1. Offertoria
         totius anni, 1-15. M 3.Z545

         Nicolas Zieleński, Opera omnia, v. 2. Offertoria
         totius anni, 16-35.

         Nicolas Zieleński, Opera omnia, v. 3. Offertoria
         totius anni, 36-56.

Introductory essays as well as critical notes are
printed in both Polish and English.

Reviews: Elżbieta Głuszcz-Zwolińska, *Muzyka* 14, no. 3
(1969): 114-16; *Muzyka* 24, no. 4 (1979): 93-96.

587.   Marcin Mielczewski: Opera Omnia 2. Konzerty
        wokalno-instrumentalne, ed. Zygmunt M. Szweykowski.
        Kraków: Polskie Wydawnictwo Muzyczne, 1976.
        M 3.M64

588.   Marcin Mielczewski. Canzony instrumentalny, ed.
        Zygmunt M. Szweykowski. Kraków: Polskie
        Wydawnictwo Muzyczne, 1986.

        Each volume contains a preface in both Polish and
        English. The editorial notes which accompany the scores
        are also presented in both of these languages.

589.   Series D. Bibliotheca Antiqua.

        Facsimile editions of Latin treatises published in the
        original size. Only a short note of introduction is
        provided, in both Polish and English.

        Vol. 1. Monetarius, Stefan. *Epitoma utriusque musicae
            practicae* (1515).

        Vol. 2. Kromer, Marcin. *Musicae elementa* (1532).

        Vol. 3. Gallinius, Marcin. *Ad venerabilem virem*
            (1535).

        Vol. 4. Sebastian z Felsztyna. *Opusculum musices
            noviter congestum* (1534).

        Vol. 5. Sebastian z Felsztyna. *Modus regulariter*
            (1518).

        Vol. 6. Liban, Jerzy. *De accentuum ecclesiasticorum*
            (1539).

        Vol. 7. Liban, Jerzy. *De philosophiae laudibus*
            (1537).

Vol. 8.   Liban, Jerzy.   *De musicae laudibus oratio*
(1540).

Reviews: *Revue de musicologie* 69, no. 1 (1983): 107-8;
Piotr Poźniak, *Muzyka* 22, no. 3 (1977): 119-21;
Gareth R.K. Curtis, *Early Music* 6, no. 3 (1978): 453-
55; *Revue de musicologie* 62, no. 2 (1976): 305-6.

590. *Musica antiqua polonica.* Kraków: Polskie Wydawnictwo
      Muzyczne, 1969- . M 2.M6375

Vol. 1.   The Middle Ages, ed. Jerzy Morawski.

Vol. 3.   Baroque, ed. Zygmunt M. Szweykowski.

Reviews: Bolesław Bartkowski, *Muzyka* 19, no. 2 (1979):
101-5; Stanisław Dąbek, *Muzyka* 21, no. 3 (1976): 93-
100.

591. *Muzyka polskiego odrodzenia. Wybór utworów z XVI i
      początku XVII wieku,* ed. Józef M. Chomiński and
      Zofia Lissa. Kraków: Polskie Wydawnictwo Muzyczne,
      1953.

      *Music of the Polish Renaissance: A Selection of Works
      from the XVIth and the Beginning of the XVIIth
      Century,* ed. Józef M. Chomiński and Zofia Lissa.
      Kraków: Polskie Wydawnictwo Muzyczne, 1955. 370 pp.
      M 2.C616 M82

      English version has extended introduction in English
      and translates the texts of Polish vocal music.
      Includes instrumental music for organ and keyboard
      dances, especially from the Jan z Lublina tablature.
      Vocal selections are from cantionals, the Gomółka
      Psalms, and works by Zieleński.

592. Pawlowska, Harriet M. *Merrily We Sing. 105 Polish
      Folksongs.* Detroit: Wayne State University Press,
      1961. 263 pp. M 1762.P2897 M5

Songs were collected by Americans both in the United
States and Poland. Polish and English texts to songs
are printed; the music features only the melody.
Tunes are presented in the book loosely classified by
the theme of text. Indexes of titles in English and
Polish. Provides commentaries on songs with
references to versions in Polish collections. The
notes offer a short analysis of musical characteristics
of the selected folksongs.

593. Smialek, William, ed. *The Symphony in Poland*. The
Symphony 1720-1840, F7. New York: Garland
Publishing, 1982. 358 pp. ISBN 0824038207
M 1001.S986

Reproduces scores of symphonies by Michał Orłowski,
Jakub Pawłowski, Karol Pietrowski, Bazyli Bohdanowicz,
Jakub Gołąbek, and Jan Wański from the series *Symfonie
polskie* (item 594). Additionally, includes an edition
of Ignacy Feliks Dobrzyński's *Symphony No. 2*. Begins
with an essay on the history of the Polish symphony in
the eighteenth and early nineteenth centuries. Provides
a thematic index of symphonies by the seven composers
considered, critical notes to the Polish publications,
and a bibliography.

594. *Symfonie polskie*. Zygmunt M. Szweykowski, gen. ed.
Kraków: Polskie Wydawnictwo Muzyczne, 1964- .

Publishes full scores of early Polish symphonies with
short introductions about the composers and their
works. Translates the introductions into English,
sometimes in abbreviated form. Provides critical notes
in Polish and English. The series includes works by:

1. Paszczyński, G. *Symfonia Es*.

2. Pietrowski, Karol. *Symfonie D, D*.

3. Pawłowski, Jakub. *Symfonie B, F, Es*.

4. Orłowski, Michał. *Symfonia F*.

5. Namieyski. *Symfonia D*.

6. Bohdanowicz, Bazyli. *Symfonia d.*

7. Engel, Jan. *Symfonie F, B, G.*

8. Engel, Jan. *Symfonie F, B (II), d.*

9. Mirecki, Franciszek. *Symfonia.*

595. Szweykowski, Zygmunt M., ed. *Muzyka w dawnym Krakowie*
      [Music in Old Cracow]. Kraków: Polskie Wydawnictwo
      Muzyczne, 1964. 326 pp. M 2.S97 M8

      Offers selected music of the fifteenth through
      eighteenth centuries. The music includes short pieces
      from organ and lute tablatures, as well as instrumental
      and vocal works in full score. The volume is
      ornamented with plates of Cracow art works and
      architecture. Prints an introduction in both Polish
      and English. Provides English revisional notes in a
      separate pamphlet.

596. *Szymanowski, Karol: Dzieła,* ed. Józef M. Chomiński, *et
      al.* Kraków: Polskie Wydawnictwo Muzyczne, 1922- .
      M 3.S99

      Series A, vol. 1. Concerto overture, op. 12.

      Series A, vol. 3. Symphony No. 3.

      Series A, vol. 4. Symphony No. 4 (Concertante), op.
         60.

      Series A, vol. 5. First Violin Concerto.

      Series A, vol. 6. Second Violin Concerto.

      Series A, vol. 7. Stabat mater.

      Series A, vol. 8. Veni creator, op. 57; Litania do
         Marii Panny, op. 59.

      Series A, vol. 9. Agawe, op. 38 (facsimile); Demeter,
         op. 37bis.

      Series A, vol. 10. Songs with orchestra.

Series A, vol. 11. String Quartets.

Series A, vol. 12. Violin works.

Series B, vol. 14. Piano works.

Series B, vol. 15. Piano works. Metopy, op. 20;
   Maski, op. 34.

Series C, vol. 17. Vocal works.

Series D, vol. 23. Król Roger, op. 46.

Series D, vol. 24. Dramatic works.

Review: (Vol. 7, Stabat mater): Adam Neuer, *Muzyka* 11,
no. 2 (1966): 175-77.

597. *Szymanowski, Karol: Dzieła/Karol Szymanowski: Complete
      Edition,* ed. Teresa Chylińska. Kraków: Polskie
      Wydawnictwo Muzyczne, 1968- . M 3.S985

Series A, vol. 2. Third and Fourth Symphonies.

Series A, vol. 3. First and Second Violin Concertos.

Series A, vol. 5. Songs with orchestra.

Series B, vol. 7. Piano works.

Series C, vol. 12. Six Kurpian Songs.

Series D, vol. 14. King Roger.

598. *Wieniawski, Henri: Dzieła,* ed. I. Dubiska and E. Umińska.
      Kraków: Polskie Wydawnictwo Muzyczne, 1962- .

Vol. 1. Concerto No. 1 for violin in F-sharp major,
   op. 14.

Vol. 2. Concerto No. 2 for violin in D minor, op. 22.

599. *Wydawnictwo dawnej muzyki polskiej*, ed. Adolf
     Chybiński (vols. 1-22), Hieronim Feicht (vols. 23-
     50), Hieronim Feicht and Zygmunt M. Szweykowski
     (vols. 51-67), and Zygmunt M. Szweykowski (vols.
     68-). Warszawa: Stowarzyszenie Miłośników Dawnej
     Muzyki, 1928-38; Kraków: Polskie Wydawnictwo
     Muzyczne, 1947- .

     1. Szarzyński, Stanisław. *Sonata a due violini e
        basso pro organo.*

     2. Mielczewski, Marcin. *Deus in nomine tuo.*

     3. Rożycki, Jacek. *Hymni ecclesiastici.*

     4. Pękiel, Bartłomiej. *Audite mortales.*

     5. Szarzyński, Stanisław Sylwester. *Pariendo non
        gravaris.*

     6. Mielczewski, Marcin. *Canzona a 3.*

     7. Gorczycki, Grzegorz Gerwazy. *Missa Paschalis.*

     8. Anonymous. *Duma.*

     9. Wacław z Szamotuł. *In te domine speravi.*

     10. Szarzyński, Stanisław Sylwester. *Jesu spes mea.*

     11. Jarzębski, Adam. *Tamburetta.*

     12. Zieleński, Mikołaj. *Vox in Rama.*

     13. Stachowicz, Damian. *Veni consolator.*

     14. Gorczycki, Grzegorz Gerwazy. *Illuxit sol.*

     15. Jarzębski, Adam. *Nova casa.*

     16. Rożycki, Jacek. *Magnificemus in cantico.*

     17. Pękiel, Bartłomiej. *Missa Pulcherrima.*

     18. Podbielski, Jan. *Preludium.*

     19. Pękiel, Bartłomiej. *Magnum nomen Domini, Resonet
        in laudibus.*

20. *Tańce z tabulatury organowej Jana z Lublina*
    [Dances from the organ tablature of Jan of Lublin].

21. Jarzębski, Adam. *Chromatica.*

22. Polak, Jakub. *Preludia, fantazje i tańce na lutnie*
    [Preludes, fantasies, and dances for lute].

23. Długoraj, Wojciech. *Fantazje i villanelle na
    lutnie* [Fantasies and villanelles for lute].

24. Cato, Diomedes. *Preludia, fantazje, tańce i
    madrygały na lutnie* [Prelude, fantasias, dances and
    madrigals for lute].

25. Szarzyński, Stanisław Sylwester. *Ave Regina.*

26. Szarzyński, Stanisław Sylwester. *Ad hymnos ad
    cantus.*

27. Jarzębski, Adam. *Bentrovata.*

28. Wacław z Szamotuł. *Pieśni* [Sacred songs].

29. Mielczewski, Marcin. *Canzoni a 2.*

30. Pękiel, Bartłomiej. *40 utworów na lutnie* [40 works
    for lute].

31. Zieleński, Mikołaj. *Domus mea.*

32. Jarzębski, Adam. *Sentinella.*

33. Sządek, Tomasz. *Dies est laetitiae.*

34. Bazylik, Cyprian. *Pieśni* [Sacred songs].

35. Leopolita, Marcin. *Missa Paschalis.*

36. Zieleński, Mikołaj. *Exiit sermo inter fratres,
    Si consurrexisti cum Christo.*

37. Gorczycki, Grzegorz Gerwazy. *Laetatus sum.*

38. Mielczewski, Marcin. *Veni Domine.*

39. Jarzębski, Adam. *5 Canzoni.*

40. Lilius, Franciszek. *Jubilate Deo omnis terra.*

41. Zieleński, Mikołaj. *Justus ut palma florebit.*

42. Mielczewski, Marcin. *Vesperae Dominicales.*

43. Rohaczewski, Andrzej. *Canzon a 4.*

44. Rożycki, Jacek. *Exsultemus omnes.*

45. Zieleński, Mikołaj. *4 Communiones.*

46. Rohaczewski, Andrzej. *Crucifixus surrexit.*

47. Gomółka, Mikołaj. *Melodie na Psalterz Polski,* I. [Melodies for the Polish Psalter].

48. Gomółka, Mikołaj. *Melodie na Psalterz Polski,* II.

49. Gomółka, Mikołaj. *Melodie na Psalterz Polski,* III.

50. Szarzyński, Stanisław Sylwester. *Veni Sancte Spiritus.*

51. Jarzębski, Adam. *4 Concerti a 2.*

52. Pękiel, Bartłomiej. *2 Patrem.*

53. Zieleński, Mikołaj. *In monte Olivetti.*

54. Rożycki, Jacek. *Magnificat.*

55. Kobierkowicz, Józef. *Ego mater.*

56. Lilius, Franciszek. *Tua Jesu dilectio.*

57. Jarzębski, Adam. *2 Concerti a 2.*

58. Pękiel, Bartłomiej. *Missa Paschalis.*

59. Jarzębski, Adam. *Concerti a 3.*

60. Rożycki, Jacek. *Confitebor.*

61. Mielczewski, Marcin. *Canzoni a 3.*

62. Pękiel, Bartłomiej. *Missa Brevis.*

63. Gorczycki, Grzegorz Gerwazy. *Os iusti mediabitur, Justus ut palma florebit.*

64. Żebrowski, Marcin Józef. *Magnificat.*

65. Gorczycki, Grzegorz Gerwazy. *Missa Rorate.*

66. Mielczewski, Marcin. *Benedictio et claritas.*

67. Cato, Diomedes. *Preludia, fantazje, tańce i madrigały na lutnie* [Prelude, fantasies, dances, and madrigals for lute].

68. Żebrowski, Marcin Józef. *Salve Regina.*

69. Pękiel, Bartłomiej. *Missa a 14.*

70. Zieleński, Mikołaj. *Communiones a 3.*

71. Gorczycki, Grzegorz Gerwazy. *4 Hymny.*

72. Szarzyński, Stanisław Sylwester. *Litania cursoria.*

73. Żelechowski, Piotr. *Fantasia.*

74. Pękiel, Bartłomiej. *Missa concertata La Lombardesca.*

76. Szarzyński, Stanisław Sylwester. *Completorium.*

Reviews: John Glowacki, "Editions of Early Polish Music." *Musical Quarterly* 44 (1958): 106-12. Assesses volumes 28-32.

600. *Źródła do Historii Muzyki Polskiej,* ed. Zygmunt M. Szweykowski. Kraków: Polskie Wydawnictwo Muzyczne, 1960- .

Editions of Polish music from the Renaissance and early Baroque suitable for performance. Some volumes have introductions in other languages, such as Russian, French, German, or English. The Polish introductions are often a recapitulation of research to date on the composer and music. Some editions include facsimiles.

1. *Tańce polskie z Vietoris-Kodex* [Dances from the Vietoris-Codex].

2. *Tańce polskie z tabulatur lutniowych. I.* [Polish dances from lute tablatures].

3. Gołąbek, Jakub. *Symfonie D, D, C.*

   Review: Jan Prosnak, *Muzyka* 9, no. 1-2 (1964): 141-44.

4. Gołąbek, Jakub. *Partita.*

5. Wański, Jan. *Dwie symfonie D, G* [Two symphonies].

   Review: Jan Prosnak, *Muzyka* 7, no. 4 (1962): 101-4.

6. *Tańce polskie ze zbioru Anny Szirmay-Keczer* [Polish dances from the collection of Anna Szirmay-Keczer].

7. Gorczycki, Grzegorz Gerwazy. *Completorium.*

8. Wronowicz, Maciej. *Koncerty wokalno-instrumentalne* [Vocal-instrumental conertos].

9. *Tańce polskie z tabulatur lutniowych. II.* [Polish dances from lute tablatures].

10. Habermann, Jan Piotr. *Utwory wokalno-instrumentalne* [Vocal-instrumental works].

11. *Polonezy z XVIII wieku na zespoły instrumentalne* [Eighteenth-century polonaises for instrumental ensembles].

12. *Pastorele staropolskie. I.* [Old Polish pastorelles].

13. *Polonezy ze zbiorów Anny Marii Sąskiej. I.* [Polonaises from the collections of Anna Maria Saska].

14. Zwierzchowski, Mateusz. *Requiem.*

15. *Plankty polskie* [Polish laments].

16. *Muzyczne Silva rerum z XVII w.* [Musical Silva rerum from the seventeenth century].

17. *Polonezy ze zbiorów Anny Marii Sąskiej. II.* [Polonaises from the collections of Anna Maria Sąska].

18. Janiewicz, Feliks. *Trio.*

19. Saltus Polonici, *Polonaises, Lengjel, Tańtzok z I połowy XVIII wieku* [Polonaises, Lengjel, and Tańtzok from the first half of the eighteenth century].

20. Maffon, Franciszek. *Madrygał i Greghesca na chor a cappella. Fantazja na lutnie* [A Madrigal and greghesca for a cappella choir. Fantasie for lute].

21. *Polonezy ze zbiorów Anny Marii Sąskiej. III.* [Polonaises from the collections of Anna Maria Sąska].

22. Pietrowski, Karol. *Veni Creator. Benedictus sit Deus.*

23. *Polonezy, kozaki, mazury z przełomu XVIII na XIX w.* [Polonaises, kozaks, and mazurs from the turn of the eighteenth and nineteenth centuries].

24. Brant, Jan. *Utwory zebrane na zespóły wokalne* [Collected works for vocal ensemble].

26. Scacchi, Marco. *Madrigały.*

28. Krener, Jan. *Veni sponsa Christi. Contere Domine.*

DISCOGRAPHY

601. Anonymous. Prelude and fugue from the Warsaw Tablature; O przedziwna gładkości; Nie złodziejem; Dobranoc anusieńko. "Music of the Royal Castle in Warsaw." Musica antiqua polonica. Musicae Antiquae Collegium Varsoviense: Stefan Sutkowski, director. Muza SXL 0295.

602. Bacewicz, Grażyna. Mały tryptik (1966). "Four centuries of solo piano music by women composers." Marciano, piano. Turnabout TV-34685.

603. _____. Musica sinfonica (1965); Pensieri notturni (1961); Konzert na orkiestrę (1962); Uwertura (1943). Warsaw National Philharmonic Symphony Orchestra: Rowicki, conductor. Muza XL 0274.

604. _____. Quintet, piano and strings, no. 1. Warsaw Piano Quintet. Muza SCL 0608.

605. _____. Regina Smendzianki plays works by Grażyna Bacewicz. Muza SCL 0977.

606. _____. Sonata no. 2. "Keyboard music by women." Fierro, piano. Avant AV-1012.

607. _____. Ten studies, nos. 2 and 8 only; Triptych for piano. "Piano music by five women composers." Eskin, piano. Musical Heritage Society MHS-4236.

608. Badarzewska-Baranowska, Thekla. La prière d'une
      vierge. "Salon music--Musical decor for the
      fashionable 19th century home." Kann, piano.
      Musical Heritage Society MHS-1139.

609. Baird, Tadeusz. Chanson des trouvères; Four songs;
      Epiphany music; Four novelettes. Krystyna Szostek-
      Radkowa, mezzosoprano; Warsaw National Philharmonic
      Symphony Orchestra: Witold Rowicki, conductor.
      Muza 0462.

610. _____. Ekspresje; Egzorta; Erotyki. Muza XL 0177.

611. _____. Elegeia (1973). Prague Radio Symphony
      Orchestra: Kasprzyk, conductor. Supraphon 1410.2734.

612. _____. Jutro. Muza SX 1057.

613. _____. Suite: Colas Breugnon. Bartkiewicz, flute;
      Pluzek, bassoon; Kammerorchester Leopoldinum,
      Wrocław: Pijarowski, conductor. Polyphonia POL-
      63014.

614. _____. Symphony No. 3. Warsaw National Philharmonic
      Symphony Orchestra: Jan Krenz, conductor. Muza
      SX 0571.

615. Bohdanowicz, Bazyli. Symphony in D major. "Polish
      eighteenth-century symphonies." Musica antiqua
      polonica. Poznań Chamber Orchestra: Robert
      Satanowski, conductor. Muza SXL 0523.

616. "Boże Narodzenie w Polsce." Bolechowska, Raczowski,
      Woźniak. Muza XL 0184.

617. Borek, Krzysztof. Missa "Te Deum laudamus." Cantilena
      Men's Choir: Edmund Kajdasz, conductor. Veriton
      SXV 760.

618. Buczyński, Walter. Monogram (1978). Kubalek, piano.
      Centrediscs CMC-0382.

619. Cato, Diomedes. Chorea Polonica. "Music of the Royal
      Castle in Warsaw." Musica antiqua polonica.
      Musicae Antiquae Collegium Varsoviense: Stefan
      Sutkowski, director. Muza SXL 0295.

620. _____. Fantasia; Favorito; Villanella. "European
      Lute Music." Andreas Kecskes, lute. Hungaraton
      SLPX 11721.

621. _____. Fantasia. Harmonia Mundi HMF 704.

622. _____. Fantasia; Motet and fugue. Joachim Grübich,
      organ. Muza SXL 0235.

623. _____. Fantasia. "Italian Composers in Poland."
      Musica antiqua polonica. Musicae Antiquae Collegium
      Varsoviense: Stefan Sutkowski, director. Muza 0537.

624. _____. Favorito; Galliards; Praeludium. "Lute Music
      of Hungary and Poland." Konrad Ragossnig, lute.
      Archiv 2533 294.

625. Christmas carols. "Przy stole wigilijnym." Śląsk:
      Stanisław Hadyna, conductor. Muza SX 0347.

626. Chrzanowa, Mikołaj. Protexisti me Deus. Harmonia
      Mundi HMF 704.

627. _____. Protexisti me Deus. Wrocław Radio Choir:
      Stanisław Krukowski, conductor. Muza SXL 0818;
      Erato ERA 9130/6.

628. Długoraj, Wojciech. Ballet; Chorea Polonica; Hajdu
      dance. Andreas Kecskes, lute. Harmonia Mundi
      HMF 796.

629. _____. Carola Polonesa; Chorea Polonica; Fantasia;
     Finale; Kowały. "Lute Music of Hungary and Poland."
     Konrad Ragossnig, lute. Archiv 2533 294.

630. _____. Chorea Polonica; Fantasia; Finale; Villanella
     Polonica. "European Lute Music." Andreas Kecskes,
     lute. Hungaraton SLPX 11721.

631. _____. Chorea Polonica. "Music for lute--Poland and
     Eastern Europe." Ragossnig, lute. Deutsche
     Grammophon Archiv 2533.294.

632. _____. Fantasia. "Lute music--16th -17th Centuries."
     Hungaraton SLPX-11721.

633. _____. Fantasia; Villanella. "Lute Music from the
     Royal Courts of Europe." Julian Bream, lute.
     RCA GL 42952, AS26.41068.

634. _____. Villanella Polonica. Barbara Strzelecka,
     harpsichord. Muza SXL 0614.

635. _____. Villanella Polonica. "Music of the Royal
     Castle in Warsaw." Musica antiqua polonica. Musicae
     Antiquae Collegium Varsoviense: Stefan Sutkowski,
     director. Muza SXL 0295.

636. "Echos of the Fatherland." A collection of popular folk
     and army songs. Polish Radio Choir and Orchestra:
     Jerzy Kolaczkowski, conductor. Muza SX 0204.

637. Gołąbek, Jakub. Symphony No. 1 in D major; Symphony
     No. 2 in D major; Symphony in C major. Musica
     antiqua polonica. Poznań Philharmonic Chamber
     Orchestra: Robert Satanowski, conductor. Muza XL
     0288.

638. Gomółka, Mikołaj. Melodies from the Polish Psalter.
     Boys and Men's Choir of Poznań Philharmonic: Stefan
     Stuligrosz, conductor. Muza SXL 0234; Musical
     Heritage Society/Orpheus OR-361.

639. _____. Melodies from the Polish Psalter. Veriton
     SXV 753/6.

640. _____. Melodies from the Polish Psalter. "Passion
     Meditations and Lenten Hymns from Poland." Veriton
     SXV 731.

641. _____. Melodies from the Polish Psalter. Muza SXL
     0521.

642. Gorczycki, Grzegorz Gerwazy. Completorium; Missa
     Paschalis. Musica antiqua polonica. Muza SXL 0277.

643. _____. Ecce nunc benedicite. Veriton SXV 810.

644. _____. Illuxit sol; In virtute tua; Judica me Deus;
     Laetatus sum. "Music in Old Cracow." Musica
     antiqua polonica. Wrocław Radio Chorus and
     Orchestra: Edmund Kajdasz, conductor. Muza SXL 0368.

645. _____. Laetatus sum. "From the Musical Treasury of
     the Polish Millennium." Muza SXL 0100.

646. Górecki, Henryk Mikołaj. Epitafium, op. 12; Scontri,
     op. 17; Genesis II, op. 19; Refrain, op. 21. Jan
     Krenz, conductor. Muza XL 0391.

647. _____. Symphony No. 3 (Symphony of sorrowful songs).
     Woytowicz, soprano; Berlin Radio Symphony Orchestra:
     Kamirski, conductor. Schwann VMS-1615.

648. Haczewski, A. Symphony in D major. "Polish symphonies
     of the eighteenth century." Musica antiqua polonica.
     Poznań Chamber Orchestra: Robert Satanowski,
     conductor. Muza SXL 0523.

649. Jan z Lublina. "Dance music from the tablature of Jan
     of Lublin." Pohlert Lute Ensemble. Musical
     Heritage Society MHS-1420.

650. _____. "Dance music of the Renaissance, from the
     tablature of Johannes von Lublin." Hubert
     Schoonbrodt, organ. Musica Mundi VMS-2002; Musical
     Heritage Society MHS 1323.

651. _____. Dances mon mary. "Music to entertain the
     Kings of Hungary, 1490-1526." Camerata Hungarica
     with Ars Rinata: Czidra, conductor. Hungaraton
     SLPX-11983-84.

652. Jarzębski, Adam. Canzoni; Sentinella; Nova casa;
     Tamburetta; Bentrovata. "Instrumental music of the
     Polish Baroque." Musica antiqua polonica. Musicae
     Antiquae Collegium Varsoviense: Stefan Sutkowski,
     director. Muza XL 0200; Erato Era 9130/6.

653. _____. Complete Canzoni and Concerti. Veriton SXV
     818/820.

654. _____. Canzona. Muza SXL 0303.

655. _____. Susanna videns. "Music of the Royal Castle
     in Warsaw." Musica antiqua polonica. Musicae
     Antiquae Collegium Varsoviense: Stefan Sutkowski,
     director. Muza SXL 0295.

656. "Jazz Studio Orchestra of Polish Radio." Muza SXL 0569.

657. Jezierski, Kazimierz. Vigiles pastores. Veriton
     SXV 710.

658. Karłowicz, Mieczysław. Concerto, violin, A major,
      op. 8. Wiłkomirska, violin; Warsaw National
      Philharmonic Orchestra: Witold Rowicki, conductor.
      Musical Heritage Society MHS-1103.

659. _____. Concerto, violin, A major, op. 8; Smutna
      opowieść, op. 13. Wiłkomirska, violin; Rowicki,
      conductor. Muza XL 0179.

660. _____. Symphonic poem no. 3, "Lithuanian Rhapsody,"
      op. 11; Symphonic poem no. 6, "An Episode during a
      Masquerade," op. 14. Silesian Philharmonic Symphony
      Orchestra: Jerzy Salwarwoski, conductor. Wifon
      LP-064.

661. Kobierkowicz, Józef. Dormi mei redemptio; Musae piae.
      Veriton SXV 710.

662. _____. Ego mater. Musica antiqua polonica. Musicae
      Antiquae Collegium Varsoviense: Stefan Sutkowski,
      director. Muza SXL 0496.

663. Kotoński, Włodzimierz. Cato for 18 instruments. "New
      Music for chamber orchestra." Mainstream MS-5008.

664. Kurpiński, Karol. Concerto, clarinet. Muza XL 0231.

665. Leopolita, Marcin. Missa paschalis. Musica antiqua
      polonica. Polish Radio Wrocław, Mixed Choir: Edmund
      Kajdasz, conductor. Muza XL 0188.

666. _____. Ricecare; Resurgente Christe Domino. Muza
      SXL 0235.

667. _____. Cibavir eos. "Music at Wawel Castle." Muza
      SXL 0296.

668. _____. Mihi autem. Muza SXL 0818; Erato Era 9130/6.

669. Liban, Jerzy. Ortus de Polonia. Muza SXL 0818;
     Erato Era 9130/6.

670. Lilius, Franciszek. Missa brevissima. Musica antiqua
     polonica. Muza SXL 0548.

671. _____. Jubilate Deo omnis terra. "Music in Old
     Cracow." Musica antiqua polonica. Wrocław Radio
     Chorus and Chamber Orchestra: Edmund Kajdasz,
     conductor. Muza SXL 0368.

672. Lutosławski, Witold. Chain of straw; Dance preludes
     for clarinet, strings, harp, piano, and percussion
     (1955); Funeral music; Little suite for small
     orchestra; Overture for string orchestra. Candide
     CE-31035.

673. _____. Concerto for orchestra; Five songs; Jeux
     vénitiens; Paroles tissées; Prelude no. 1; Prelude
     and fugue; Symphony No. 1; Symphony No. 2; Trois
     poèmes d'Henri Michaux. "Orchestral Music." Polish
     Chamber Orchestra, Polish National Symphony
     Orchestra: Lutosławski, conductor; Kraków Radio
     Chorus and soloists. EMI Electrola 1C-165.03231-36.

674. _____. Concerto for orchestra; Jeux vénitiens. Warsaw
     National Philharmonic Orchestra: Witold Rowicki,
     conductor. Muza XL 0132; Muza XW 263/64; Philips
     65000628.

675. _____. Concerto for orchestra. Chicago Symphony
     Orchestra: Ozawa, conductor. Angel S-36045; EMI
     Electrola 1C 063-02118.

676. _____. Concerto for orchestra. L'Orchestre de la
     Suisse Romande: Kletzki, conductor. London CS-6665;
     Decca SXL 644.

677. Lutosławski, Witold. Concerto, violoncello.
Rostropovich, violoncello; Orchestre de Paris:
Lutosławski, conductor. Angel S-37146; EMI Electrola
1C 065-02687Q.

678. _____. Concerto, violoncello; Dance preludes; Concerto
for oboe, harp, and chamber orchestra. Schiff,
violoncello; H. Holliger, oboe; U. Holliger, harp;
Brunner, clarinet. Symphonie-Orchester des
Bayerischen Rundfunks: Lutosławski, conductor.
Philips 416817-2 PH.

679. _____. Concerto, violoncello. Perenyi, violoncello;
Budapest Symphony Orchestra: Lehel, conductor.
Hungaraton SLPX-11749.

680. _____. 5 Dance preludes for clarinet and piano. "The
virtuoso clarinet." Milosovich, clarinet; Dresden,
piano. Musical Heritage Society MHS-1473.

681. _____. Dance preludes. James Campbell, clarinet;
York, piano. Crystal S-336.

682. _____. Dance preludes (1954). "20th century classics
for clarinet and piano." University of Michigan
Records SM-0018.

683. _____. Dance preludes (third version, 1959). West
Jutland Chamber Ensemble. BIS LP-87.

684. _____. Dance preludes (1955). Dangain, clarinet;
Koerner, piano. Calliope CAL-1668.

685. _____. Double concerto for oboe, harp, and chamber
orchestra. H. Holliger, oboe; U. Holliger, harp;
Cincinnati Symphony: Gielen, conductor. Vox Cum
Laude D-VCL-9064; MCD-10006.

686. Lutosławski, Witold. Epitaph. Maximilien, piano.
     Composers Recordings SD-501.

687. _____. Les espaces du sommeil; Symphony No. 3. John
     Shirley-Quirk, baritone; Los Angeles Philharmonic:
     Esa-Pekka Salonen, conductor. CBS Records M2K 42271
     (CD).

688. _____. Livre pour orchestre. Eastman Philharmonic
     Orchestra: Effron, conductor. Mercury SRI-75141.

689. _____. Livre pour orchestre. Warsaw National
     Philharmonic Symphony Orchestra: Witold Rowicki,
     conductor. Muza SX 1370.

690. _____. Livre pour orchestre. Warsaw National
     Philharmonic Symphony Orchestra: Jan Krenz,
     conductor. Muza SXL 0571.

691. _____. Muzyka żałobna. Landesjugendorchester
     Nordrheinland-Westfalen: Stephani, conductor. Da
     Camera 91605.

692. _____. Mi-parti. Prague Radio Symphony Orchestra:
     Kaspryk, conductor. Supraphon 1410.2734.

693. _____. Paroles tissées. Pears, tenor; London
     Sinfonietta: Lutosławski, conductor. Decca HEAD-3.

694. _____. Paroles tissées; Symphony No. 2. Warsaw
     National Philharmonic Symphony Orchestra: Lutosławski,
     conductor. Muza SXL 0453.

695. _____. Prelude and fugue for thirteen strings.
     Warsaw Philharmonic Chamber Orchestra: Lutosławski,
     conductor. Muza SXL 1145; Aurora AUR-5059.

696. Lutosławski, Witold. Quartet, strings. La Salle
     Quartet. Deutsche Grammophon 2530.735.

697. _____. Quartet, strings. New Budapest Quartet.
     Hungaraton SLPX-11847.

698. _____. Quartet, strings. Warsaw String Quartet.
     Da Camera Magna SM-92418.

699. _____. Quartet, strings. Wilanowski Quartet. Veriton
     SXV 811-12.

700. _____. Symphony No. 1; Symphony No. 2. Warsaw Radio
     Symphony: Jan Krenz, conductor; Southwest German
     Radio Orchestra: Bour, conductor. Wergo 60044.

701. _____. Symphony No. 3; Les espaces du sommeil.
     Fischer-Dieskau, baritone; Berliner Philharmonic:
     Lutosławski, conductor. Philips 416387-2 PH.

702. _____. Trois poèmes d'Henri Michaux; Postludium;
     Symfonia. Wielka Orkiestra Symfoniczna Polskiego
     Radia: Jan Krenz, conductor. Chor Polskiego Radia
     w Krakowie: Lutosławski, conductor. Muza SXL 0237;
     Wergo 60019.

703. _____. La Valse; Variations on a theme of Paganini.
     Le Duc and Engel, duo pianists. Orion ORS-76238.

704. _____. Variations on a theme by Paganini. Neal and
     Nancy O'Doan, duo pianists. Orion ORS-78289.

705. _____. Variations on a theme of Paganini. Argerich
     and Freire, duo pianists. Philips 6514.369.

706. Maxylewicz, Wincenty. Gloria tibi trinitas. "Music in
        Old Cracow." Musica antiqua polonica. Wrocław
        Radio Chorus and Orchestra: Edmund Kajdasz,
        conductor. Muza SXL 0368.

707. "Mazowsze: the Polish song and dance ensemble." Muza
        SXL 0189.

708. Mielczewski, Marcin. Benedictio et claritas; Triumphalis
        dies. Muza SXL 0548.

709. _____. Canzoni. Muza SXL 0303.

710. _____. Canzona. "Instrumental Music of the Polish
        Baroque." Musica antiqua polonica. Warsaw National
        Philharmonic Chamber Orchestra: Karol Teutsch,
        director. Muza SXL 0200; Erato Era 9130/6.

711. _____. Canzoni; Magnificat. Veriton SXV 704.

712. _____. Deus in nomine tuo; Canzona seconda. "Music
        of the Royal Castle in Warsaw." Musica antiqua
        polonica. Musicae Antiquae Collegium Varsoviense:
        Stefan Sutkowski, director. Muza SXL 0295.

713. _____. Deus in nomine tuo; Veni Domine. "Baroque
        Sacred Concertos." Musica antiqua polonica.
        Musica Antiqua Wrocław: Eugeniusz Sąsiadek, director.
        Muza SXL 0975.

714. _____. Vesperae dominicales. Wrocław Radio Chorus
        and Chamber Orchestra: Edmund Kajdasz, conductor.
        Muza SXL 0358; Musical Heritage Society/Orpheus
        OR-371.

715. Milwid, Antoni. Sinfonia Pastorella "Tuba mirum."
        Veriton SXV 766.

716. Mikołaj z Krakowa. Alec nade mna wenus. Muza SXL
      0893/4.

717. _____. Choreas I and II; Ad novem soltus; Rex;
      Zakłułam się tarnem. Muza SXL 0521.

718. _____. Hayducky Dance; Praeludium; Ave Jerarchia.
      Muza SXL 0235.

719. _____. Music of the Polish Renaissance. "Sounds of
      celebration." Irma Rogel. Protone S-147.

720. _____. Salve Regina; Wesel się Polska korona. Muza
      SXL 0818, Erato Era 9130/6.

721. _____. Wesel się Polska korona. "Music from the
      Royal Court of Kraków." Concentus Musicus CM-S80-
      895.

722. Moniuszko, Stanisław. Concert Overture; Concert
      Polonaise; Mazurkas; Overtures. "Compositions for
      Orchestra." National Philharmonic Symphony Orchestra:
      Witold Rowicki, conductor. Muza XL 0229.

723. _____. Flis. Slonicka, Nikodem, Hiolski. Muza
      XL 0145.

724. _____. Halka. Zagorzanka, soprano; Racewicz, mezzo-
      soprano; Ochman, tenor; Hiolski, baritone; Ostapiuk,
      bass. Classic Produktion Osnabruck 999 032-2.

725. _____. Halka. Dawecka; Domieniecki; Wozniczko;
      Kossewski. Muza XEPN 0113-0115.

726. _____. Halka [Highlights]. Soloists, chorus, and
      orchestra of the Warsaw State Opera House: Zdzisław
      Gorzyński, conductor. Muza SXL 0252.

727. Moniuszko, Stanisław.   "I wish I were a Lark" from
      Halka. "Teresa Żylis-Gara--Arias from Slavic Operas."
      Rodolfe RP-12402.

728. _____. Krakowiak (transcribed by Sabatini); Mazurka
      from the Haunted Castle; Polonaise caracteristique;
      Three waltzes; Vilanella mazur weselny; Polish
      dances. Sabatini, piano. Dynamic DS-4011.

729. _____. Mass in E-flat major; Motet "Ne memineris";
      Psalm "Vide humilitatem." Warsaw Chamber Orchestra:
      Edmund Kajdasz, conductor. Veriton SXV-713.

730. _____. Piano works; Quartet, strings, no. 1. Regina
      Smendzianka, piano; Rezler String Quartet. Muza
      SX 0546.

731. _____. Quartet, strings, no. 1 in C minor; Quartet,
      strings, no. 2, in F major. Warsaw String Quartet.
      Le Chant du Monde LDC 278 832/3 [CD].

732. _____. Songs. Teresa Żylis-Gara, soprano; Ivaldi,
      piano. Rodolphe RP-12424.

733. _____. Songs. Wiesław Ochman, tenor; Jerzy Gaczek,
      piano. Muza SX 1744.

734. _____. Songs. A. Hiolski, baritone; S. Nadrzyzowski,
      piano. Muza 0545.

735. _____. Songs from the Songbooks for Home Use. Bożena
      Betley, soprano; Jerzy Marchwinski, piano. Muza
      SX 1052.

736. _____. Straszny dwór. Kawecka; Kostreszewska;
      Paprocki. Muza XEPN 0109-0112.

737. Moniuszko, Stanisław. Straszny dwór [Highlights].
     Soloists, chorus, and orchestra of the Warsaw State
     Opera House: Witold Rowicki, conductor. Muza SX
     0253.

738. _____. Works for orchestra. National Philharmonic
     Symphony Orchestra: Witold Rowicki, conductor.
     Muza SXL 0229.

739. _____. Verbum nobile. Chorus and orchestra of the
     Poznań State Opera: Robert Satanowski, conductor.
     Muza SX 0526-27.

740. Noskowski, Zygmunt. Cztery Pory roku. Muza XL 0398-9.

741. _____. Step, op. 6; Szkice węglem; Polonez Elegijny;
     Morskie Oko, op. 19. Warsaw National Philharmonic
     Orchestra: Rowicki, conductor. Muza SX 0259.

742. _____. Works for orchestra. Warsaw National
     Philharmonic Symphony: Witold Rowicki, conductor.
     Muza XL 0259.

743. Ogiński, Michał Kleofas. Nineteen polonaises. Kann,
     piano. Musical Heritage Society MHS-3784.

744. Organ recital. Includes works by J. Podbielski, M.
     Surzyński, F. Raczkowski, F. Nowowiejski, and W.
     Bakfark. Muza XL 0299.

745. Paderewski, Ignace Jan. Concerto, piano, A minor, op.
     17; Fantasie polonaise, op. 19. Wild, piano;
     London Symphony Orchestra: Fiedler, conductor.
     RCA LSC-3190, LSC-3080, AGL-1-2876.

746. _____. Concerto, piano, A major, op. 17; Ballad for
     piano and orchestra. Rożycki, conductor. Muza
     XL 0196.

747. Paderewski, Ignace Jan. Fantasie polonaise, op. 19.
       Blumenthal, piano; Innsbruch Symphony Orchestra:
       Robert Wagner, conductor. Turnabout TVS-34345;
       Everest 3376.

748. _____. Légende, op. 16, no. 1. "Sic transit gloria
       mundi--a recital of forgotten Romantic gems."
       International Piano Archives IPA 102.

749. _____. Légende, op. 16, no. 1. Sigismond Stojowski
       and Luisa Stojowska. International Piano Archive
       IPA 115.

750. _____. Mélodie, op. 16, no. 2; Minuet, G major, op.
       14, no. 1; Prelude and mazurka. "Fritz Kreisler--
       vol. 3." Camerata CMTX-1503.

751. _____. Melody, op. 6, no. 3. "Itzak Perlman plays
       Fritz Kreisler, vol. 3." Perlman, violin; Sanders,
       piano. Angel SZ-37630.

752. _____. Minuet, G major, from *Humoresques de concert*.
       "Salon music--Musical decor for the fashionable 19th
       century home." Musical Heritage Society MHS-1139.

753. _____. Minuet, G major, op. 14, no. 1. "Piano
       personalities--Alicia de Larrocha, vol. 1." Vox
       SVBX-5800; previously Epic and MHS.

754. _____. Minuet, G major, op. 14, no. 1. "Sergei
       Rachmaninoff plays Concert III." Klavier KS-123.

755. _____. Minuet, G major, op. 14, no. 1. "The complete
       Rachmaninoff, vol. 3." RCA ARM-3-0294.

756. _____. Un moment musical, op. 16, no. 6. "Music of
       the Romantic pianist-composer, vol. 2." Musical
       Heritage Society MHS-4246.

757. Paderewski, Ignace Jan. Polonaise Fantasy for piano
     and orchestra; Variations symphoniques for piano.
     Regina Smendzianki, piano. Muza XL 0114.

758. _____. Sonata, piano, E-flat minor, op. 21; Variations
     and fugue, op. 23. Kubalek, piano. Citadel CT-7001,
     Musical Heritage Society MHS-4103.

759. _____. Sonata, violin, A minor, op. 13. Granat,
     violin; Gray, piano. Desmar DSM-1004.

760. _____. Theme with variations, A major, op. 16, no. 3.
     Nicolaisen, piano. Klavier KS-501.

761. _____. Variations and fugue in E-flat minor, op. 23;
     Sonata in E-flat minor, op. 21. Andrzej Stefanski,
     piano. Muza SX 0570.

762. Panufnik, Andrzej. Autumn music; Heroic overture;
     Nocturne; Tragic overture. "Panufnik concert."
     London Symphony Orchestra: Horenstein, conductor;
     Peebles, piano. Unicorn RHS-306.

763. _____. Concertino for timpani, percussion, and strings;
     Concerto festivo; Katyń epitaph; Landscape--interlude
     for string orchestra. London Symphony Orchestra:
     Panufnik, conductor; Goedicke, timpani; Frye,
     percussion. Unicorn/Kanchana DKP-9016.

764. _____. Symphony No. 1 (Sinfonia rustica); Symphony
     No. 3 (Sinfonia sacra). Monte Carlo Opera Orchestra:
     Panufnik, conductor. Unicorn RHS-315, UNS-257,
     UNS-315, UN-1-75026.

765. _____. Symphony No. 5 (Sinfonia di sfere); Symphony
     No. 6 (Sinfonia mistica). London Symphony
     Orchestra: Atherton, conductor. Decca HEAD 22.

766. Panufnik, Andrzej. Thames Pageant; Invocations for
      Peace. King's House School Choir; Thames Youth
      Ensemble: Stuckley, conductor. Unicorn UNS 264.

767. _____. Universal prayer. Unicorn RHS-305.

768. "Pieśni, tańce i padwany; anonymus XVII wiek."
      Musica antiqua polonica. Muza SXL 0612.

769. Pękiel, Bartłomiej. Audite mortales. Veriton SXV 704.

770. _____. Dulcis amor. "Music of the Royal Castle in
      Warsaw." Musica antiqua polonica. Musicae Antiquae
      Collegium Varsoviense: Stefan Sutkowski, director.
      Muza SXL 0295.

771. _____. Magnum nomen Domini; Resonet in laudibus.
      "Choral works." Bartók Chorus of Eötvös Loránd
      University: Baross, conductor. Hungaraton SLPX-
      12019.

772. _____. Magnum nomen Domini; Resonet in laudibus.
      "Music from the Treasury of the Polish Millennium."
      Muza SXL 0100.

773. _____. Missa brevis. Veriton SXV 735.

774. _____. Missa pulcherima. Musica antiqua polonica.
      Polish Radio Wrocław Mixed Choir: Kajdasz, conductor.
      Muza XL 0188.

775. Penderecki, Krzysztof. Actions for free jazz orchestra.
      New Eternal Rhythm Orchestra: Penderecki, conductor.
      Everest 3484; Philips 6305 153 D.

776. Penderecki, Krzysztof. Anaklasis (1959); The
     awakening of Jacob. Prague Radio Symphony
     Orchestra: Kasprzyk, conductor. Supraphon 1410.2734.

777. _____. Anaklasis for strings and percussion (1960);
     Florescences for orchestra; Psalms of David; Sonata
     for cello and orchestra; Stabat Mater. Mace MXX-
     9090.

778. _____. Anaklasis; Symphony No. 1; Threnody. London
     Symphony Orchestra: Penderecki, conductor. EMI
     Electrola SHZE 393.

779. _____. Anaklasis (1960); De natura sonoris, no. 2
     (1971); Florescences; Kosmogonia. Warsaw National
     Philharmonic Symphony Orchestra: Markowski,
     conductor. Muza SXL 0260; Wergo 60020; Philips
     6500.683.

780. _____. Cantata for 2 mixed choruses and orchestra;
     Canticum canticorum salomnis; Strophes.
     Philharmonic Orchestra and Chorus of Kraków: Jerzy
     Katlewicz, conductor. Muza SXL 1151.

781. _____. Canticum canticorum. Polish Radio Symphony
     Orchestra: Penderecki, conductor. EMI Electrola
     1C 065-02484.

782. _____. Capriccio for Siegfried Palm. "Contemporary
     works for 'cello and piano." Palm, violoncello;
     Aloys Kontarsky, piano. Deutsche Grammophon
     2530.562.

783. _____. Capriccio for Siegfried Palm. Christenssen,
     violoncello. Gasparo GS-102.

784. _____. Capriccio for violin and orchestra, no. 2;
     Emanations for 2 string orchestras; Partita for
     harpsichord and orchestra. "Penderecki conducts

Penderecki--vol. 2." Polish Radio Symphony
Orchestra; Wiłkomirska, violin; Blumenthal,
harpsichord. Angel S-36950.

785. Penderecki, Krzysztof. Capriccio no. 2 for violin and
     orchestra; De natura sonoris. Zukofsky, violin;
     Buffalo Philharmonic: Foss, conductor. Nonesuch
     71201.

786. _____. Concerto for violin and orchestra. Isaac
     Stern, violin; Minnesota Orchestra: Skrowaczewski,
     conductor. CBS 76-739; M-35150.

787. _____. Concerto for violin and orchestra. Andrzej
     Kułka, violin; Polish Radio Symphony Orchestra:
     Penderecki, conductor. Muza SX 1840.

788. _____. Concerto for violoncello and orchestra; De
     natura sonoris, no. 2; Fonogrammi for flutes and
     chamber orchestra; Kanon for orchestra and tape.
     "Penderecki conducts Penderecki--vol. 1." Polish
     Radio Symphony Orchestra; Palm, violoncello.
     Angel S-36949.

789. _____. Concerto for violoncello and orchestra, no. 2.
     Iwan Monighetti, violoncello; Polish Radio National
     Symphony Orchestra: Antoni Wit, conductor. Muza
     SX 2256.

790. _____. De natura sonoris (1966); Dies irae; Polymorphia.
     Cracow Philharmonic: Czyż, conductor; Woytowicz,
     soprano; Ochman, tenor; Ładysz, bass. Philips
     839.701LY.

791. _____. De natura sonoris no. 2. Louisville Orchestra:
     Mester, conductor. Louisville Orchestra LS-722;
     EMI Electrola C 193-02386-7.

792. Penderecki, Krzysztof. Dies irae. Woytowicz, Ochman,
     Ładysz, Kraków Philharmonic Symphony Orchestra and
     Chorus: Czyż, conductor. Philips 839/701 LY.

793. _____. The Devils of Loudon. Troyanos, mezzo-soprano;
     Ahlin, mezzo-soprano; Boese, contralto; Thieme,
     soprano; Krüger, soprano; Steiner, contralto; Hiolski,
     baritone; Ładysz, bass; Sotin, bass; Wilhelm, tenor;
     Wiemann. Philips 6700.042.

794. _____. Ecloga VIII. King's Singers. MMG 1142.

795. _____. Emanations for two string orchestras; Miserere;
     Miniatures for violin and piano; Quartet for strings;
     Stabat Mater; Sonata for cello and orchestra.
     Candide CE-31071.

796. _____. Lacrimosa and Te Deum. Podles, mezzo-soprano;
     Ochman, tenor; Hiolski, baritone; Gadulanka,
     soprano; Polish Radio Orchestra and Chorus of Cracow:
     Penderecki, conductor. Angel DS-38060.

797. _____. Magnificat. Lagger, bass; Polish Radio Chorus
     of Kraków; Polish Radio National Symphony Orchestra:
     Penderecki, conductor. Angel S-37141; EMI Electrola
     C 065-02483.

798. _____. Three miniatures. "Music for clarinet and
     piano." Stevensson, clarinet; Knardahl, piano.
     BIS LP-62.

799. _____. Three miniatures. "The composer's clarinet."
     Schweickardt, clarinet; Cobb, piano. Coronet
     LPS-3116.

800. _____. Three miniatures. "Melvyn Warner, clarinet."
     Warner, clarinet; Reynolds, piano. Crystal S-335.

801. Penderecki, Krzysztof. Psalms of David; Sonata for
     Cello and Orchestra; Anaklasis; Stabat Mater;
     Flourescences. Warsaw National Philharmonic
     Choir; Poznań Philharmonic Orchestra. Muza XL 0260.

802. _____. Quartet, strings, no. 1. Warsaw String
     Quartet. Da Camera Magna SM-92418.

803. _____. St. Luke Passion. Woytowicz; Hiolski; Ładysz;
     Herdegen; Kraków Philharmonic Symphony Orchestra and
     Chorus: Czyż, conductor. Muza XL 0325-6; Philips
     802 771-2 AY.

804. _____. St. Luke Passion. Woytowicz; Hiolski; Ładysz;
     Bartsch; Cologne Radio Orchestra and Chorus: Czyż,
     conductor. RCA VICS-6015.

805. _____. Stabat Mater. Musical Heritage Society MHS-
     1187.

806. _____. Symphony No. 2 (Christmas Symphony). Polish
     Radio National Symphony Orchestra: Kasprzyk,
     conductor. Muza SX 2310; Pavane ADW-7100.

807. _____. Threnody, To the Victims of Hiroshima. Warsaw
     National Philharmonic Symphony Orchestra: Rowicki,
     conductor. Muza XL 0171; Philips 839260 DSY,
     A 02383 L.

808. _____. Utrenja, the entombment of Christ. Woytowicz,
     soprano; Meyer, mezzo-soprano; McCoy, tenor; Ładysz,
     bass; Lagger, bass. Temple University Choirs and
     Philadelphia Orchestra: Ormandy, conductor. RCA
     LSC-3180.

809. _____. Utrenja, the entombment of Christ and the
     resurrection. Ambroziak, soprano; Woytowicz,
     soprano; Szczepańska, mezzo-soprano; Pustelak, tenor;
     Denysenko, bass; Ładysz, bass; Carmeli, bass; Lagger,

bass; Pioneer Choir; Warsaw National Philharmonic
Chorus and Symphony Orchestra: Andrzej Markowski,
conductor. Philips 6700.065.

810. Pietrowski, Karol. Symphony in D major. "Polish
     eighteenth-century symphonies." Musica antiqua
     polonica. Poznań Chamber Orchestra: Robert
     Satanowski, conductor. Muza SXL 0523.

811. Podbielski, Jan. Praeludium. "Baroque program music,
     toccatas, and dances for harpsichord." Kind,
     harpsichord. University of Washington Press UWP-
     2002.

812. _____. Praeludium in D minor. Muza SXL 0614.

813. _____. Praeludium in D minor. "Words and music from
     the Baroque." Jecklin JD 521.

814. _____. Praeludium in D minor. Muza SXL 0235.

815. Polak, Jakub. Branle; Courante; Galliard. Barbara
     Strzelecka, harpsichord. Muza SXL 0614.

816. _____. Courante. "European Lute Music." Hungaraton
     SLPX 11721.

817. _____. Praeludium. "Lute Music of Hungary and Poland."
     Archiv 2533 294.

818. Poldowski [Irene Regine Wieniawska]. Impression fausse.
     "Woman's work." Gemini Hall RAP-1010.

819. _____. Tango. RCA ARM-4-0946.

820. "Polish instrumental music of the seventeenth century."
      Musica antiqua polonica. Muza SXL 0303; Orpheus
      OR 347 S.

821. "Polish modern music." Composers represented: Baird,
      Bogusławski, Dobrowolski, Rudziński, Kotoński.
      Warsaw Philharmonic Orchestra: Rowicki, conductor.
      Muza SL 0336.

822. "Polish organ music of the sixteenth and seventeenth
      centuries." Musica antiqua polonica. Joachim
      Grübich, organ. Muza SXL 0235.

823. "Polish romantic organ music." Works by A. Freyer, F.
      Nowomiejski, J. Furmanik, J. Surzyński, S. Moniuszko,
      W. Zeleński, G. Roguski, and S. Kazaro. Feliks
      Raczkowski, organ. Muza XL 0301.

824. "Polnische Avantgarde." Composers represented: Baird,
      Bacewicz, Górecki, Paciorkiewicz. Muza 0586.

825. Radomia, Mikołaj. Et in terra pax; Magnificat;
      Patrem omnipotentem. "At the origin of Polish Music."
      Muza SXL 0294; Erato Era 9130/6.

826. _____. Hystorigraphi Acie. Harmonia Mundi HMF 704.

827. "Renaissance motets." Muza SXL 0818.

828. Rożycki, Jacek. Confitebor; Magnificat; Magnificemus in
      cantico. "Baroque Sacred Concertos." Musica
      antiqua polonica. Musica Antiqua Wrocław: Eugeniusz
      Sąsiadek, director. Muza SXL 0975.

829. _____. Magnificat. "Music of the Royal Castle in
      Warsaw." Musica antiqua polonica. Musicae Antiquae
      Collegium Varsoviense: Stefan Sutkowski, director.
      Muza SXL 0295.

830. Scacchi, Marco. Vivat et Floreat Rex. "Music of the
      Royal Castle in Warsaw." Musica antiqua polonica.
      Musicae Antiquae Collegium Varsoviense: Stefan
      Sutkowski, director. Muza SX 0295.

831. Scharwenka, Xaver. Polish dances, op. 3; Polish dances,
      op. 40; Theme and variations, op. 48. Trenkner,
      piano. Orion ORS-76230.

832. Sebastian z Felsztyna. Alleluia ave Maria; Alleluia
      felix es sacra vergo Maria. Muza SXL 0818; Erata
      Era 9130/6.

833. _____. Alleluia felix es sacra vergo Maria. "Music
      from the time of Copernicus." Muza SXL 0893/4.

834. Serocki, Kazimierz. Sonatina for trombone and piano.
      "Ralph Sauer, trombone." Sauer, trombone; Carno,
      piano. Crystal S-384.

835. _____. Sonatina for trombone and piano. "Henry
      Charles Smith plays trombone." Coronet 1410M.

836. _____. Sonatina for trombone and piano. "The
      burlesque trombone." Lundberg, trombone; Pontinen,
      piano. Bis CD-318 [CD]/LP-318 [LP].

837. _____. Works for orchestra. Polish Radio Symphony
      Orchestra: Krenz, conductor. Muza XL 0267.

838. Skrowaczewski, Stanisław. Concerto for English horn
      and orchestra. Minnesota Orchestra: Skrowaczewski,
      conductor. Desto DC-7126.

839. _____. Music at Night. Louisville Orchestra: Endo,
      conductor. Louisville Orchestra LS-77-8.

840. _____. Trio for clarinet, bassoon, and piano. "New
       music from Minnesota." Longo, clarinet; Miller,
       bassoon; Schoenfield, piano. Minnesota Composers
       Forum McKnight Disc 2.

841. Spisak, Michał. Duetto concertante for viola and
       bassoon; Concerto no. 2. V. Christensen, viola;
       Eifert, bassoon. Gasparo GS-104.

842. Stachowicz, Damian. Litania; Missa pro defunctis,
       Requiem; Veni redemptor. Veriton SXV 827.

843. _____. Veni consolator. "Baroque Sacred Concertos."
       Musica antiqua polonica. Musica Antiqua Wrocław:
       Eugeniusz Sąsiadek, director. Muza SXL 0975.

844. Staromieyski, Janusz. Laudate pueri. "Music of Old
       Cracow." Musica antiqua polonica. Wrocław Radio
       Chorus and Chamber Orchestra: Edmund Kajdasz,
       conductor. Muza SXL 0368.

845. Szadek, Tomasz. Missa "in melodiam moteti pisneme":
       Sanctus. "Music from the Treasury of the Polish
       Millennium." Muza SXL 0100.

846. _____. Officium Dies et laetitiae. Cantilena Men's
       Choir: Edmund Kajdasz, conductor. Veriton SXV 760.

847. Szałowski, Antoni. Sonatina (1936). "Clarinet con
       espressione." Pino, clarinet; Webb, piano. Orion
       ORS-76256.

848. _____. Sonatina (1948). "Recital music for clarinet."
       Willett, clarinet; Staples, piano. Mark MRS-32638.

849. Szamotuł, Wacław z. Ach mój niebieski Panie; Alleluja,
      chwalcie Pana; Błogosławiony człowiek; Ego sum
      pastor bonus; In te, Domine, speravi; Już się
      zmierzcha; Kryste dniu naszej świadości; Nakłoń
      Panie; Nune scio vere; Pochwalmyż wszyscy. Veriton
      SXV 807.

850. _____. Błogosławiony człowiek; In te, Domine, speravi.
      Veriton SXV 810.

851. _____. Ego sum pastor bonus; In te, Domine, speravi;
      Nune scio vere. Muza SXL 0818; Erato Era 9130/6.

852. _____. Już się zmierzcha. "Music from the Royal
      Castle of Kraków." Concentus Musicus CM-S80-895.

853. _____. Kryste dniu naszej światłości. "Music from
      the Treasury of the Polish Millennium." Muza SXL
      0100.

854. _____. Nakłoń Panie, Psalm 85. "Passion Meditations
      and Lenten Hymns from Poland." Veriton SXV 731.

855. _____. Nune scio vere. Harmonia Mundi HMF 704.

856. Szarzyński, Stanisław Sylwester. Sonata in D major;
      Pariendo non gravis. "Music from the Treasury of
      the Polish Millennium." Muza SXL 0100.

857. _____. Ave regina; Jesu spes mea. "Baroque Sacred
      Concertos." Musica antiqua polonica. Musica
      Antiqua Wrocław: Eugeniusz Sąsiadek, director.
      Muza SXL 0975.

858. _____. Ave regina; Ad hymnos ad cantus; Gloria in
      excelsis Deo; Jesu spes mea; Pariendo non gravaris;
      Veni Sancte Spiritus. Musica antiqua polonica.
      Musicae Antiquae Collegium Varsoviense: Jerzy
      Dobrzański, conductor. Muza SXL 0524.

859.   Szarzyński, Stanisław Sylwester.   Ad hymnos ad cantus.
        Muza SXL 0548.

860.   _____. Gloria in excelcis Deo.   Veriton SXV 710.

861.   Szeligowski, Tadeusz.   Concerto, piano. H.
        Siedzieniewska, piano; National Symphony Orchestra:
        S. Wislocki, conductor.   Muza XL 0205.

862.   Szymanowska, Maria.   Nocturne, A-flat major; Nocturne,
        B-flat major.   "Four Centuries of solo piano music
        by women composers." Mariano, piano. Turnabout
        TV-34685.

863.   Szymanowski, Karol.   Berceuse, op. 52; Dance from
        Harnasie, op. 51; Notturno e tarantella, op. 28;
        Romance, op. 23; Violin sonata, D minor, op. 9.
        Wiłkomirska, violin; Chmielewski, piano.   In Sync
        C-4059.

864.   _____. Chant du Roxane.   "Wanda Wiłkomirska Recital."
        Wiłkomirska, violin; Garvey, piano. Connoisseur
        Society CSQ 2070.

865.   _____. Chant du Roxane.   "The art of Steven Stark."
        Stark, violin; Boucher, piano. Orion ORS-7027/2.

866.   _____. Children's Rhymes, op. 49; Four songs, op. 11.
        Zofia Janukowicz-Pobłocka, soprano; Jerzy Lefeld,
        piano. Muza SX 1053.

867.   _____. Concerto, violin, no. 1, op. 35; Concerto,
        violin, no. 2, op. 61. Wiłkomirska, Treger, violin;
        Warsaw National Phiharmonic Symphony Orchestra:
        Rowicki, Satanowski, conductors. Muza SXL 0383;
        Aurora AUR-5063.

868. Szymanowski, Karol. Concerto, violin, no. 1, op. 35;
      Concerto, violin, no. 2, op. 61. Kułka, violin;
      Polish Radio Symphony Orchestra: Maksymiuk,
      conductor. EMI 1C 065 03597.

869. _____. Concerto, violin, op. 35. Ishikawa, violin;
      Czech Philharmonic Orchestra: Krenz, conductor.
      Supraphon 110.1639.

870. _____. Concerto, violin, no. 1, op. 35. Wiłkomirska,
      violin; Warsaw National Philharmonic Orchestra:
      Rowicki, conductor. Musical Heritage Society MHS-
      1103.

871. _____. Concerto, violin, no. 1, op. 35. Janowski,
      violin; Warsaw National Philharmonic Orchestra:
      Wislocki, conductor. Muza XL 0518; Stolart SZM-0105.

872. _____. Concerto, violin, no. 1, op. 35. Konstanty
      Andrzej Kułka, violin; Wielka Orkiestra Symfoniczna
      Polskiego Radia i Telewizji: Maksymiuk, conductor.
      EMI/Electrola 065-03.597.

873. _____. Concerto, violin, no. 2, op. 61; Sonata,
      violin, D minor, op. 9. Lack, violin; Berlin
      Symphony Orchestra: Kohler, conductor; Hirsh, piano.
      Vox Cum Laude VCL-9061; MCD-10013.

874. _____. Concerto, violin, no. 2, op. 61. Szeryng,
      violin; Bamberg Symphony Orchestra: Krenz, conductor.
      Philips 6500.421.

875. _____. Concerto overture, E major, op. 12; Harnasie--
      ballet pantomime, op. 55; Mandragora--ballet-
      grotesque, op. 43; Symphonie concertante for piano
      and orchestra; Symphony no. 2, B-flat major, op. 19;
      Symphony no. 3, op. 27 (Song of the Night).
      "Orchestral works." Polish Radio Symphony Orchestra:
      Kasprzyk, conductor; Polish Radio Symphony Orchestra

of Cracow: Wit, conductor; Polish Radio National
Symphony Orchestra, Semkow, conductor. EMI His
Master's Voice SLS-5242; EMI Electrola 1C-165.
43210-12.

876. Szymanowski, Karol. Dance from Harnasie. "Separate
but equal." Skrowronski, violin; Isaak, piano.
Eb-Sko 1001.

877. _____. Étude, B-flat minor, op. 4, no. 3 (arr.
Fitelberg); Roxana's song, from King Roger; Symphony
No. 2, B-flat major, op. 19 (rev. Fitelberg). Łódź
Philharmonic Symphony Orchestra: Czyż, conductor.
Aurora AUR-5060.

878. _____. Étude, B-flat minor, op. 4, no. 3. "My
favorite encores." Cliburn, piano. RCA LSC-3185.

879. _____. Études, op. 4; Preludes, op. 1; Mazurkas,
op. 50; Theme and variations, B-flat minor, op. 3;
Symphonie concertante, op. 60. "Piano pieces."
Blumenthal, piano; Polish Radio Symphony Orchestra
of Katowice: Kord, conductor. Unicorn RHS 347,
UN-1-75023.

880. _____. Études, op. 4; Fantasie, op. 14; Masques,
op. 34; Metopes, op. 29. "Piano works." Martin
Jones, piano. Argo ZRG-713.

881. _____. Études, op. 4; Études, op. 33; Masques, op.
34. Rosenberger, piano. Delos DEL-15312.

882. _____. Études, op. 4; Preludes, op. 1; Variation in
B-minor. Tamara Pospieszył, piano. Mixtur Sonclair
MXT S 7E 213.

883. _____. Études, op. 33. Adam Wodnicki, piano. Muza
SX 1223.

884. Szymanowski, Karol. Fontaine d'Aréthuse, op. 30, no. 1.
     Steiner, violin; Berfield, piano. Orion 75195.

885. _____. Harnasie, ballet, op. 56. Pustelak, tenor;
     Warsaw National Philharmonic Choir and Orchestra:
     Rowicki, conductor. Aurora AUR-5064.

886. _____. King Roger, op. 46. Rumowska, soprano;
     Malewicz-Madey, contralto; Nikodem, tenor; Pustelak,
     tenor; Hiolski, baritone; Dąbrowski, bass; Warsaw
     State Opera House Chorus and Orchestra: Mierzejewski,
     conductor. Aurora AUR-5061-62.

887. _____. Król Roger. Muza XL 0250, XL 9251.

888. _____. Kurpian Songs, op. 58; Songs of the Infatuated
     Muezzin, op. 42; Suleika, op. 13, no. 4; The Swan,
     op. 7. Comoy, soprano; Wladowski, piano. Solstice
     SOL-29.

889. _____. Litany to the Virgin Mary, for soprano, chorus,
     and orchestra, op. 59; Symphony No. 3, op. 27 (Song
     of the Night). Gadulanka, soprano; Mitrega,
     contralto; Witkiewicz, baritone; Lucerne Festival
     Weeks Chorus, Swiss Festival Orchestra: Rowicki,
     conductor. Woytowicz, soprano; Chorus and Orchestra
     of the Warsaw National Philharmonic: Kord, conductor.
     Schwann AMS-3538.

890. _____. Masques, op. 34. Koenig, piano. Prelude
     PMS-1503.

891. _____. Mazurkas, op. 50; Mazurkas, op. 62. Carol
     Rosenberger, piano. Delos DEL 25417.

892. _____. Metopes, op. 29. Benoit, piano. Orion ORS
     7274.

893. Szymanowski, Karol. Mythes, op. 30; Kurpian Song,
      op. 58 (trans. Kochański); Roxane's Song from *King
      Roger* (trans. Kochański). Danczowska, violin;
      Zimerman, piano. Deutsche Grammophon 2531.330.

894. _____. Mythes, op. 30; Nocturne and tarantella, op. 28;
      Romance in D, op. 23; Trois caprices de Paganini,
      op. 40. "Works for violin and piano." Hoelocher,
      violin; Beroff, piano. EMI Electrola 1C-067.46599.

895. _____. Mythes, op. 30; Nocturne and tarantella, op.
      28; Trois caprices de Paganini's opus 1; Trois
      poèmes pour violon et piano. I. Oistrakh, violin;
      Serzalowa, piano. Melodiya/Eurodisc 28363-KK.

896. _____. Mythes, op. 30. Konstanty Andrzej Kułka,
      violin; Jerzy Marchwiński, piano. Muza SX 1563.

897. _____. Nocturne and tarantella, op. 28. "Gentleman
      gypsy." Skowronski, violin; Isaak, piano. Eb-Sko
      ES-1004.

898. _____. Nocturne and tarantella, op. 28. "Violin/
      piano recital." LaFosse, violin; Simms, piano.
      Orion ORS-77277.

899. _____. Nocturne and tarantella, op. 28. Kaja
      Danczowska, violin; Lothar Broddack, piano. Schwann/
      Musica Mundi VMS 2058.

900. _____. Preludes, op. 1. Marian Filar, piano. Bruno
      32012.

901. _____. Preludes, op. 1. Tadeusz Zmudziński, piano.
      Muza XL 0335.

902. _____. Preludes, op. 1; Prelude and fugue in C-sharp
      minor; Mazurkas, op. 62; Sonata no. 3, op. 36.
      John Bingham, piano. Thorofon MTH 181.

903. Szymanowski, Karol. Quartet, strings, no. 1, C major,
          op. 27; Quartet, strings, no. 2, op. 56. Pro Arte
          Quartet. Laurel LR-123.

904. _____. Quartet, strings, no. 1, C major, op. 27;
          Quartet, strings, no. 2, op. 56. Varsovia String
          Quartet. Pavane ADW-7118.

905. _____. Quartet, strings, no. 1. Kwartet Wilanowski.
          Muza SX 1563, Veriton SXV 811.

906. _____. Quartet, strings, no. 2. Warsaw String Quartet.
          Da Camera Magna SM-92418.

907. _____. Quartet, strings, no. 2. Kwartet Wilanowski.
          Muza SX 1255.

908. _____. Romance, op. 23; Three caprices after Paganini,
          op. 40. Skrowronski, violin; Isaak, piano. Eb-Sko
          ES-1006.

909. _____. Scheherezade, from *Masques*, op. 29. Toperczer,
          piano; Slovak Philharmonic Orchestra. Royale
          ROY-2005.

910. _____. Sonata, piano, no. 1, C minor, op. 8; Sonata,
          piano, no. 2, A major, op. 21. Schmalfuss, piano.
          Thorofon Capella MTH-175.

911. _____. Sonata, piano, no. 2, A major, op. 21.
          Pleshakov, piano. Orion ORS-73111.

912. _____. Sonata, piano, no. 1; Sonata, piano, no. 3.
          Alasdair Graham, piano. Musical Heritage Society
          MHS 3136.

913. Szymanowski, Karol. Sonata, violin, D minor, op. 9.
      Franco Gulli, violin; Enrico Cavallo, piano.
      Musical Heritage Society MHS 3123.

914. _____. Sonata, violin, D minor, op. 9 (arr. viola).
      Kosmala, viola; Snyder, piano. Orion ORS-79349.

915. _____. Sonata, violin, D minor, op. 9. Lachert,
      violin; Bloom, piano. Telarc S-5033.

916. _____. Songs. Krystyna Szostek-Radkowa, mezzo-
      soprano; Jerzy Lefeld, piano. Muza SYL 0980.

917. _____. Songs to the poems of James Joyce, op. 54.
      Andrzej Bachleda, baritone; Jerzy Marchwiński, piano.
      Muza SX 1546.

918. _____. Songs to the poems of James Joyce, op. 54.
      Magdalena Bojanowska, soprano; Barbara Halska, piano.
      Veriton SXV 788.

919. _____. Stabat Mater, op. 53. Woytowicz, Szczepańska,
      Hiolski, National Philharmonic Symphony Orchestra
      and Chorus: Rowicki, conductor. Muza SX 1564.

920. _____. Stabat Mater, op. 53; Symphony No. 3.
      Woytowicz, Szczepańska, Hiolski, National Philharmonic
      Symphony Orchestra and Chorus: Rowicki, conductor.
      Muza SX 2352.

921. _____. Symphony No. 2, op. 19; Symphony No. 3, op. 27
      (Song of the Night). Detroit Symphony Orchestra:
      Dorati, conductor; Karczykowski, tenor; Kenneth
      Jewell Chorale. London LDR-71026; Decca SXDL KSXDC
      7524.

922. Tansman, Alexandre. Alla polacca e galliarde.
     "Jonathan Taylor-- Debut." Taylor, guitar. Mark
     56/840.

923. _____. Cavatina. "Contemporary Music for the Guitar."
     Bitetti, guitar. Music Guild MS-871.

924. _____. Mouvement perpetuel, from 5 pieces for violin
     and piano. "The Heifitz Collection, vol. 5 1946-
     1949, The end of an era." RCA ARM-4-0946.

925. _____. Sonatina for bassoon and piano. "The virtuoso
     bassoon." Sonstevolo, bassoon; Krardahl, piano.
     Bis LP-122.

926. _____. Sonatina for bassoon and piano. "Arthur
     Grossman plays bassoon." Grossman, bassoon;
     Hokanson, piano. Coronet S-2741.

927. _____. Sonatina for flute and piano. "Sounds of Gold."
     Thomas, flute; Croshaw, piano. Golden Crest RE-7095.

928. _____. Spirituel and blues-fox-trot, from *Sonatine
     transatlantique*. "American piano music by European
     composers." J. Smith, piano. Musical Heritage
     Society MHS-7035.

929. _____. Suite for bassoon. "The virtuoso bassoon."
     Grossman, bassoon; Hokanson, piano. Ravenna RAVE-
     761.

930. Wański, Jan. Symphony in D major; Symphony in G major.
     Poznań Philharmonic Orchestra: Satanowski, conductor.
     Muza XL 0194.

931. Wieniawski, Henryk. La cadenza, op. 10, no. 7.
      "Virtuoso music for solo violin." Ricci, violin.
      Columbia M-35159.

932. _____. La cadenza, op. 10, no. 7; Variations on an
      original theme, op. 15. "The virtuoso violin."
      Szabadi, violin; Gulyaś, piano. Hungaraton SLPX-
      12514.

933. _____. Caprice, A minor, op. 18, no. 4. "Itzhak
      Perlman plays Fritz Kreisler, vol. 2." Perlman,
      violin; Sonder, piano. Angel S-37254.

934. _____. Caprice, A minor, op. 18, no. 4. Sitkovetsky,
      violin; Canino, piano. Orfeo S-048831A.

935. _____. Capriccio-valse, E major, op. 7; Kujawiak;
      Légende, op. 17; Obertass-mazurka, op. 19, no. 1;
      Polonaise no. 2, A major, op. 21; Polo; Souvenir
      de Moscou, op. 6; Variations on an original theme.
      "Virtuoso showpieces." Ricci, violin; Gruenberg,
      piano. Deutsche Grammophon 2531.305.

936. _____. Capriccio-valse, E major, op. 7. "Cho-liang
      Lin -- Bravura." Lin, violin; Rivers, piano. CBS
      IM-39133.

937. _____. Concert polonaise. Rosand, violin; Luxembourg
      Radio Orchestra: De Froment, conductor. Turnabout
      TVS-34629.

938. _____. Concerto, violin, no. 1, F-sharp minor, op. 14.
      David, violin; Prague Symphony Orchestra: Halvácek,
      conductor. Supraphon 110.1837.

939. _____. Concerto, violin, no. 1, F-sharp minor, op. 14.
      Rabin, violin; Philharmonia Orchestra: Boult,
      conductor. Angel 35484; Seraphim S-60342.

940. Wieniawski, Henryk. Concerto, violin, no. 1, F-sharp
      minor, op. 14. Muza XL 0168.

941. _____. Concerto, violin, no. 1, F-sharp minor, op. 14.
      Pikaizen, violin; Moscow Radio Symphony Orchestra:
      Rozhdestvensky, conductor. Melodiya-Angel SR 40185.

942. _____. Concerto, violin, no. 1, F-sharp minor, op. 14;
      Concerto, violin, no. 2, D minor, op. 22. Krysa,
      violin; Warsaw National Philharmonic Symphony
      Orchestra: Satanowski, conductor. Wiłkomirska,
      violin; Warsaw National Philharmonic Symphony
      Orchestra: Rowicki, conductor. Musical Heritage
      Society/Orpheus OR-366.

943. _____. Concerto, violin, no. 1, F-sharp minor, op. 14;
      Concerto, violin, no. 2, D minor, op. 22. Perlman,
      violin; London Philharmonic Orchestra: Ozawa,
      conductor. Angel S-36903.

944. _____. Concerto, violin, no. 2, D minor, op. 22.
      Rabin, violin; New Philharmonia Orchestra: Goosens,
      conductor. Seraphim S-60222; Capitol SP-8534.

945. _____. Concerto, violin, no. 2, D minor, op. 22;
      Thème original varié, op. 15; Légende, op. 17;
      Polonaise no. 1 in D major, op. 4. Brodsky, violin;
      Polish Radio National Symphony Orchestra: Michalak,
      conductor. Musical Heritage Society MHS 4983H.

946. _____. Concerto, violin, no. 2, D minor, op. 22.
      Stern, violin; Philadelphia Orchestra: Ormandy,
      conductor. Odyssey ML 5208; MS-6277, Y-35225.

947. _____. Concerto, violin, no. 2, D minor, op. 22.
      Zukerman, violin; Royal Philharmonic Orchestra:
      Foster, conductor. Columbia M-30644.

948. Wieniawski, Henryk. Concerto, violin, no. 2, D minor, op. 22. Szeryng, violin; Bamberg Symphony Orchestra: Krenz, conductor. Philips C500.421.

949. _____. Concerto, violin, no. 2, D minor, op. 22. Perlman, violin; Orchestre de Paris: Barenboim, conductor. Deutsche Grammophon 410.526-1.

950. _____. L'ecole moderne: Études-caprices, op. 10. Ricci, violin. Dynamic DS-4028.

951. _____. Études-caprices, op. 18, no. 1, G minor and no. 2, E-flat major. "Duets for violins." Perlman, Zukerman, violins. Angel S-37406.

952. _____. Études-caprices for 2 violins, op. 18; Legende, op. 17; Mazurka, op. 19, no. 2; Polonaise, D major, op. 4; Scherzo tarantelle, op. 16. "Works for violin." Staryk, violin; Kotowska, piano. Musical Heritage Society MHS 1131.

953. _____. Fantasy on themes from Gounod's Faust, op. 20. "Ruggiero Ricci--Opera paraphrases for violin and orchestra." Ricci, violin; Orchestra of Radio Luxembourg: De Froment, conductor. Turnabout QTV-34720.

954. _____. Fantasy on themes from Gounod's Faust, op. 20. "Diana Steiner--Operatic fantasies." Steiner, violin; Berfield, piano. Orion ORS-78313.

955. _____. Légende, op. 17. Oistrakh, violin; Yampolsky, piano. Angel 35334, Seraphim S-60259.

956. _____. Légende, op. 17. "Virtuoso violin." Neikrug, piano. CBS M-36689.

957. Wieniawski, Henryk. Légende, op. 17. "Rare works for
      virtuoso violin." Bobesco, violin; Bemant, piano.
      Desto DC-7204.

958. _____. Légende, op. 17; Polonaise no. 1, D major,
      op. 4; Thème original varié, op. 15; Concerto,
      violin, no. 2, D minor, op. 22. Brodsky, violin;
      Polish Radio National Symphony Orchestra: Michalak,
      conductor. Musical Heritage Society MHS-4983.

959. _____. Légende, op. 17. "Vintage Menuhin--the
      legendary early recordings." Orion ORS-7271.

960. _____. Mazurka, G major, op. 19, no. 1; Polonaise
      brillante, no. 2, A major. "Wanda Wiłkomirska
      Recital." Wiłkomirska, violin; Garvey, piano.
      Connoisseur Society CSQ 2070.

961. _____. Obertass-Mazurka, op. 19, no. 1; Polonaise
      brillante, no. 2, A major. "Itzak Perlman--Encores."
      Perlman, violin; Sander, piano. Angel S2-37560.

962. _____. Polonaises; Dudziarz; Kujawiak; Scherzo-
      Tarantella G minor. Gumpel, Rezler. Muza XL 0104.

963. _____. Polonaise brillante, no. 1, D major, op. 1.
      "Violin encores." Weiner, violin; Demoulin, piano.
      Musical Heritage Society MHS-3294.

964. _____. Polonaise brillante, no. 1, D major, op. 4;
      Scherzo-tarantelle, op. 16. "Eugene Fodor--violin
      recital." Fodor, violin; Feldman, piano. RCA
      ARL-1-0735.

965. _____. Polonaise, D major, op. 4. "Recital by Pinchas
      Zukerman." Zukerman, violin; London Symphony
      Orchestra: Mackerras, conductor. Columbia MS-7422.

966. Wieniawski, Henryk. Polonaise de concert, op. 4;
      Scherzo tarentelle, op. 16. "Philharmonic solo--
      Concertos in contrast." Dicterow, violin; Los
      Angeles Philharmonic Orchestra: Mehta, conductor.
      London CS-6967.

967. _____. Romance from Concerto, violin, no. 2, D minor,
      op. 22. "Romances sans paroles." Suk, violin;
      Prague Symphony Orchestra: Smetacek, conductor.
      Supraphon 110.2199.

968. _____. Romance from Concerto, violin, no. 2, D minor,
      op. 22; Légende, op. 17. "Violin romances."
      Grumiaux, violin; New Philharmonia Orchestra:
      de Waart, conductor. Philips 6580.047.

969. _____. Romance from Concerto, violin, no. 2, D minor,
      op. 22. "Romance." Stern, violin; Columbia
      Symphony Orchestra: Brieff, conductor. Columbia
      M-31425.

970. _____. Scherzo-tarentelle, op. 16. "The Heifitz
      collection, vol. 2, 1925-1934, The first electrical
      recordings." RCA ARM-4-0943.

971. _____. Scherzo-tarentelle, op. 16. "Itzak Perlman,
      virtuoso violinist." Perlman, violin; Sander,
      piano. Angel S-37456.

972. _____. Scherzo-tarentelle, op. 16. "Gerard Poulet
      plays violin favorites." Poulet, violin; Blanchot,
      piano. Musical Heritage Society MHS-3236.

973. _____. Scherzo-tarentelle, op. 16. "Heifitz encores."
      RCA LSC-3233.

974. _____. Variations on the Austrian National Anthem.
      "Bravura." Ricci, violin. Decca DL-710172.

975. Wislocki, Stanisław. Concerto, piano. H.
      Siedzieniewska, piano; National Symphony Orchestra:
      S. Wislocki, conductor. Muza XL 0205.

976. Zarębski, Juliusz. Quartet, piano, G minor, op. 34.
      Muza XL 0178.

977. _____. Works for piano. Ryszard Bakst, piano. Muza
      XL 0255.

978. Zarzycki, Aleksander. Mazurka, op. 26 (arr. Dubiska).
      Oistrakh, violin; Yampolsky, piano. Seraphim
      S-60259; Angel 35334.

979. Żebrowski, Marcin Józef. Magnificat. Musica antiqua
      polonica. Musicae Antiquae Collegium Varsoviense:
      Stefan Sutkowski, director. Muza XL 0496.

980. Zeidler, Józef. Vespers. Musica antiqua polonica.
      Muza XL 0289.

981. Zelechowski, Piotr. Fantasia. Joachim Grübich, organ.
      Muza SXL 0235.

982. Żeleński, Władysław. Works for orchestra. Warsaw
      National Philharmonic Symphony Orchestra: Witold
      Rowicki, conductor. Muza XL 0259.

983. Zieleński, Mikołaj. Benedicamus Deum caeli; Deus in
      simplicitate. Muza SXL 0302; Erato Era 9130/6.

984. _____. Fantasia. Muza SXL 0303.

985. _____. In monte Oliveti. Muza SXL 0548.

986. Zieleński, Mikołaj. In monte Oliveti. "Music from the
     Treasury of the Polish Millennium." Muza SXL 0100.

987. _____. Offertorium XXX. "Choral works." Bartók
     Chorus of Eötvös Loránd University: Baross, conductor.
     Hungaraton SLPX-12019.

988. _____. Offertoria; Magnificat; Communiones. Muza
     SXL 0302.

989. Zwierzchowski, Mateusz. Requiem. Musica antiqua
     polonica. Muza XL 0275.